NATIONAL MYTHS IN GREECE

SOCIETY AND POLITICS SERIES: 10

National myths in Greece

By Hercules Millas

Copyright © 2023 Transnational Press London

First published in 2023 by Transnational Press London in the United Kingdom, 13 Stamford Place, Sale, M33 3BT, UK.
www.tplondon.com

Transnational Press London® and the logo and its affiliated brands are registered trademarks.

Requests for permission to reproduce material from this work should be sent to:
sales@tplondon.com

Paperback
ISBN: 978-1-80135-099-0
Digital
ISBN: 978-1-80135-100-3

Cover Design: Nihal Yazgan
Cover image: Nikolaos Gyzis, "Greek school in the time of slavery", popularly known as "To krifó scholió", Oil painting, 1885/86.

Transnational Press London Ltd. is a company registered in England and Wales No. 8771684.

NATIONAL MYTHS IN GREECE

Hercules Millas

TRANSNATIONAL PRESS LONDON

2023

To Eleanor, James, Iris and Alexandra

CONTENTS

ACKNOWLEDGEMENT

Five close friends read this text when it was in draft form and communicated encouraging me with their useful comments. Uğur Aker, Christos Clairis, Christos Elmatzoglou, Alexis Heraclides and Vasilis Sakellariou. I thank them warmly.

I thank the editor Prof. Dr. Ibrahim Sirkeci for his prompt and warm willingness to publish my work

The greatest indebtedness is to Evy, my sixty-year partner, who reads everything I write corrects my English, suggests improvements and enencourages in general.

Naturally, all mistakes and shortcomings are mine.

ABOUT THE AUTHOR

Hercules Millas (born 1940) has a Ph.D. degree in political science and a B.Sc. in civil engineering. In the years 1968-1985, he worked as engineer in various countries such as Turkey, Greece, Indonesia, Saudi Arabia, and others.

During the period 1990-2010 he taught at various Turkish and Greek universities Greek and Turkish language and literature, history based on the bilateral relations of these countries, political science, literary criticism and conflict resolution.

He participated in many international meetings and projects related to the above topics. He was a moderator in the Turkish-Greek Civic Dialogue Project (supported by the European Commission, 2002-2004) and he participated as organizer in a project to assist minority youth in matters of education in Western Thrace, Greece (2005-2012).

His publications, many books and articles, cover fields such as literature, language, historiography, textbooks, political science and interethnic perceptions. He translated more than twenty books, mainly Greek and Turkish poetry.

He received the 'Abdi Ipekçi Peace Award' in 1992, the 'Dido Sotiriou' award of the Hellenic Authors' Society in 2004 and the award of Free Thinking by Publishers' Association of Turkey in 2005. His documentary (jointly with N. Dinç), The Other Town, on how Greeks and Turks perceive each other received the Spectators Award in the Thessaloniki Film Festival in 2011. His novel The Family Grave received the "Orhan Kemal best novel award" for the year 2021 in Turkey.

PART ONE

SOME GREEK NATIONAL MYTHS

PREFACE: WHAT IS A MYTH?

As a Greek resident in Greece I have often been confronted with various national myths that cover a very wide range of issues but mostly they are about "our" superiority – accompanied with the degradation of some "other" ethnic groups. These myths are encountered in various spheres such as historiography, textbooks, literature, media, political speeches, etc. I am aware that this nationalistic discourse is a worldwide phenomenon but it is some time now that I am interested in the Greek case, mainly because of my proximity to this environment.

Being brought up in Turkey as a member of the Greek minority and probably due to that, I often felt opposed to these extremist views and otherings; and I thought of choosing the most recurrent and widely believed of these myths, deconstruct them and expose their mythical, i.e. mistaken character. Initially, the whole enterprise seemed a very simple one. Whenever I discussed this issue with my colleagues and my friends we readily agreed on the erroneous and naïve aspect of these stereotypes and legends. It was only needed to show the contradictions, the inconsistencies and/or the absence of evidence and the myths would be exposed and annulled.

However, when I made the very first step by starting putting my arguments on paper and imagining what the possible objections to my views could be by the wider society, I realized that my views would not be accepted as self understood realities beyond my familiar circle. For the wider public the erroneous side has to be demonstrated and proved. This does not seem to be as easy as talking to friends. Exposing some ideas was not enough. It became clear to me that it is a different situation to discuss an issue with people that we share similar opinions than trying to talk to people who have strong opposing beliefs. In the first case all the members of the groups confirm each other and reaffirm their shared opinions. In the second case one confronts total resistance and opposition. What is a myth for me is a reality for others.

It was clear that I needed to develop persuasive arguments that will falsify some widely believed "truths". Furthermore, the meanings that I attributed to my terms when I discussed the myths with my close friends were not

7

understood in the same way by many others. Gradually, as I came to think of what I had to do, the scope of "showing some national myths" has widened.

I felt the need to see what has been said on similar studies and what the probable counter opinions could be. I met ambiguities. First, it was not clear what the issue and the problem in question really were. There were various definitions of "myths". Why was there such a resistance to my "common sense" views? Was it because of lack of historical knowledge, was it because of harmful ideologies, of ethnocentric education, of a special psychological disposition, of low IQ? And why was it so difficult to keep an effective and productive dialog going on similar issues? Is it possible that my common sense understanding was also a kind of a personal subjective opinion, even a myth? Why is sometimes a simple argument about the popular myths, especially the sensitive national ones, seen as a challenge? And what does "national" mean?

To try to prove one's "self-understood" truths is an oxymoron in the first place! The use of a term like "undeniable reality" infers the non-acceptance of any dispute in this domain and even an indirect confession that such truth cannot be proved. It is a priori declaration of a "truth". And realities of this kind hardly change after a dialog.[1]

Actually, in a discussion with an "unbeliever" about "our" truth, one is lost in the various meanings of the expressions and the utterances mutually used. The "opponent" at a certain point will dispute even the good intentions and the integrity of his adversary. The whole situation will look like trying to persuade a Muslim about the righteousness of Christianity – and vice a versa - or a nationalist of his fanaticism. These ends are almost never attained.[2]

On the other hand, my basic need and my initial purpose were to warn and persuade those who "went astray" following their national myths and those who, according to my and to my friends' understanding, could not see what is self-evident, the obvious truth. I have not lost hope yet, even though now I realize that the whole enterprise is a complex one.

Eventually, I decided to approach the whole issue starting from the basics: What and how this issue of myths is handled in general and how the lexicon used created difficulties of communication. Here below I will discuss the following:

1- How the national myths are discussed and studied in so many different

---

[1] It was clever and very practical to say, "We hold these truths to be self-evident, that all men are created equal, that they are endowed by their creator with certain unalienable rights...etc", since to try to "prove" these truths would have required time and effort that would have delayed action.
[2] Some people may follow different understanding of reality, e.g., a particular theocentric religion and some others may be followers of science. Irrespective of the theoretical dispute on the relativity or objectivity of "reality", in practice people very often are unable to reach to a consensus on what is valid.

academic fields that the whole issue is perplexed within this abundance. I will try to reach to an understanding on the followed methodology and I will recount my experience on similar issues.

2- The terms "national" and "myths" bear so many different meanings and connotations that a sensible dialog is hindered at the outset. I will try to define my terms.

3- I will occasionally present and discuss my academic efforts in related issues since the whole enterprise is initiated by my personal query.

4- Finally, having set my framework and definitions, hopefully establishing a ground hospitable enough to enable communication, I will present the Greek national myths.

5- Naturally, at the end the "myths" will be explained and will be evaluated anew.

1- The plethora of academic approaches

At a certain stage I felt as if I had taken a too daring decision to get involved with national myths. I started by checking the existing literature so that I would not repeat what is already known. What I encountered amounted to hundreds of books and articles with all kinds of ideas. But worse, these studies do not belong to the same academic discipline. It was difficult for me to make a synthesis out of the various approaches and opinions and reach to a fairly comprehensible explanation of what a "myth" and "national" mean.

The biggest difficulty is the incongruence of the academic disciplines. Myths and national phenomena are being studied by various branches of academic/scientific disciplines. Some are: history, philosophy, anthropology, political science, psychology, sociology, cultural theory etc. Each one of these disciplines is subdivided to more specialized groups. There are tens of philosophical schools that express various interpretations on "beliefs". Political scientists are in disagreement according to their political and/or ideological starting points. Psychology and/or social psychology may vary as much as cognitive psychology differs from psychoanalysis. Cultural studies can be seen as a series of "disciplines" such as structuralism, Marxism, postmodernism, etc. with many competing theories. Sociologists show a great variety, too.[3]

In a list of "academic disciplines" I found five main groups: Humanities, social sciences, natural sciences, formal sciences and applied sciences. Each

---

[3] By "plethora of academic approaches" I do not mean a situation akin to Kuhn's "incommensurability" of concepts between scientific theories, an issue which has been widely discussed the last decades; I mean the different and limited scope and approach in each discipline.

of them is subdivided into three to seven subgroups which are each subdivided again into ten to fifty groupings. The total is approximately 1220 – I might have missed some as I counted![4]

The real problem is not that the readers are asked to make an effort and decide on their own as to what is valid or wrong, making their own synthesis as of what a national myth is. Such a requirement is probably legitimate and the effort to synthesize may even prove to be a very useful exercise. The worry is that there is an intrinsic flaw in the whole enterprise in approaching the said issue in these various disciplines. The following:

Academic and/or scientific disciplines are recognized as the learned societies and academic departments or faculties within colleges and universities to which their practitioners belong. Various terms are used for "academic discipline": Academic field, field of study, field of inquiry, research field, scientific discipline, branch of knowledge, etc. In all cases when a study is associated to a discipline it is understood that the study is carried out according to that *particular* discipline and not to *some other*.

When an issue, in this case the "national myth" (say, issue A), is worked out within a discipline successfully and fully complying with the standards of that discipline (say, within discipline 1), to what degree is the issue A covered and studied? This question arises when one considers that the issue A may be studied also by disciplines 2, 3, 4, etc. Then the end result seems to be: "Discipline 1 has covered only (tiny) part of the issue A".

This is a very common occurrence. The researcher normally specifies a "method" and this method naturally will be in compliance with one's discipline - history, sociology, psychology etc. The other "fields of thought" would be absent and/or silenced. Silencing would mean either rejection due to irreverence or due to negligence because the other disciplines' input is considered irrelevant or due to unawareness of the alternative disciplines.

In other words, the problem is not only the readers' who have to find their answers searching among disciplines, but the basic worry should belong to the academic/scientist/researcher: It is as if one begins working on a subject having decided at the start that the work will be done only "partly". In short, if one accepts that each prospective discipline has something to offer, then each discipline covers only a part of the whole.

Once the conviction "only our method/discipline is valid" is rejected as a too haughty claim, the next obvious alternative is to resort to inter/multi/trans/cross disciplinary methods. In some cases the term "polymethodist approach" is used, too. These methods basically link and

---

[4] https://en.wikipedia.org/wiki/Outline_of_academic_disciplines

relate different disciplines. There are nuances between them but almost all seek the same target, to create a holistic approach by making use of many disciplines, even sometimes non-scientific ones in dealing with a single subject.

Just for brevity I will use here below the prefix "multi" to indicate all methods that use various disciplines at the same time. Actually, these "multi" approaches indirectly recognize a shortcoming, too: that a single "discipline", on its own, may not produce a total description of a phenomenon and will not answer all relevant questions. The need of a "multi" approach is appreciated and this recognition is a positive move.

However, these "multi" approaches are open to many questions. They correctly propose *in general* a "multi" approach but in practice this intention does not lead to a method. It is a vague directive. How many "more disciplines" does one have to choose and consult? When will a "multi" method be considered necessary and by whom? Is there going to be a hierarchy among these disciplines? How will the "portion" of each be determined? When these and other similar questions are not answered, what is left of a "multi" disciplinary approach is only some vague advice. In the last resort, the researcher will follow her own impromptu decision.

Naturally one may find many successful multidisciplinary studies. Also it is normal to expect that a "multi" approach will produce richer and multi-perspective results. The problem is that voicing the principle of "multi" does not secure its application. The frequency and the degree of the "multi" use will depend on a personal decision and especially on the ability of the researcher. Whereas a "method" should operate as a guide and not only as a general intent.[5]

In the case of "National myths in Greece" one may use a big number of "disciplines". Firstly, history and philosophy are indispensible since all issues have their own history and all cases can be discussed from a philosophical perspective. I overlook the complexity of choosing the proper schools of philosophy and historiography. Theology should somehow be introduced since myths, mythology and beliefs are interlinked. Of course anthropology and sociology is a must. Psychology and social psychology is also important. In all these cases one has to decide between groups and subgroups. Since national myths are linked to the concept of "nation", political science (subgroup: nationalism) is also required. Statistics go with sociology and political science. In order to see the hidden meanings of the discourses

---

[5] The Merriam Webster dictionary defines "method" as 1- "a systematic procedure, technique, or mode of inquiry employed by or proper to a particular discipline or art" and as 2- "a systematic plan followed in presenting material for instruction". The Cambridge dictionary's definition is: "a particular way of doing something".

linguistics is also needed.

How are these "disciplines" going to be integrated within a study? Another question may be more interesting: Are there studies that are *not* "multi"? Is it ever possible to study any social topic, i.e., any issue that is related to human existence, without referring to various "disciplines"? Consider the following paragraph which I have purposely constructed to show that various disciplines – shown in parenthesis - are set in motion usually prior to a conscious decision on a "method". (Assuming a study on the Greeks, their "national" beliefs and especially their perceptions about the Other.):

> "Starting right after the founding of the Greek modern nation-state (history), in most Greek novels (statistics, literature), the past Greek-Turkish relations (international relations) were narrated with symbolic references (philosophy/semiotics) to the roles that the Greek heroines had played (cultural and gender studies). Related studies have shown (sociology) that in some remote villages of the country, especially the old people still sing patriotic songs (anthropology, nationalism) imagining (psychology) those old days of absence of freedom (political science)."

The issue of "disciplines" and their "multi" use is a very intricate one. It is not a matter of putting together a number of disciplines and methods. Mostly because any human situation exists as a total (as a holistic) phenomenon that incorporates all phases of life at the same time. All the parameters which are the subjects of the above mentioned "disciplines" play a role simultaneously. An effort to go "deeper and deeper" on a specific discipline, keeping a distance from the other branches, produce important knowledge. But this may turn up to seeing the trees missing the forest. Each discipline may be seen as a brick, the basic material to build the wall, but the wall is different from the bricks.

On the other hand, the "total knowledge" I refer to, would not have existed in my mind if I had not previously somehow studied each particular discipline as a separate branch. There is not a wall if bricks are absent. I do not infer that I am against in having different disciplines. My concern is the way they are used: the selection of one as if the other's existence is secondary.

2- A case of a "multi" approach

I came to think about the above mentioned problematic of academic disciplines for the first time when I started working on my PhD. In 1998 and at an advanced age of 58 I received my doctorate at Ankara University, Department of Political Science. Prior to that I had a MA in Civil Engineering (1966) from Robert College of Istanbul (later named Boğaziçi University).

Between the two studying periods I worked as an engineer in various countries, I lived in both Turkey and Greece and as a hobby I was interested in the relations between these two societies. Before my PhD I had already published a book on the Greek-Turkish relations and various articles about the perceptions of these nations.

As a PhD research, I suggested the following topic: "A comparative study of nationalism and identities as these are expressed in the Turkish and Greek literary texts and through the images of the Other". I had to convince my professors that this would be a PhD of "political science". Actually, I was interested in studying this particular issue and political science was not my concern! Being a minority member in Turkey I was curious to find out how nationalist sentiments were created and experienced and how the majorities perceived the minorities. On the other hand, since I was a student of a specific department, I had to follow the curriculum and its "method".

The PhD research looked like being in harmony with the academic requirements and with political science in particular. What I believe that I actually did, however, was to read many Turkish and Greek novels of various periods and to check through the texts how each side perceived the Other. At the end I reached some conclusions that were numbered from 1 to 86.[6]

I was satisfied with the results and the books were well received in both countries. But I cannot say to which discipline(s) my thesis really belongs. Officially it was a study of political science since it was related to national perceptions and identities of two nations. On my part I felt it was closer to imagology since literary texts and images were involved. But here now I want to narrate how this study started, developed and was concluded. Because I think this process gives some clues about the possible answers (my answers) to issues of "methods" and multi-disciplinary approaches. This story goes as follows:

It was the early 1990s, I was hosted in Istanbul by a friend and as I went to sleep, I took a book from the shelf to read for a while. It was the short stories of Yakup Kadri (1889-1974), a well known Turkish writer, diplomat and member of the parliament. I was shocked by the way he portrayed the Greeks: murderers, barbarians, treacherous, etc. All were alike without exceptions. In those years the complete works of Yakup Kadri were just published. I was curious to see if his other books were the same and I read his nine novels, two volumes of short stories and five volumes of memoirs. The Greeks in the literary texts were all negative personalities.

Was he an exception? I then read the complete works of Halide Edip and

[6] This study was published in Turkey and in Greece see in bibliography: Millas 2000, 2001 and 2005. For articles in English that reflect some of these findings see: Millas, 1996, 2016.

Ömer Seyfettin, both well-know writers in Turkey of the first half of the 20th century. The Greeks were the same, very negative and the Greek women on top mostly prostitutes. I knew that Sait Faik (1906-1954) liked the Greeks, "us", but I wanted to have an opinion based on a critical reading and on numbers. In his complete works, mostly short stories, the Greeks were lovely and exemplary positive personalities (Millas, 2000, p. 179-185; 2001. p. 225-229).

How can one evaluate these findings and what kind of conclusions can one reach? An opportunity was given to me during my PhD studies. When I presented some of the above mentioned findings in class the Turkish students and my professor were shocked, too. They did not know that the image of the Greeks was so bad in these texts – which they almost all had read, in whole or at least partly! Why didn't they notice what I saw clearly? And how should one explain Sait Faik who was so different? This experience drove me to suggest "The image of Greeks in Turkish literature" as a PhD. I knew I was in a virgin area.

At the start I did not know what I was going to find, even though I had a vague idea of what I could meet with. During my readings I tried not to be selective and I chose the literary texts "at random". So I was justified to reach to some *statistical results*. I had to have a thorough idea of the *history* of the two countries to understand what the writers were referring to and *international relations* came to the agenda, too. *Philosophy of history* was needed to understand why the two sides differed so much in evaluating their common past. For the national stereotypes many (standard) books on *nationalism* had to be read. Prejudices necessitated the basics of *psychology*: defense mechanisms, projection, phobias, paranoia. *Literary criticism* was part of my approach. I knew that this kind of political worldviews were based on a special "education" that contributes to the creation of prejudices. All these texts (with negative and positive Others) influenced the political atmosphere, and *political science* was part of the study. The way Monsieur Jourdain spoke prose for forty years without knowing it, I had completed a PhD dissertation without knowing I was probably following the methodology of imagology! To be more precise, the closest I can get to as a discipline is this one, probably, with some additions to it.

But to where do all these lead method-wise? To assign a method to this study or to make a list of disciplines and identify it as a "multi"-disciplinary work limited to these disciplines looks like begging the question. The whole enterprise started and was completed on a different basis. It started as a curiosity from my part and with a set of questions. The method followed. Actually it was as if the "method" imposed itself. It was shaped gradually as new findings came to the fore. I started "looking at my material" and then trying to describe and if possible to explain the phenomena. There was not any particular discipline in mind but only some questions and "all my knowledge". The extent and the richness of the study depended on and were limited by the capacities of the researcher, irrespective of any method and/or discipline.[7]

Now, after two decades, as all the above problematic comes to the fore and I look back trying to give a meaning to the final result of my study, I realize that I had somehow followed a "method". It is a "multi" one indeed. I am reluctant, however, to consider it as a study that belongs to the "humanist studies" or "social sciences" per se. I will outline it, in some details to clarify my point.

EMPATHY

Apart from the disciplines, the scientific fields and the related knowledge some additional qualifications are needed when the issues to be studied have to do with the human understanding and behavior. Based almost solely on my own experience and not being very confident of my judgment, I suspect that what is also needed is a kind of aptitude.[8] Aptitude may be seen like something one has to have in order to be, for example, an opera singer; that I would never be one was clear when I was ten!

Empathy may be one of the required abilities. Many have a clear knowledge of the feelings of others, especially the psychologists, but empathy is something different. It means to "feel" the Other. "Today there are many definitions of empathy. Most clinical and counseling psychologists, however, agree that true empathy requires three distinct skills: the ability to share the other persons' feelings, the cognitive ability to intuit what another person is feeling, and a 'socially beneficial' intention to respond compassionately to that person's distress." (Decety, p. 19)

Actually empathy has two components/sources: one is the experience (and education) one gets during lifetime and the other, say, the mysteries of the brain. About the first I have some observations but I am reluctant to reach general conclusions based on my limited personal observations. On the other hand, I see no reason not to share my experience with others.

---

[7] This evaluation of my study should not be seen as a repetition of Paul Feyerabend's understanding expressed in *Against Method*. It is an effort to describe a method, but beyond some exclusionary academic approaches causing monodisciplinary isolationisms. Also "looking at it without having a particular discipline in mind" should not be read as Jacques Derrida's "suspension". However, I might have been influenced by similar discourses on an unconscious level, i.e., by E. Husserl and his phenomenology and by the sophists in general!

[8] The word I chose to name what I "suspect" – aptitude – is not so important. I could as well have used words such as talent, gift, competence, ability, frame of mind, inclination, emotional condition, mind-set, personality, emotional quotient (EQ), etc. The *meaning* that I attribute to these words are more important.

Almost all the people that I met who were interested and able in studying cases that were directly or indirectly related to issues of "perceptions"[9] were sentimentally attached to and empathic towards their "subject". These people had been somehow familiar with resembling situations themselves. It was as if they had experienced cases where "perceptions" played a role in their lives. For example, there were brought up in ethnically or religiously mixed families, or in a multicultural turbulent environment, or they belonged to ideologically persecuted groups or to discriminated minority groups or they were ethnically or gender-wise marginalized personalities. When I conversed with them they expressed themselves as if sometimes in their past they had felt uncomfortable under the staring of others.

I often suspected that they chose this "academic field" due to the questions they had in mind for a time. They were not detached, apathetic, impartial and objective researchers. They were involved. The people I met and worked with on the field of "perceptions" in Turkey and in Greece have been active in human and women rights movements; some were ethnically, religiously, politically or sexually marginalized; others leftists, atheists, Jews, Caucasians, Georgians or persons that had married an "Other". Some were "normal", i.e., they belong to the conformist "majority", but their family history was not: There had family secrets that had to do with social marginalization, e.g., refugee grandparents that did not speak the language of the host country or who once had been converted to the "proper" religion of the majority.

Lately I was positively surprised to read that a clinical professor of psychiatry specialized on empathy related her interest to her life experience. On the very first page of her book on empathy she explained how she came to get attached to this field. Her family, migrants to USA after the Second World War, had faced all kinds of persecutions and discrimination during their lifetime: ethnically and religiously. They were "judged" because of their accents. "As a child, I got very upset when my classmates ridiculed others because of things they could not control, such as color of their skins, where they lived, or their family situations." (Riess, p. 1, 2)

The case of Claude Levi-Strauss seems to be of the same category. He was born to French Jewish parents. During the First World War he was assigned as a liaison agent to the Maginot Line. After the French capitulation in 1940, he was employed at a *lycée* in Montpellier, but then was dismissed under the Vichy racial laws. By the same laws, he was denaturalized (stripped of French citizenship). Years later as he narrated (in *Tristes Tropiques*) how he came to become an anthropologist (who fervently tried to show how close people of

---

[9] I will use the word "perceptions" as a shortened substitute to "beliefs, prejudices, stereotypes, images, and the like".

different cultures were, and I suspect, re-constructing his past) he wrote:

> "Anthropology affords me an intellectual satisfaction: it rejoins at one extreme the history of the world, and at the other the history of myself, and it unveils the shared motivation of one and the other at the same moment. In suggesting Man as the object of my studies, anthropology dispelled all my doubts: for the differences and changes which we ethnographers deal in are those which matter to all mankind, as opposed to those which are exclusive to one particular civilization and would not exist if we choose to live outside" (Levi-Strauss, 1961, p. 62).

All these people ought to have felt what othering is. They were sensitive vis-à-vis situations that had to do with "perceptions"; they were receptive to the related findings. On my part, on one hand, I feel reasonably confident of this judgment of mine, on the other hand, I am hesitant. I may be projecting my own history and feelings to others, being myself a minority member with a history of exclusions. And with a family secret: my grandmother from my mother side was a Catholic who had converted to Greek Orthodoxy! Or maybe there are actually very few people who are religiously, ethnically, ideologically, gender wise "pure" and almost all of us are somehow mixed, marginalized and "different". And, therefore, all my observations might have been a coincidental statistical unavoidability.

Whatever the case is, empathy is a complex phenomenon and plays an important role in the study of "perceptions". To understand human beings means mostly to know how they think, feel and imagine. Sociobiology shows that other animals, too, exhibit actions that resemble some social behaviors of humans, such as altruism (Wilson). Frans de Waal showed that monkeys and especially chimpanzees exhibit empathy (De Waal). Neuroscience understands empathy as an innate capability of the human brain that works unconsciously, yet it can be trained for special cases. Neuroscientists have discovered that people scoring high on empathy tests have especially busy mirror neuron systems in their brains. This means that in cases of a "physical/biological anomaly" empathy is hampered. Actually the autistic people are short in exhibiting empathic symptoms (Schuster, Sacks). Daniel Kahneman, too, associates absence of empathy with autism (Kahneman, p. 76).

It is as if neuroscientists and philosophers reach the same "understanding" with respect to the "reality" even though they have different starting points. Some neuroscientists reminded the close relationship between their discoveries of the neurons and especially of the mirror neurons and the philosophical school of phenomenology. For them, philosophers like Franz

Brentano, Edmund Husserl and Martin Heidegger "criticized the classical philosophical approach as being seduced by the holy grail of discovering the very essence of phenomena and thus getting bogged down in musing about abstractions... The phenomenologists proposed to pay close attentions to the objects and phenomena of the world and to our own inner experience of these objects and phenomena (Iacoboni, p.16)."

Looking at the same process from the philosophical point of view we read the following: "Husserl proposed a radical new phenomenological way of looking at objects by examining how we, in our many ways of being intentionally directed toward them, actually 'constitute' them (to be distinguished from materially creating objects or objects merely being figments of the imagination); in the phenomenological standpoint, the object ceases to be something simply 'external' and ceases to be seen as providing indicators about what it is, and becomes a grouping of perceptual and functional aspects that imply one another under the idea of a particular object or 'type'. The notion of objects as real is not expelled by phenomenology, but 'bracketed' as a way in which we regard objects—instead of a feature that inheres in an object's essence founded in the relation between the object and the perceiver."[10]

This scientific explanation of empathy is pessimistic. Especially the absence of empathy is seen as a function of a brain defect or as a special brain case. From the point of any study on "perceptions" where empathy is considered indispensable in order to approach the feelings of people, the issue transcends academic disciplines. It becomes one of a human capacity – an aptitude - which in everyday language may be called being "good natured", "considered" etc. But at the same time it is as if one accepts that some people cannot display empathy due to their "nature".[11]

IMMUNITY TO NATIONALISM

There is an additional non-academic requirement that may be critical in any scientific study of our times, humanistic or social: immunity to nationalism. Our era is one of the nation-states and ethnic groupings. Almost all carry a national identity or at least a citizenship associated to a nation-state.

---

[10] https://en.wikipedia.org/wiki/Edmund_Husserl
[11] This kind of an understanding – to have or not to have empathy or similar feelings - is seen in some wordings of ancient texts. For example, the sayings "Blessed are the poor in spirit" (Matthew 5:3) or "Allah has set a seal upon their hearts and upon their hearing, and over their vision is a veil" (Koran, Bakara 2/7) are as if they mean that some people are doomed due to way they were created! My worry is that, after all these about empathy, one should conclude that in between the two extremes, i.e., the people with empathy and those, say, autistics who do not have that feeling, there should be a wide range of gray area. Which means that when academics are evaluated in matters of "perceptions" and on their related capabilities a scale of empathy will come to the agenda! Some may even think of an "empathy test" in order to employ experts on empathy!

How efficient can ever a researcher be who is a nationalist, or, at least, is under the appeal of national sentiments, in a study on "perceptions", especially ones associated with ethnic issues?

I think the presence of empathy and the absence of national attachment are prerequisites for a successful approach to "perceptions". The good quality of a study dealing with "national perceptions" is directly proportional to empathy and indirectly proportional to national feelings.[12]

I once experienced a surprise that made it clear to me that "seeing" is not as simple as looking! When I finished my dissertation on images, I handed the manuscript for review to a Turkish political scientist and a good friend of mine. In a chapter titled "contradictions and silencing" I had listed various categories of inconsistencies. For example, some writers in their introductions stated that they were impartial since they approached the issues "scientifically" but then they portrayed the Other almost in a racist way; others "missed" or "forgot" important but not flattering historical incidents caused by "us", etc. One category was about the contradictions within a single sentence. In one case, my friend wrote in the margin "I do not see any contradiction". The sentence was this: "[You Greeks] show the basest infidelity to the masters of this noble nation, to the Turks and Muslims who for centuries have shown excess of respect to you and fed you in this country, and whom you served for centuries as slaves..."(Millas, 2005, p. 292). One needs to have empathy and absence of "national sensitivities" to understand how a member of an ethnic group feels when he is portrayed as a "centuries-long respected slave".

I think that a study on ethnic/national issues should not be limited with academic principles and disciplines. It has to incorporate, from the start, the awareness of the identity of the researcher and her way of thinking and feeling. "Scientific approach" does not secure an impartial approach.[13] One may demonstrate this with hundreds of examples: one may think, for example, the big number of scientists and academics who disagree and contradict each other when they act – of course unconsciously - as members of different and rival ethnic/national/religious/ideological groups. This is a well known phenomenon. In these cases "science" may even turn into a pretext, a fallacy and a self-deception.[14]

As of how this kind of difficulties could be dealt with is another issue. But

---

[12] It is self-understood but I still feel the need to add an additional requirement in addition to all other essentials because it is rarely remembered: A successful study requires a certain level of a kind of IQ on the part of the researcher!

[13] By "impartiality" I mean a relative objectivity. No human being can be as impartial as a computer.

[14] Hobsbawm, too, comments on the "nationalist beliefs" of a researcher: "No serious historian of nations and nationalism can be a committed political nationalist, except in the sense which believers in the literal truth of the Scriptures, while unable to make contributions to evolutionary theory, are not precluded from making contributions to archeology and Semitic philology" (Hobsbawm, p. 12).

first I will define some of the terms I will be using.

3- The meaning of words: National / myth

Naturally these words mean different things to different people. For example, some people attribute 1) positive characteristics to "nation/national/nationalism", such as patriotism and love for the home country and its citizens; others may see 2) a negative fanatical ideology; historians and academics have developed other approaches: they see 3) a new historical development and identity related to a new kind of a state, the nation state.

I identify myself with the second and third group, but I am interested in the first. The social developments are mostly shaped by the beliefs of the majorities, especially in democratic societies. There are many myths related to "nation", too, which is the main topic of my present endeavor. Therefore, even though what is true is important, what people believe as true may prove in practice more important and decisive.

NATION/NATIONAL

There are disagreements among social scientists and historians about the definitions and the origin of nationalism and nation-states. For example, according to Ernest Gellner "It is nationalism which engenders nations, and not the other way around… In a nationalist age, societies worship themselves brazenly and openly" (Gellner, 1983, p. 55-56). Anthony Giddens explains that "nationalism feeds upon, or represents an attenuated form of those 'primordial sentiments' … of tribal societies and village communities" (Giddens, 1981, p.193). Benedict Anderson defined nation as "an imagined political community – and imagined as both inherently limited and sovereign"; and elsewhere "as shared feelings of attachments to symbols which identify the members of a given population as belonging to the same overall community (Giddens, 1982, p. 163). (Anderson, p. 15)[15]. Anthony Smith does not agree with the completely "modern" appearance of the nations: "If there was no model of past ethnicity and no pre-existent ethnie, there could be neither nations nor nationalism" (Smith, 1989, p. 214). Seton-Watson sees that eventually all nation-states somehow converge to a resembling model: "I am driven to the conclusion that no 'scientific definition' of a nation can be devised; yet the phenomenon has existed and exists… a nation exists when a significant number of people in a community consider themselves to form a nation, or behave as if they form one" (Seton-Watson, p.5). All these were written in the mid 20th century; Ernest Renan said a similar thing in 1882

---

[15] This definition by B. Anderson indirectly assumes the existence of the Other: by "limited" inferring the line where the other society starts and by "sovereign" the other societies' non-interference.

(Renan).

Among the various academic definitions and explanations of nationalism I have my preferences, but here my intention is to avoid getting involved in these discussions. I will present my own definition of nation/nationalism so that my approach vis-à-vis my main issue, "national myths", becomes clearer. With my definitions I try to give a meaning to some contradictions that I often notice when "nationalism" is discussed. My definition and explanation – this sentence is a tautology! – is what I understand of nation and nationalism.

An old study on the images of Turkey as expressed in the Greek press, on the one hand, revealed a sort of a national consensus on what "Turkey" is, but on the other, there were various fluctuating opinions, influenced by the particular political events of the time. (Millas, 1999). I had then concluded that the first, the general trend, operates within the sphere of (what I called) *consensual nationalism*, i.e., the manifestation of the minimum national consensus that enables the existence of a group (a nation) called "the Greeks". This communality secures the grouping. The second, the varying and fluctuating evaluations, may be seen as a *contingent nationalism*, and it operates as a political program, liable to changes according to local and international contingencies.

Thus there may be short-term different opinions within a nation-state about the Self and the Other, but this "split" does not challenge the first "sphere". Contingent nationalism may elicit sudden and/or frequent changes, whereas consensual nationalism displays durability. For example, a nation may, for a period of time, be willing to fight for a cause and then later may change its program, say, due to a defeat in the front, and decide to be in favor of peace and cooperation with its neighbors. If the groups choose aggression or war sometimes this is called "negative/extreme/racist nationalism." A "program", however, that is peaceful or aggressive does not influence the national identity and the basic beliefs of the nation. The nation and the related national identity continue to exist as before.

Some speak of a "nationalism in the good sense" (εθνικισμός με την καλή έννοια, in Greek - pozitif milliyetçilik, in Turkish) versus "racism" or "chauvinism". Yet, it is more constructive to see national identity as a belief that can incorporate various political programs. With this differentiation in mind, it becomes possible to understand how nations and nation-states change their political targets, also keeping intact their national stories (myths) and all the related feelings towards the "Other": These occurrences take place in different spheres.

National identity is associated with national myths about the "Self" as well as the "Other". In this sense, together with "us", the "Other" also obtains a timeless past. This is why stereotypes about the "Other" persist, even though people declare that they do not feel ill-will towards the "specific/concrete/real" "Other".[16] The specific "Other" is not enough in order to change the image of the "historical/imagined/abstract Other", who forms the basis of consensual nationalism. These two different definitions of national perceptions are helpful in explaining the difference between what is said, on one hand, and what exists "deep below" and actually done, on the other. "Nations" – in this case, the great majority of the Greeks – are far from having transcended their historical beliefs and myths. These beliefs constitute the main dynamics that secures the existence of a nation-state.

How should racism be defined? The political movements that usually are called racist are part of nationalism, precisely of the contingent one.

> "The most important overlaps between the history of racial and of national thought predate and postdate the romantic 19th century. Even before 1800, the concepts of "race" and of "nation" were never rigidly systematized, let alone distinguished, in the different European languages… After 1900, nationalism and pseudo-scientific racism converged." (Leerssen, 2018, p. 76)

Nationalism and racism share a basic belief: the unbroken continuity of the nation. The element that (supposedly) secures this time-long continuity changed during the history of nationalism. Different explanations were proposed. For example, the common "blood", the "language", the "culture" and religion, the "ethnicity", the "consciousness" were some of the constituents that were thought to be the basic reason that preserved the "nation".[17] But whatever the reason is, once an "uninterrupted continuity" is accepted, at least one element that does not change in time has to be accepted, too.

Race is only one of these elements. A racist explanations implies that a community with common characteristics perpetuates its existence through history, unbroken and unchanged. These racist/national characteristics are positive for the "self" and negative for the "Other". Naturally, the same "racist" implications will follow if one substitutes "race" with any of the other "elements", since the "uniformity and the continuity" of the community could be still claimed.

Racism than may be seen as an aspect of contingent nationalism: a political

---

[16] The difference of the concrete versus imagined Other is explained in Millas (2000 and 2001) (see bibliography) under the title "3- Summary of a study on images".

[17] Racists who try to bypass criticism sometimes resort to more "scientific" explanations: They base the continuity of the nation to the "culture" of the nation. This is an unfalsifiable argument because the continuity of the culture needs first to be proven, and prior to that the definition of culture is needed. The continuity of culture is normally "proved" by selecting few traditions, which mostly are "invented".

program with a specific interpretation of the nation(s). In our days, racism is still being practiced, without, however, mentioning "blood", "genes" or "DNA", but instead, other parameters: "national history and tradition", "national character", "national destiny and vision", "national culture ", etc. Also, racism and nationalism may be practiced in a disguised way, e.g., with a Marxist phraseology or by references to religious texts. (Millas, 2008, p.103-105)

The best expression that I ever met in a text clearly disclosing what are consensual nationalism and its related myths, legends and beliefs, is in a paragraph by Ilias Venezis (1904-1973), a well-known Greek novelist. Venezis, who in his novels is impartial when he portrays the Turks, addresses to the Turks in an article, in a period when the two nation states had signed a peace agreement:

"From old times come the memories, the stories and the tears . . . The [Greek] mothers narrated stories of . . . massacres and hunger to their babies to put them to sleep . . . Everything here exists in order to remind us of the past. We are a nation of memories. This is the source of our sorrow and of our pride . . . So we address the other side of the Aegean and we say [to the Turks]: 'If you expect us to forget our history, our martyrs, we cannot do that. But we can do something else which is honest and deep: we may not feel hate. So we will help the brotherhood of nations without wiping our history: On one side we will place our sufferings, our pain that lasted for centuries and on the other side our love for peace…" (Venezis, p.156-157).

Thus, in a single paragraph, the two "spheres", a conciliatory contingent national discourse (love for peace) and classic consensual nationalist myth (centuries-long national pain caused by the Other) can harmoniously coexist.

Summarizing the above, nationalism can be seen as a new historical understanding that secured the unity of a group of people based on a new identity. The old loyalties, such as religious, regionalist, ethnic bondages and attachment to leaders etc., were somehow superseded and the "nations" came to the fore. This *consensual nationalism*, is deeply rooted and exists horizontally in a society/nation as long as there are people who self-identify themselves as members of that nation. This belief is shared by all in a nation, irrespective of these citizens' possible different political, religious and ideological views and visions.[18]

---

[18] An efficient way to understand what consensual nationalism and national identity mean is to think of the absence of these loyalties. When the movement of nationalism had not yet appeared, say in the Middle Ages, the question "what are you?" was not answered by a national adjective: e.g., Greek, English, French,

When the word "nationalism" is used without making this distinction between the two spheres, it becomes difficult to explain how people who are politically and ideologically on different camps, share the same feelings in a football match as they cheer "their" team or when they join the army to fight for "the" homeland. What causes the unity, if it is not the common identity based on consensual nationalism?

In Greece the term "nationalism in the good sense of the word" is heard often. Actually, they refer to a peaceful political program or something akin to that. But the basic constituents of (consensual) nationalism are still there: "we are a superior group with a history of thousand years" – which means some others are not –, "we share some national characteristics which are unique and positive, the ones of the Others are negative"… The Greek national myths are related to both the apparent contingent nationalism and also to the hidden, the unconscious, the consensual one. (Nationalism will be discussed again in the context of myths here below in Chapter 2.)

HOW "MYTH" IS UNDERSTOOD

When I set out to deal with the "national myths of the Greeks" I felt the need to define some words, e.g., national and myth, and to comment on some issues of methods and disciplines. An assessment will follow, but first I have some remarks on "myth", a word of primary importance for my present enterprise.

A few years back a Greek firm advertised a beer that carried the label Mythos, meaning myth in Greek, apparently a "positive" word. Then the slogan "Live your Myth in Greece" was popularized to encourage tourism. Again, in this case, too, "to live a myth" bears a positive connotation. Does it mean anything, though? How does one *live* a myth? Myth here is "positive" probably because it alludes recollections that touch some Greek sensitivities: Maybe mythology (the oldest reference of the nation?), the mythical periods of ancient grandeur, the mythical heroes, even the mythical myths!

So many different things are understood by "myth" that one doubts if it really means anything! According to the Greek dictionaries myth is defined as: 1) A narration of a mythical tradition about real or imaginary events used to explain a phenomenon or a social practice (mind the wide spectrum, from "real" to "imaginary". 2) Allegorical and didactic stories (e.g., Aesop's fables,

---

etc. Other pre-nationalism "identities" were voiced. For example, Christian, Muslim, Greek (speaking) Orthodox, Protestant; or some geographically determined identities such as Cretan, Venetian; or legacies to rulers; or an identity of a relatively small religious or language group: Karamanlis, Sabataist, etc. These were the kinds of "identities" prior the appearance of nationalism, which show what "nationalism" has incurred.

which are named "myths" in Greek). 3) Metaphorically, a (modern) story that is imaginary, not true. 4) Metaphysical way of thinking. 5) The plot of a story (in Greek the novel is called "mythistorima", a "myth-story",). 6. A part of Greek mythology, 7. A false statement, a lie, gossip.

As for the word "mythical", it is understood as "imaginary or false" and as "the one that transcends the normal, in a positive way". The derivatives of myth may bear negative meanings – e.g., mythevma, mythoplasia, mythomania refer to creating false stories - or positive ones like mythistorima (novel) and mythographos (story-writer). The word "thrylos" (close to "legend") is used sometimes as a synonym of myth but solely in a positive sense.

THE HISTORIANS

Internationally and academically "myth" has various meanings, too. In general it means a traditional story, especially one concerning the early history of a people (folk tale, legend, fable) or a widely held, mostly a false belief. Limiting the issue to national myths I noticed that historians may attribute three different characteristics to the word "myth".

1- A story which is false, contrary to historical reality/truth and which is better to be rejected.

2- A story which is needed and useful in order to compose the "grand narrative" (myth of origin) of a nation.

3- As number 2 above, but which is to be correctly defined and historically explained so that nations and nationalism are better understood and confronted and even "nationhood" is transcended.

As an example of the first I present a case from Central Europe. Prof. Herwig Wolfram characterizes "master narratives of historical myths" the way the Middle Ages of Austrians are presented by some dignitaries and suggest that "by realizing and analyzing the fact that these stories and myths are themselves part of history, strategies can be developed to overcome them… If, … one wishes to invoke beginnings in our present day and age, it needs to be the *logical* beginnings and not the myths or 'eternal recurrence' that are actively sought… But it has to be logical, that is, it needs to be goal-oriented, freed from its mythical baggage and isolation, and become scientific through the objectivity developed during the Enlightenment" (Wolfram, p. 237).

The Greek historian Alkis Aggelou, too, in his book *The Secret School*, which is about the story of secretive schools during the Ottoman period which Greek children attended because the Ottomans had allegedly prohibited the study of Greek, calls this story a "myth" and even a "Modern Greek

Mythology". He is clearly against the teaching of this kind of stories (Aggelou, p. 70).

The definition of "nation" of Anthony Smith may be an example of the second group: "A named and self-defined human community, whose members cultivate shared myths, memories symbols, values, and traditions, reside in and identify with a historic homeland, create and disseminate a distinctive public culture and observe shared customs and common laws." Further on it is explained that the "sacred elements of ethnic myths, memories" etc., secure nationalism as a secular religion (Smith, 2008, pp. 19, 46).

The criticism of Chris Lorenz on myths and historiography (the third case) is an "endoscopy": "National historians have not, to any significant extent, reflected on the temporal structure of their histories or on the 'mythical', 'unhistorical' component of historical thinking" (Lorenz, 2008, p.29). Peter G. Bietenholz points to the relation between history and *fabula*:

> "All historical thought is concerned both with things that actually happened – we shall call this here *historia* – and with things that are only supposed to have happened; ... this we shall call here *fabula* (Bietenholz, p. 1)... *Historia* and *fabula* do not part company, They did not in the nineteenth century and probably never will (p. 336)... Michelet's greatest mythical creation was France herself a female collective *persona* he would call *La France, la nation* or *le peuple* (p. 347)... Michelet's Joan [of Arc] was at the same time the reincarnation of Christ and the model of the French nation (p. 349)... Powerful incentives for the retention of historical myths, and even the creation of new ones, came from nineteenth-century nationalism. The potential of mythistory for the nurturing of national sentiment had been discovered in the Renaissance, if not earlier... Politically and ideologically motivated mythmaking would also flourish in the twentieth century (p. 400)... *Fabula* thus is the constant companion of *historia* (p. 404)... [I]t is precisely the necessity to interpret, to digest, to adapt the past to one's needs, which offers an incentive to go beyond factuality or even ignore it" (Bietenholz, p. 405).

Joep Leeressen, too, points to the close relation of historiography and literary creation.

> "The urgent need for a national mythology is manifested most ironically by the art of contrivance: filling lacunae in the cultural record by means of fiction or forgery. Historical novels and occasional speculative flights of fancy in romantic history writing are two modes of patching up the imperfections of positive historical knowledge."

(Leerssen, 2016)

"Historians wrote moral essays, like Michelet, or novels, like the Portuguese Alexandre Herculano. Frequently, their historical work went in tandem with the *imaginaire* of culture at large, in that historians investigated the topics which creative writers were to develop as potent cultural myths. Social and literary myths, such as Robin Hood (King Arthur, King Alfred) in England, Jeanne d'Arc in France, El Cid in Spain, were all developments and spin-offs of sources made available or accessible by historians" (Leerssen, 2008, p. 84). ??

The close relation of historiography and literary creation was often pointed:

"The Romantic views of history was given enduring presence in public space in the form of commemorative … The histories of the Romantic generation perpetuated their allure and vision through their lasting influence on other cultural fields, from the novel and grand opera to the monumental and decorative arts" (Baar, p. 127).

Post-structuralist and post-modernist thinkers like Roland Barthes, Jacques Derrida and Michel Foucault, starting from the 1960s blurred the demarcation line between historiography and literary narrative. The "text" gains prominence to "academic discipline". "Foucault has questioned the traditional generic divisions between literary, historical and scientific texts, particularly with reference to texts antedating that mode of division which belonged largely to the nineteenth century" (Leerssen, 1996, p. 9).

Remaining within the realm of historiography one may remind Hayden White. For him, it is as if history and a story (say a myth) can be evaluated on a literary basis: "[T]he master historians of the nineteenth century wrote history in the modes of Metaphor, Metonymy, Synecdoche and Irony…" (White, p. 428).

On my part, I am not surprised to see that big bookshops still display the books on history and on literature in different sections. This makes sense to me and I can foresee the kind of texts that I will find in each. Still, I see an interesting link between the two. In the cases that I had a chance to study – Greek and Turkish – and in some crucial issues, it was first the novelists that developed the "grand national stories" and then the historians "documented" them. Maybe the main difference between a history book and a novel (which deals with the past) is not so much in the interpretation of the past, but in the *style* used to portray that past.

For example, in the Greek case it was the philologist Spyridon Zambelios (1815-1881) who first voiced the Greek "national narrative" – the uninterrupted existence of the Greek nation through Antiquity, the Byzantine Empire and Modern – and then the historian Konstantinos Paparrigopoulos (1815-1891) turned the idea to a historical thesis. In the Turkish case novelists and short story writers, like Namık Kemal, Ömer Seyfettin, Cevat Şakir and Kemal Tahir inspired Turkish historians to develop various theories on Turkish historical past and national identity (Millas 2001b).

THE ANTHROPOLOGISTS

The anthropologists in general have been more interested in "myths" than the academics of the other disciplines. Their understanding of "myth", however, does not help reaching a consensus on its definition. Anthropologists seem ambivalent as to what a "myth" means. For example, Sir James Frazer (1854-1941), who is considered one of the fathers of this discipline, dedicates many pages to the "myths" of Adonis, Attis, Osiris and Dionysus, he explained how Attis was born miraculously by a virgin, who conceived by putting a ripe almond or a pomegranate in her bosom and how Attis (like Adonis) was resurrected as god (Frazer, 1993, p. 347). He writes that the similarities between these myths and Christianity are many and that the similarity cannot be a coincidence: "it appears that… Christians and pagans alike were struck by the remarkable coincidence between the death and resurrection of their respective deities…" (p. 361). But Frazer does not include the story of Christ in his list of "myths". Also, contrary to his use of the terms "pagan religions" and "myths" for various beliefs, he prefers the word "religion" for Christianity.[19] Other anthropologists see a mythological dimension in the case of Jesus, claiming that there is no historical evidence of his existence (Eliade & Couliano, p. 249/32.2).

An explanation of this inconsistent use of the words "myth" versus "religion" may be that what is still being believed by "us" (and also by those that we acknowledge the privilege to have their own faith, e.g., Islam, Buddhism, etc.) is seen as a "religion", whereas the beliefs of the Others as "myths". If this explanation is correct, then a definition of "myth" may be, simply, "the belief of the Other".[20] I will come back to this issue.

---

[19] See: *The Golden Bough, abridged version* where the issue of Adonis and Attis is identical with the original version of this study: Frazer, 1914. According to Frazer culture passed through three stages, moving from "magic", to "religion", to "science". But what he called "myth of Attis, of Osiris, etc.," are presented as "religions" in his text and they are compared to Christianity (but not calling *this* religion, Christianity, a "myth".) On the issue of beliefs he does not seem to be impartial, but rather bears stereotypes related to "ethnic characteristics": "[Sacred dramas, i.e., death and resurrection of Christ] are well fitted to impress the lively imagination and to stir the warm feelings of a susceptible southern race, to whom the pomp and pageantry of Catholicism are more congenial than to the colder temperament of the Teutonic peoples" (Frazer, 1993, p, 345).

[20] The belief of the Other versus "ours" may be experienced as a confrontation. In that case the words used

Franz Boas (1858-1942), the "father of American anthropology", was a German who emigrated to USA when he was twenty-nine. His grandparents were Jews. He experienced the growing anti-Semitism and nationalism in Germany. In1906, at the invitation of W. E. B. Du Bois, in his commencement address to Atlanta University he said: "Even now there lingers in the consciousness of the old, sharper divisions which the ages had not been able to efface, and which is strong enough to find - not only here and there - expression as antipathy to the Jewish type." Apparently, he was sensitive to the issues of othering like Levi-Strauss that we saw above.

Boas is associated with the movement known as Cultural Relativism. He has been against racist theories, popular in the early 20th century. Boas argued that culture developed historically through the interactions of groups of people and the diffusion of ideas and that, consequently, there was no process towards continuously "higher" cultural forms. He taught that all humans see the world through the lens of their own culture and judge it according to their own culturally acquired norms. Like some other anthropologists of his time he was interested basically in the primitive societies which he approached with interest and understanding.

> "It is vain to try to understand primitive science without and intelligent knowledge of primitive mythology. 'Mythology', 'theology' and 'philosophy' are different terms for the same influence which shape the current human thought, and which determine the character of the attempts of man to explain the phenomena of nature". "In primitive life, religion and science; music, poetry and dance; myth and history; fashion and ethics appear inextricably interwoven... [Primitive man] associates them with other ideas, often of a religious, or at least of a symbolic nature" (Boas, pp. 197-225).

Boas, undeniably an anti-racist of his time, had to cope with Gobineau-like racist theories that propagated the idea of biological racial characteristics and consequently of some superior (white) nations. So he tried to document that all races, the "primitives" included, have their own cultures, but more importantly that this culture was not inferior to what was then called "civilized" and "modern". In a long section titled "The mind of primitive man and the progress of culture" in his book *The Mind of Primitive Man* he challenged many arguments that supported the theory of "advanced culture".

---

to name the beliefs are important. The believers would not like to have the same name for their belief with the belief of the Other. "Myth-versus- religion" is one case. But among Christians, too, the same tendency may occur. Some Greek Orthodox Christians do not want to call their "true belief" a "religion", similar to all the others. They say that "Greek Orthodoxy is not a religion but a communion" or a "revelation", presumably to show their special superiority. See, for example, some Greek Orthodox blogs which voice this opinion: https://agonistes.gr/2018/02/13/είναι-ο-χριστιανισμός-θρησκεία/ and https://www.pemptousia.gr/2013/07/o-christianismos-ine-ekklisia-ochi-thr/

He chose societal values, such as intellect, knowledge, social organization, social strata, poverty, cultural achievements, arts, wealth of inventions, technical skill, tools used, the way achievements are shared in a society, etc., and he used them to defy the "advance theory". He made use basically of two arguments: First, he tried to show that any "positive" trait of the modern man also exists in some remote primitive society, –even though sometimes a little differently to suit the requirement of that society- and second, in cases where a similar trait did not exist in the primitive society, it was argued that that particular trait actually was not needed. For example, the numeral system of the Eskimo which did not exceed the number ten and did not include higher numbers, was explained by the argument that "there was not many objects that they have to count."

And he concluded that mythology and philosophy both explain the phenomena of nature. In this sense, a "myth" is a term of human thought, like philosophy, that does not bear a special different value and essence. The mathematical skills of an Eskimo and of Archimedes both originate from the same source, served the same purpose, satisfying equally the needs of their society. In a sense they were "equal": "We are, therefore, justified in assuming that 15,000 or 20,000 years ago the general cultural activities of man were not different from those of today".[21]

It is true that many human needs were not "different" in the last millenniums; but the way these needs were satisfied varied. Boas, equates (or rather confuses) the human drives and needs with the human accomplishments. There is logic behind this: At an era where the racists tried to prove that human beings were different by birth on a biological basis, and that consequently some races were superior to others, the counter argument appeared as "basically all humans have the same drives and capabilities, there are no communities with inabilities." The key word seems to be the "abilities". With reference to the numerals that do not exceed ten, for example, we read: "[Primitive] Members of a war expedition may be known by name, and may not be counted. In short, there is no proof that the lack of the use of numerals is in any way connected with the inability to form the concepts of higher numbers when needed." This is the rational that equates any Eskimo with Einstein: The theoretical ability is equated to the practical (and historical) accomplishment.[22]

---

[21] Pinker explains clearly our "fear of inequality", i.e., the unwillingness to accept the existence of differences in the social and individual bases, out of our good will to fight racism, but which is contrary to reality, too (Pinker, pp.141-158).
[22] There may be also other ways to "equate" phenomena. Imagine me high-jumping 1 meter and the world record holder 2.45 meters. If one does not compare the outcome but the act itself (jumping), the intention (to compete) and the effort given (the maximum of one's ability) than we are "equal", we do the "same thing"!

The everlasting needs, drives and abilities may be almost the same along the ages; but the different ways that the societies satisfied these innate wants, gave birth to different social structures. Actually, the different approaches in coping with situations can be perceived as different cultural environments.

Boas by choosing to approach societies on the basis of "they are equal" bypasses another sensitive issue: the evaluation of different societies as primitive/advanced or lower/higher. Had he chosen other parameters to compare ancient societies with modern ones, for example, life expectancy, safety in everyday life, medical facilities, etc. he would have to accept that some societies are more efficient and preferable – to human beings of course.

Due to these reservations of mine, the use of "myth" by the "fathers" of anthropology does not seem helpful: it is vague. Below I will refer to Bronislaw and Levi-Strauss and their approach to similar issues, but prior to that, I want to state a peculiarity of the said studies and of the era, i.e., the beginning of the 20th century.

It is correctly stated that past societies and old generations should be evaluated and judged based on their own time and understanding. Indeed, the effort should be in this direction. At the same time, however, it should be recognized that the present-day researcher of the past, faces the same limitation: he judges the past based "on the past time's point of view", but he does that as a modern person. In other words, apart from the intentions, the era one belongs to cannot be ignored as if it does not shape and limit one's judgment. When the present-day researcher judges the past "based on the point of view of that time" she does it based on the point of view of her time and her personal perceptions. To keep this in mind, means to be on the safe side when one reaches to conclusions about the past: the doubt about one's objectivity keeps one at a safer distance from subjectivity.

As for "objectivity", which sometimes with self-confidence is presented and defended as "scientific objectivity", reveals a shortage of self-knowledge. Human beings are not only rational; they are emotional beings, too. For example, for the Nobel Prize winner Daniel Kahneman we are all, humans and other mammals, emotionally driven due to our evolutionary history (Kahneman, pp. 408-418). In connection to that, empathy does not operate upon our will but it acts automatically and when it is expressed "scientifically" it works unconsciously. Some practices of our great-grand parents, e.g., sacrificing prisoners of war to secure sunrise, slave trade, female genital mutilation and the like, rarely can be studied "objectively"; we are not "neutral" in these cases. As modern actors we judge accordingly. In the same token, I confess that, being totally subjective, I marvel "Venus of Milo" and not so much "Venus figurine".

I will close this reference to Franz Boas with a long passage from a speech of his. One may see: 1) how the period we live in influences our understanding and our wording, 2) how in spite of one's self-perception (self-image) one may be something else, 3) how empathy sometimes is directed mostly to the "in-group", 4) how difficult it is to transcend ethnic and religious stereotypes.

Some passages from the opening speech at Atlanta University addressing to "Negro" students in 1906 reveal the "anti-racism" of the early 20th century.[23] My comments are in parentheses. I imagine that some of the students might have "heard" messages akin to what I gathered from the address.

I have accepted with pleasure the invitation to address you on this day, because I believe that the broad outlook over the development of mankind which the study of the races of man gives to us, is often helpful to an understanding of our own everyday problems, and may make clear to us our capacity as well as our duty. ("Races have capacities and duties.")

If you did accept the view that the present weakness of the American Negro, his uncontrolled emotions, his lack of energy, are racially inherent, your work would still be a noble one. ("These are your present weaknesses, but they are not racially inherited.")

While much of the history of early invention is shrouded in darkness, it seems likely that at a time when the European was still satisfied with rude stone tools, the African had invented or adopted the art of smelting iron... It seems not unlikely that the people that made the marvelous discovery of reducing iron ores by smelting were the African Negroes. Neither ancient Europe, nor ancient western Asia, nor ancient China knew the iron, and everything points to its introduction from Africa. ("Your ancestors once had marvelous inventions.")

Domesticated animals were also kept; in the agricultural regions chickens and pigs, while in the arid parts of the country where agriculture is not possible, large herds of cattle were raised. It is also important to note that the cattle were milked, an art which in early times was confined to Africa, Europe and northern Asia, while even now it has not been acquired by the Chinese... The occurrence of all these arts of life points to an early and energetic development of African culture.

---

[23] Atlanta University opened on October 13, 1869. The University offered training for African American students of all ages including kindergarten, grade school, normal, industrial, academy and college.

African ethnology is such that it should inspire you with the hope of leading your race from achievement to achievement. Shall I remind you of the power of military organization exhibited by the Zulu, whose kings and whose armies swept southeastern Africa. Shall I remind you of the local chiefs, who by dint of diplomacy, bravery and wisdom united the scattered tribes of wide areas into flourishing kingdoms, of the intricate form of government necessary for holding together the heterogeneous tribes. (You should not despair, you had a great past.)

In short, wherever you look, you find a thrifty people, full of energy, capable of forming large states. You find men of great energy and ambition who hold sway over their fellows by the weight of their personality. That this culture has, at the same time, the instability and other signs of weakness of primitive culture, goes without saying. (In spite of everything, your culture is a primitive culture, i.e., problematic.)

If, therefore, it is claimed that your race is doomed to economic inferiority, you may confidently look to the home of your ancestors… You may say that you go to work with bright hopes, and that you will not be discouraged by the slowness of your progress; for you have to recover not only what has been lost in transplanting the Negro race from its native soil to this continent, but you must reach higher levels than your ancestors had ever attained. ("You have two problems: first you have been transplanted here and second, you have to surpass your (problematic?) ancestors.")

The physical inferiority of the Negro race, if it exists at all, is insignificant when compared to the wide range of individual variability in each race. There is no anatomical evidence available that would sustain the view that the bulk of the Negro race could not become as useful citizens as the members of any other race. ("The bulk of this race can become "useful" citizens. This will happen in the future.")

That there may be slightly different hereditary traits seems plausible, but it is entirely arbitrary to assume that those of the Negro, because perhaps slightly different, must be of an inferior type.

Even the barbarous hordes of northern Europe, who at the time of the ancient Romans were tribal groups without cultural achievements, have become the most advanced nations of our days. ("So, there were, after all, some barbarous groups in history without cultural achievements.")

The best example [of discrimination], however, is that of the Jews of Europe… Even now the feeling of inequality persists and to the feeling of many the term Jew assigns to the bearer an exceptional position. And this is so, although … in industry, commerce, science, and art, the Jew holds a respected place. ("The Jews, too, were discriminated, *although* they held respected places in many fields. So respect goes with the respected place of each race.")

In France, that let down the barriers more than a hundred years ago, the feeling of antipathy is still strong enough to sustain an anti-Jewish political party. I have dwelt on this example somewhat fully, because it illustrates the conditions that characterize your own position. ("Your position is worse than the Jews', you do not hold respected places.")

You must, therefore, recognize that it is not in your power, as individuals, to modify rapidly the feelings of others toward yourself, no matter how unjust and unfair they may seem to you, but that, with the freedom to improve your economic condition to the best of your ability, your race has to work out its own salvation by raising the standards of your life higher and higher, thus attacking the feeling of contempt of your race at its very roots. ("The present-day contempt is due to the standards of your life. As for the bad feelings against you, in this matter the responsibility rests with you, not the wider community.")

When they [your own people] learn how to live a more cleanly, healthy and comfortable life, they will also begin to appreciate the value of intellectual life, and as their intellectual powers increase, will they work for a life of greater bodily and moral health. (You do not live a cleanly, healthy life; try harder.)

The vastness of the field of improvement and the assurance of success should be an ever present stimulus to you, even though it will take a long time to overcome the inertia of the indolent masses. (If you work hard, in the far future the masses will accept you.)

If, therefore, you want to overcome the old antagonism, you have to be on your watch all the time. Your moral standards must be of the highest. (As black people you have to be on your watch all the time.)

Looking at your life work thus, everything should combine to make you happy idealists. A natural goal has been set before you, which - although it may lie in the dim future - will be attained, if every one of you does his or her duty; in the fulfillment of which you are supported by the consciousness of your responsibility. May happiness and success be the reward of your endeavors! (If you accept your responsibilities in the dim future happiness and success will be your award.)

Boas, no doubt, fought against racism and today's relative improvement is due to people like him. Maybe he was more empathic with the Jews and less with the Blacks who did not hold "respected places" in the society. He was clearly against racism, but I also ponder if he had a clear idea of what national stereotypes were. As for "myths", probably he had some of his own!

Bronislaw Malinowski (1884-1942), another "father" of anthropology, also shows signs of contradictions, on one hand, between his interest for the "primitive" societies with their own cultural values, and on the other, the "higher" capabilities of his own academic trade and, eventually, society. Malinowski was a Polish/Austrian who eventually lived in England and with apparent sensitivity to issues of "othering". His interest was to show the unique culture of different primitive societies mostly of the New Guinea area. Here is how he saw "his role" compared to the natives':

> "The natives obey the forces and commands of the tribal code, but they do not comprehend them; exactly as they obey their instincts and their impulses, but could not lay down a single law of psychology... In our society, every institution has its intelligent members its historians and its archives and documents, whereas in a native society there is none of these (Malinowski, p.17) ... [The natives] have no knowledge of the *total outline* of any of their social structure. They know their own motives, know the purpose of individual actions and the rule which apply to them, but how, out of these, the whole collective institution shapes, this is beyond their mental range... For the integral picture does not exist in his mind [in the mind of the most intelligent native]; he is in it, and cannot see the whole from the outside. The integration of all the details observed, the achievements of a sociological synthesis of all the various, relevant symptoms, is the task of the Ethnographer" ... [who] has to *construct* the picture of the big institution, very much as the physicist constructs his theory from the experimental data, which always have been within reach of everybody, but needed a consistent interpretation" (Malinowski, p. 52).

It is apparent that Malinowski especially esteems his own and his societies' capabilities when these are compared to the natives'. As for the "myth", it seems the Malinowski understands to mean a legend and/or a story that is believed but not true.

"[T]he natives would have a tendency, when meeting with an extraordinary and to them supernatural event, either to discard it as untrue, or relegate it into the regions of the *lili'u*. ["*Lili'u*" is close to "mythical", HM] This does not mean, however, that the untrue and the mythical are the same or even similar to them. Certain stories told to them, they insist on treating as *sasopa* (lies), and maintain that they are not *lili'u*... [T]his distinction is based on the fact that all myths are labeled as such and known to be such to all natives... The supernatural is believed to be true, and this truth is sanctioned by tradition, and by the various signs and trace left behind by mythical events, more especially by the magical powers handed on by the ancestors who lived in time of *lilu's*... Myth has crystallized into magical formula, and magic in its turn bears testimony to the authenticity of myth" (p. 166).

"Thus we can define myth as a narrative of events which are to the native supernatural. In this sense, he knows well that to-day they do not happen. At the same time he believes deeply that they did happen then." (p. 167).

Interestingly, in the mind of the "primitive man" the relation of "true" history and the "fictitious" myth are not differentiated – like a post-modern trend! "All past events are placed by them on one plane, and there are no gradations of 'long ago' and 'very long ago'... the line of demarcation between myth and history does not coincide with any division into definite and distinct period of time" (p.165).

Assessing the views of the "fathers of anthropology" – the "sons and daughter" are different – I reckon the following:

1- The three well-known anthropologists belong to the same era and they died almost in the same year: James Frazer (1854-1941), Franz Boas (1858-1942), and Bronislaw Malinowski (1884-1942). They seem, naturally, to have been influenced by their era:

2- All three focused on "primitive" societies. This seems a direct Jean-Jacques Rousseau (1712 – 1778) and Johann Gottfried Herder (1744 – 1803) influence of romanticism. In search of the human character and societies, the "savage", the "primitive" and the "non-civilized" communities were chosen for their studies.

3- Apart from Frazer, they belong to "out-groups" and they were influenced by their personal histories. I add here Claude Levi-Strauss (1908-2009), too, even though he is of a younger generation. The two were persecuted as Jews and they openly stated their related complaints, pointing to the ethnic/religious prejudices that they had to cope with. Malinowski was a Polish/Austrian who eventually ended up in England and USA. They shared related sensitivities.

4- They coped with the racism of their time and they reacted to it. Basically, they tried to show that the "backwardness" of primitive societies was not hereditary. In their time, the intricate and indirect paths of ethnic othering were not known yet, nor the unconscious expressions of the prejudices. They did not fight against ethnic, nationalist and religious stereotypes *per se*, but rather against the racist understanding.

5- In spite of their good will, and their tendency to stress the similarities of "primitive" societies with the "modern" ones, signs of an unconscious superiority syndrome of the "cultured/superior", or the "Western/white race" can be seen in their texts. In spite of their will, the discrimination of the "primitive" existed in an unconscious level. Indirectly, they voiced the "difference" of the "primitive" from the "civilized".

6- All, in their own ways, stated the "equal status" of civilized and uncivilized societies. They stressed the injustice done by (the racist) looking down upon the "savage" and the "primitive". Some stressed that all societies think the same way and others that "we (the "civilized") have something to learn" from "them". However, they had been ambivalent on the meanings such as "equal", "different", "primitive", "developed", "civilized", "ancient", "modern", "rural", "urban".

7- A similar ambivalence is seen in the case of the meaning of "myth", too. It varied from a "false perception of reality" to "a way of thinking like philosophy".

Claude Levi-Strauss (1908-2009), one of the most important figures of anthropology, precisely the founder of structural anthropology, is of a later generation. He was connected however, with the "fathers" of his domain, James Frazer and Franz Boas. Actually, the latter happened to die in the hands of Levi-Strauss in 1942. As I wrote above, he was of a Jewish family and he had experienced traumatic ethnic and religious discrimination. His work reflects his reaction to these. He tried to show that the differences between human beings and especially between cultures is of a less importance than the structural similarities. He had a universal understanding of Man.

> "Probably, there is nothing more than that in the structuralist approach; it is the quest for the invariant, or for the invariant elements among superficial differences." (Levi-Strauss, 2003, p.6)

To demonstrate that human beings and cultures share similarities to a great degree he emphasized not the existing situations and the end results of the various societies but the "capability" and potential capacity of human beings - just as Franz Boas had done. "The human mind is everywhere one and the same and that it has the same capacities. (2003, p. 15).

What he wrote about the meaning of myth suggests ambivalence. He makes a distinction between the scientific thinking and the mythical one: "We are able, through scientific thinking, to achieve mastery over nature... while, of course, myth is unsuccessful in giving man more material power over the environment. However, it gives man, very importantly, the illusion that he can understand the universe and that he *does* understand the universe. It is, of course, only an illusion" (2003, p. 13) So myths are illusions, but myths of the primitive people are like the thinking of the philosopher and/or the scientist: "[The 'primitive people'] are perfectly capable of disinterested thinking; that is, they are moved by a need or a desire to understand the world around them, its nature and their society. On the other hand, to achieve that end, they proceed by intellectual means, exactly as a philosopher, or even to some extent a scientist, can and would do." (2003, p. 12)

Levi-Strauss tries – through structuralism – to find the order in the societies, which bears a universal validity. This order has to encompass the whole humanity. "[I] try to find an order behind this apparent disorder... It is, I think, absolutely impossible to conceive of meaning without order" (2003, p. 9). In *The Naked Man,* he associates the order with the myths. "[T]he myths tell us nothing instructive about the order of the world, the nature of reality of the origin and destiny of mankind... On the other hand, they help to lay bare their inner workings and clarify the *raison d'etre* of beliefs, customs and institutions, the organizations which were at first sight incomprehensible; lastly, and more importantly, they make it possible to discover certain operational modes of the human mind, which have remained so constant over the centuries, and are so widespread over immense geographical distances" (Levi-Strauss, 1990, p. 639).

The approach of *equating* phenomena by finding some similarities is encountered often in Levi-Strauss' texts. Something what is absurd may hide logic; myths may be both illusions but they may disclose hidden laws, too. "[A]lthough the myths, considered in themselves, appear to be absurd narratives, the interconnections between their absurdities are governed by a hidden logic" (1990, p.687) "No myth or version of a myth is identical with the others... however, taken as a whole, they all come to the same thing and, as Goethe says about plants: 'their chorus points to a hidden law'" (p. 693). The problem is that it is not clear when and under what conditions a myth is an illusion and when an expression of logic and a law.

Once the socially determined purpose, the drives and the needs are the same or similar, the phenomena are associated. If this association is called "same" or "different" depends on the way one defines these words. It is upon each of us to see mythology and history as two *different* or two *same* or *similar* practices. Levi-Strauss writes: "[I]n our own societies, history has replaced mythology and fulfills the same function, that for societies without writing and without archives the aim of mythology is to ensure that as closely as possible... the future will remain faithful to the present and to the past." (2003, p. 36).

The enterprise to demonstrate that "structurally" the myths express a universal logical order is encountered in *The Savage Mind*, too. "The mistake ... was to think that natural phenomena are *what* myths seek to explain, when they are rather *the medium through which* myths try to explain facts which are themselves not of a natural but a logical order" (Underlining in the original, Levi-Straus,1966, p.95). And again, "All these myths of origin of clan appellations are so similar that it is unnecessary to cite examples from other parts of the world" (p. 230). The similarity, on the other hand, is mostly seen not in the myths but in the *medium*; and this medium is open to doubts by those who do not see the "similarities". Words like "similarity" and "different" may be subjectively used. Any social change causes some differences with the past, but it simultaneously means that the new situation bears some similarities with the old, too. Then one may focus at will on one of these two extremes and conclude accordingly.[24] I will comment on similarities and differences below

I tried to show that the approach of the "fathers of anthropology" does not help me have a distinct idea as to what a "myth" is. There is no agreement among them and even sometimes one may notice contradictions in this topic in each of them. Naturally, there is a very wide academic world of anthropologists and one can find all kinds of understandings vis-à-vis myths.

THE PSYCHOLOGISTS

Robert. A. Segal in *Myth: A Very Short Introduction* allocates a chapter on myth and psychology (Segal). He writes: "In psychology, two theories have almost monopolized the field: those of the Viennese physician Sigmund Freud (1856–1938) and of the Swiss psychiatrist C. G. Jung (1875–1961)." He also mentions the followers of the "masters" and their basic books: Karl Abraham (*Dreams and Myths*) and Otto Rank (*The Myth of the Birth of the Hero*), Jacob Arlow (*Ego Psychology and the Study of Mythology*), Bruno Bettelheim (*The Uses of*

---

[24] Think of two sentences – about a village - , both sensible, but showing how arbitrarily the words "similar" and "same" may be used. A) "The rituals in this village give the impression that things run *almost the same way* the last hundreds of years"; B) "The habits of these villagers *somehow changed* the last few years." This is possible because "similarity" exists in a "range" its' limits of which can be drawn at will.

Enchantment), Alan Dundes (*Parsing through Customs*) and Joseph Campbell (*The Hero with a Thousand Faces*).[25]

However, all these "psychologists" belong to the school of psychoanalysis which by many it is not accepted as belonging to the "science" of psychology. Karl Popper, for example, considered psychoanalysis to be a pseudo-science because it has produced so many hypotheses that cannot be refuted empirically (Popper).[26] According to Ernest Gellner "A vigorous debate exists among philosophers whether psychoanalysis is untestable and hence unscientific, or whether it is merely false." (Gellner, 1985, p. 163). There is a wide "anti-Freudian" front, which includes psychologist Steven Pinker, linguist Noam Chomsky and many others.[27]

What interests us here, however, is how this school, and basically Sigmund Freud define "myth". According to his biographer, Sigmund Freud (1856-1939) who lived most of his life in Vienna as a Jew "where anti-Semitism prevailed in professional, academic, and governmental circles", used apart from "myth", words like "fiction" and "phantasy", too; the last one meaning "fictitious experiences" and "psychic reality" contrary to "actual reality" (Jones, 1953, pp. 293 and 266,267). "Myth-making" was seen as a tendency of mankind that built the totems; or "the religious myths – that of reward in the next world for the privations and renunciations in this one." (Jones, 1955, pp. 86, 314). According to his life-long friend, colleague, psychoanalyst and official biographer, Freud believed that "religion might be called a universal obsessional neurosis." Of course, all these theories and terms were perceived and related with an impressive imagination to sex. He could tell, for example, what the primitive man on earth did when he saw a fire for the first time: "Freud postulated that man's first impulse was to urinate on a fire he encountered, and that this symbolized a homosexual act, the rising flame being a well-known phallic symbol." (Jones, 1957, p. 353, 326).[28] It is also interesting to see that Freud used the findings of Sir James Frazer on primitive men but after sexualizing them.

In his *Totem and Taboo* Freud, based on the Australian Aborigines and making wide use of *Golden Bough* of Frazer, in Chapter 1 (Freud, 1990), reaches to an important thesis: "The oldest and most important taboo prohibitions are these two basic laws of totemism: namely not to kill the totem animal; and

---

[25] They are all, but the last one, Jews or of Jewish origin.
[26] Dreams according to Prophet Muhammad are messages from Allah! How can one prove this thesis wrong? Popper points to the requirement of "falsifiability" for each scientific claim.
[27] See, for example: a) https://www.bbvaopenmind.com/en/science/research/psychoanalysis-science-or-pseudoscience/ and B) https://www.ncbi.nlm.nih.gov/pmc/articles/PMC5459227/. C) Misra, Pushpa. D) Crews, Frederick.(in bibliography).
[28] Freud did not tell us how he visualized the first woman who saw a fire for the first time. Did she urinate, having in mind the positional difficulty in her case?

to avoid sexual intercourse with totem companions of the other sex. It would therefore seem that these must have been the oldest and strongest desires of mankind". Further on, he locates the beginnings of the Oedipus complex. His understanding of "myth" is rather commonplace: he uses the word together with and connected to "cult", "legend", "fairy tales", "mythology", "Christian myths", "demons", "primitive animism" and "fantasies".

The same use and understanding of "myth" and "mythology" and their relation with our dreams are apparent in *The Interpretation of Dreams*, too.

"If the Oedipus Rex is capable of moving a modern reader or playgoer no less powerfully than it moved the contemporary Greeks, the only possible explanation is that the effect of the Greek tragedy does not depend upon the conflict between fate and human will, but upon the peculiar nature of the material by which this conflict is revealed. There must be a voice within us which prepared to acknowledge the compelling power of fate in the *Oedipus*... His fate moves us only because it might have been our own, because the oracle laid upon us before our birth the very curse which rested upon him. It may be that we were all destined to direct our first sexual impulses toward our mothers, and our first impulses of hatred and violence toward our fathers; our dreams convince us that we were... [We] become aware of our inner selves, in which the same impulse are still extant, even though they are suppressed" (Freud 1950, p.161).

Going back to Segal's work on myth and psychology – actually on myth and psychoanalysis – one notices basic similarities among all the above mentioned "Freudians" as well as some differentiations on the understanding of "myth" and on other issues which will not be of our main concern here. "Freud's key myth is Oedipus Rex story interpreted as Oedipus who wants to kill his father and sleep with his mother. Here the myth is about the fulfillment of the Oedipus Complex in the male myth-maker or reader, who identifies himself with Oedipus. By identifying themselves with Oedipus, neurotic adult males secure a partial fulfillment of their own lingering Oedipal desires. In this sense myth and dreams exist in parallel. Both Abraham and Rank follow their master in comparing myths with dreams. Jacob Arlow sees myth as contributing to normal development rather than to the perpetuation of neurosis. That is to say, contemporary Freudians take myth positively rather than, like classical ones, negatively. Bruno Bettelheim says much the same as Arlow but says it of fairy tales rather than of myths. Classical Freudians tend to see myths and fairy tales as akin, just as they do myths and dreams. It is contemporary Freudians who contrast myths to fairy tales, but usually they favor myths over fairy tales, seeing myths as serving the ego or the superego and seeing fairy tales as serving the id. Where for classical Freudians myths are like dreams, for contemporary Freudians myths are unlike them. Dreams still serve to satisfy wishes, but myths serve either to deny or to sublimate them. For Alan Dundes myth fulfils rather than renounces or sublimates repressed wishes. Hence it represents id, not ego, for the most part. Dundes delights in demonstrating the hidden, antisocial wishes vented by myths – wishes that are as often anal as Oedipal, as often homosexual as heterosexual, and at times completely nonsexual. Sexual desire for the mother is likewise a means of returning to the womb, not of securing Oedipal satisfaction. Jungians analyze all kinds of myths, not just hero myths, and interpret other kinds heroically. Creation myths, for example, symbolize the creation of consciousness out of the unconscious. For Freud, the unconscious is the product of the repression of instincts. For Jung, it is inherited rather than created and includes far more than repressed instincts. As Rank's hero kills his father and, if usually only latently, marries his mother, so Campbell's hero, even if often in reverse order, marries the goddess and fights, even if not kills, the god."

The above long paragraph is the result of copy-paste form Segal's chapter and by thus summarizing it I harmed the cohesion of the original text. But still it gives an idea of how the psychoanalysts discuss myths: Together with dreams and sometimes with legends and fables, they express the sexual desires – where parents and sons are the actors. Within the Freudian paradigm sexuality, mostly unconscious, sublimated or repressed is the basis of myths. It is clear that the definition of "myth" of the psychoanalysts differs substantially from the definition of any other discipline.[29] Plus, the

---

[29] Having been involved with Freudian analysis, sexuality and subconscious impulses, I think we have, too, the right to look at these matters by trying to guess the subconscious drives behind these ideas. According to his life-long friend, colleague, psychoanalyst and official biographer Ernest Jones, there is a "Fliess Period" in the life of Freud in the years 1887-1902. (Jones, 1953, pp. 287-318). The writer called this period "extraordinary". "Freud destroyed the letters Fliess had written to him, but Fliess preserved Freud's". These letters were saved almost miraculously having passed through various "owners" and E. Jones managed to read them. Fliess, two years younger than Freud, for a long time tried to prove some strange theories. For example he found two numbers, 28 and 23 "the first was evidently derived from menstruation… he laid great stress on the bisexuality of all human beings, and on the whole the number 28 referred to the feminine component, the 23 to the masculine one." Based on these numbers Fliess tried to explain the life of all organisms but also astronomical movements!
Freud met Fliess in 1887 in Vienna for the first time. Their friendship gradually ripened in 1893 and onwards. "The two men met fairly often in Vienna, and occasionally in Berlin, but whenever possible they would meet for two or three days elsewhere away from their work, when they could concentrate on the development of their ideas. Freud half jocularly, half sadly called these special meetings 'Congresses'." In 1898 Freud wrote to Fliess "After each of our Congress I have been newly fortified" and again "No one can replace the intercourse with a friend that a particular – perhaps feminine – side of me demands." Jones evaluates these meetings: "Whatever help the meetings with Fliess gave Freud, it must have been essentially that of psychological encouragement; the purely intellectual assistance could only have been minimal." We know that Freud had an "anxiety attack" in the Berchtesgaden train station in 1890 as he was leaving Fliess after their first "Congress". This friendship ends in 1905 after some ups and downs. In 1912 Freud in a meeting in Munich in the presence of Jones, "fell on the floor in a dead faint". Freud, later, in a letter to Jones mentioned two similar fainting events six and four years ago, adding: "I saw Munich first when I visited Fliess during his illness and this town seems to have acquired a strong connection with my relation to that man. There is some piece of unruly homosexual feeling at the root of the matter."

psychoanalysts do not represent the psychologists.

4- A tentative assessment

If a word has a very wide range of meanings it may not mean much. Its use may not be helpful, either. I started to find out how "myth" is used by the historians, the anthropologists and the psychologists and I ended up with an uncontrolled number of definitions. Apart of the above mentioned various "definitions", I will now summarize the findings of Robert A. Segal, too, to demonstrate that this approach, i.e., trying to find out what has been said about "myth" in different disciplines and within each discipline does not lead to a practical end.

Segal in a text of about fifty thousand words examines how "myth" is explained and characterized in connection to various fields: science, philosophy, religion, rituals, literature, psychology, structure and society. The reader obtains a good picture about what has been said about "myth" in the last decades but I doubt if one gets an idea about what eventually "myth" is. In the introduction the sentence "To analyze a myth is to analyze it from the viewpoint of some theory" is of importance to me. I read it as "what myth is depends on the theory one chooses", which in turn means that if one wants to reach to a definition to one's liking, one only has to choose the appropriate theory the way we choose the color of the curtains in our living room.

For "myth and science" we read that "modern critics dismiss myth for explaining the world as unscientifical." However, "for Creation scientists, it is evolution that is untenably scientific. In any clash between the Bible and modern science, modern science must give way to biblical science, not vice versa." "A much tamer defense against the challenge of modern science has been to reconcile myth with that science." This is done by considering myth "a primitive science". Thus a "modern myth" is considered a self-contradiction. "Tylor subsumes myth under religion and in turn subsumes both religion and science under philosophy...There is no primitive science. Modern philosophy, by contrast, has two subdivisions: religion and science." According to the American anthropologist David Bidney "One reason Tylor pits myth against science is that he subsumes myth under religion. For him, there is no myth outside religion, even though modern religion is without myth. Because primitive religion is the counterpart to science, myth must be as well. Because religion is to be taken literally, so must myth be." Apart from all these there are "those who read myth symbolically, poetically, or metaphorically." "Where Tylor and Frazer subsume both religion and science under philosophy, Lévy-Bruhl associates philosophy with thinking freed from mystical identification with the world." "Where for Frazer primitives use myth in place of science, which, again, is exclusively modern, for Malinowski primitives use myth as a fallback to science." "Where Lévy-Bruhl asserts that primitives seek to commune with nature rather than to explain it, Malinowski asserts that primitives seek to control nature rather than to explain it" "Lévi-Strauss is severely critical of Tylor, for whom primitives create myth rather than science because they think less critically than moderns. For Lévi-Strauss, primitives create myth because they think differently from moderns – but, contrary to Lévy-Bruhl, still think and still think rigorously... Myth is primitive science, but not thereby inferior science." "Popper maintains that there are scientific as well as religious myths... For Popper, science emerges out of myth – not, however, out of the acceptance of myth but out of the criticism of it: Thus, science must begin with myths, and with the criticism of myths."

Segal's study on myth and various "areas" – psychology, science etc – is illuminating in showing the plethora of theories and disciplines on "myth". It does not help in obtaining an opinion of what myth is; only that it is a term that has stirred rival explanations. The section "myth and philosophy" is also rich with contradictory evaluations of what "myth" is called. I will only limit myself to mention few names and a few citations to give an idea of what prevails in this domain.

According to Segal there is a great "array of positions held on the relationships between myth and philosophy: that myth is part of philosophy, that myth is philosophy, that philosophy is myth, that myth grows out of philosophy, that philosophy grows out of myth, that myth and philosophy are independent of each other but serve the same function, and that myth and philosophy are independent of each other and serve different functions." The names mentioned in this part include Paul Radin, Ernst Cassirer, Levy-Bruhl, Hanri and H.A. Frankfort, Rudolf Bultmann, Hans Jonas and Albert Camus. The reader is given the choice to select his favorites. My tentative choice is "mythic thinking is primitive, emotional and part of religion; and there are modern myths which amount to ideologies"

I will not elaborate on Segal's endeavor. My point was to show that the many disciplines, theories and approaches do not lead to a simple understanding of "myth". As Ernst Cassirer wrote:

> "[A]n established authority to which one might appeal no longer existed. Theologians, scientists, politicians, sociologists, biologists, psychologists, ethnologists, economists all approached the problem [of what man is] from their own viewpoint. To combine or unify all these particular aspects and perspectives was impossible. And even within the special fields there was no generally accepted scientific principle" (Cassirer, 1944, p. 39-40).

The reason for this shortage is not very easy to show. There are few possibilities: 1) The "results" may not depend on the method and/or the discipline but on other factors – beliefs, ideologies, various feelings that limit or direct cognition; 2) The different evaluations of "myth" may be an illusion. As I will discuss the matter below, there may be many different phenomena which traditionally are all incorporated in a single word, myth; i.e., we may be discussing unrelated situations under the same title.

Until this point I tried to see and to show how "myths" were understood and treated by various researchers of various academic disciplines. The sources are many but the ones referred above seem sufficient in order to show the main trend: An agreement on the meaning of "myth", even a consensus on this issue seems unattainable. On the other hand, I need to have an initial opinion (a starting point / a working hypothesis) of what terms such as "myths" and "national" mean to deal with the question of "modern Greek myths" – my personal interest. Actually, the truth is that I have a working hypothesis of my own in my mind and this is what triggered my interest to start this study; but the point is to make it understood by other!.

First, however, some "auxiliary" issues need to be clarified. Then, I will propose a "definition" (my definition) of myth and I will propose a "method" to deal with my main issue: The Modern Greek Myths.

TO BE "SIMILAR" / "DIFFERENT" AND STATISTICAL THINKING

The myths are studied as phenomena. They are discussed based on how they came to exist, on what they do, on how they are understood, on what they mean, etc. Some developed theories about myths, others myths about myths. In all cases there is an assumption: That there is something called "myth" or for many some phenomena that are called "myth".

Whereas, they may be various different phenomena that they are named – mistakenly – by a single word, i.e., myth. On the other hand, there are other words that may be associated to "myths", such as mythology, legend, fable, story, etc. Are all these "words" understood in the same way by the "academics" and/or by the laymen? Are they all the same or are they different "things", are they different but with similarities, or are they the same with differentiations; are the similarities small enough to incorporate them under one category or are they different enough so that each constitutes something different? Do these questions make sense or are they irrelevant in a study of myths?

Language, is probably human beings' most important advantage and weapon vis-à-vis the other living organisms. Sometimes, however, it may trap thinking. Meanings like "same", "similar", "different" are words of this kind; and they are often used when dealing with "myths" and other related phenomena.

Limiting the issue to the comparison of the "primitive" societies to the "modern" ones and to the mythical thinking, the dominant argument is (especially among anthropologists) if two societies and ways of thinking are "similar", "very close" or "different" or if they are of "equal value", etc. This "problematic", as was shown above, was expressed by Franz Boas, by Claude Levi-Strauss and by many others. I tried to show that their agony was to fight the racist paradigm of their time which claimed "superior and inferior races".

This argumentation infers a discrepancy which leads this question to a dead end. Probably, the best is to say that this question is a *faute problème* or that it is open to so many answers that it is not of any practical use. My point is that whenever a comparison is attempted two phenomena are assumed:

1) First, that the compared (entities/societies/cultures/myths, etc) are somehow *different,* i.e., they are not identical. A potato is not compared to another potato; unless the other one is somehow different: more sweet or a hotter or a bigger potato, etc. Or in order to be compared it needs at least to be distinct. Any comparison means (assumes) a difference, a substantial one or a small one. We compare different cars to decide which one to buy; we compare athletes to find the best one to award, etc. And when we decide, it means we made a choice between *different* cases. My thinking is based on the assumption/understanding that *similar* does not mean *identical*; on the contrary, any comparison assumes "two" that are "comparable".

2) Second, that the compared (entities, societies, cultures, etc.) are also, somehow *related* or *similar.* They have to have something in common to be compared. No one will ever compare a potato with an astronaut who is in the outer space! We compare similar things, things that can be compared being parts of a *group*: different *cars*, best *athletes*, etc. What is common in these compared "things" is that they constitute a *"category"*: of cars or a *"group"* of *athletes.* The comparison is done within a totality and among entities that are "allowed to be compared". My thinking is based on the assumption that comparisons are possible only between "parts of groups".[30]

In other words any comparison infers that the compared are both different and similar. One may compare a potato to an astronaut if, for example, both are in outer space and they are both considered "two world organisms that

---

[30] Philosophers called this problematic of perceiving generalities, that goes as far back as to Aristotle, "Natural kind". For some this generalization is not a scientific concept, for others it is a useful practice to reach to a scientific thinking. For me it is a practice that needs to be seen how it is used when myths are involved. See, for example https://en.wikipedia.org/wiki/Natural_kind

face a new environment" and that they are out there to check their endurance. In that case both constitute *a category*: *world-organisms*. Again, both will be, in some respect, similar and different at the same time.

The problem starts in the evaluation stage. How do we prioritize these similarities and differences? A primitive society has many similarities to a modern one: e.g., both have families, beliefs (sensible or not); all people love, hate, want to live, etc.; they have a social order, a code of ethics, etc. So, one may conclude that "we are alike", "very similar" or "really close". But the two societies have differences, too: The modern society may have some laws that regulate the family relations, or it may have a police body that interferes in peoples' acts, or technically it may be "very different" using automobiles and smart phones, people there live longer, etc.

The wrong question is "What is the basic, the important, the essential aspect?" Should we prioritize the similarities or the differences as we answer a question of the sort "Are these societies different or similar?" Any either/or answer to this question will not satisfy the objection "but there are differences/similarities, too!"

Immanuel Kant (1724 – 1804) in his *Critique of Pure Reason* (1787) comments on this issue and he criticizes the either/or approach in evaluating social phenomena:

> "This distinction [of seen similarities or differences, HM] shows itself in the different manner of thought among students of nature, some of them (who are pre-eminently speculative) being almost averse to heterogeneousness, and always intent to the unity of genera; while others, preeminently empirical, are constantly striving to divide nature into so much variety that one might lose almost all hope of being able to judge its phenomena according to general principles" (Kant, p. 526).

The either/or thinking is a human trait. We daily take this kind of decisions: I will buy this pair of shoes and *not the other*; I will eventually marry her (totally, not partly!); I will not invite him, etc. These decisions finally are of the sort of either/or; but the thinking that leads to these decisions is not black and white; nor the actual situations. When I buy the pair of shoes, I hesitate between the two pairs because I like both pairs, with a small preference to the one I finally buy, say by a margin 60-40%. Yes, I will marry him, but I like the other guy, too, and it was a hard decision to make! I did not invite him – clear decision – but I regret it later! Life is much more complex than our daily either/or decisions. Statistical thinking is very recent in human history; probably only few thousand years old.

"Why is it so difficult for us to think statistically? We easily think associatively, we think metaphorically, we think causally, but statistics requires thinking about many things at once, which is something that System 1 [our intuitive thinking, HM] is not designed to do." (Kahneman, p. 13) "Contrary to the rules of philosophers of science, who advise testing hypotheses by trying to refute them, people (and scientists quite often) seek data that are likely to be compatible with the beliefs they currently hold." (Kahneman, p. 81).[31]

To equate "primitive" with the "modern" societies, or the opposite, to negate any differences between the various societies of the same species is, according to my understanding a way of thinking that is deprived of statistical capacities. D. Kahneman tried to show the homo sapiens as well as the other animals, due to their evolutionary history, they are programmed to act instinctively when they face "situations"; they did not have enough time to philosophize about. Now, we have. We are able to think calmly about our drives. And having myself transcended (I hope) racism, I am not afraid to compare societies – ancient and modern - and to express my preferences prioritizing my personal likings, too. However, being informed of all the said above, I will do that being conscious that similarities and differences are not on a black and white spectrum.[32]

In any comparison similarities and differences are not of the same importance and magnitude, especially when the case concerns two societies. Normally, the similarities of two human societies are infinite: both are made up of humans who have infinite number of bodily similarities and they have infinite human characteristics. Socially one may distinguish a great number of similarities. But it is the small number of differences that make each society "distinctive" and especially "distinguished". Similarities define totalities; the differences bring forward what is differentiated and what carries a distinct identity. In the Balkans, for example, one may find nations that share the same language, the same history and the same habits; but there may be a singular trait, e.g, their religion, that make them so "different" that they are ready to fight against the Other.[33] A wall is "a wall"; but if one paints part of it then we have "two parts": a painted one and the other. And we can distinguish

---

[31] Above (Anthropologists/ Boas) I showed how one can choose the *capability* of two societies, simultaneously ignoring their different *practical and historical accomplishment* and thus equate them. This is the rationale with which one enables himself to equate – on issues of mathematics - any Eskimo with Einstein.
[32] If there are others who share my evaluations and my prioritizing, we may then, as a group or as part of the society, start thinking that those criteria of ours are "true" and "valid" – we may even attempt to think of models, of methods and of theories!
[33] The "Karamanlis" were Greeks who lived in central Anatolia, they spoke Turkish and shared a life-style similar to the Turks/Muslims of the area. The "Turks of Crete" spoke Greek and lived like the rest of the (Greek) Cretans. These Greeks and Turks had many similarities with their neighbors Turks and Greeks, respectively. Only their religion differed. That was enough to fight to death.

them.[34]

The DNA of Homo sapiens and chimpanzees are almost 99% similar. The 1% makes the difference. If this difference is a big one or a small one is of course debatable. But small differences of this kind enable us to "see" (distinguish) an individual in a group. When we watch an army we do not distinguish the soldiers, but only when we start seeing faces or some who can be differentiated, a tall one, a wounded one, an officer that carries a different uniform, etc. Therefore, not to be inclined to stress the similarities does not mean necessarily "discriminating". The specter of Gobineau should not terrorize us and lead us astray.

I quote from Steven Pinker, known for his work in evolutionary psychology and computational theory of mind: "The fear of the terrible consequences that might arise from a discovery of innate differences has thus led many intellectuals to insist that such differences do not exist – or even that human nature does not exist, because if it did, innate differences would be possible" (Pinker, p. 141). Then he adds: "Modern biology tells us that the forces that make people alike are not the same as the forces that make people different. Indeed, they tend to be studied by different scientists: the similarities by evolutionary psychologists, the differences by behavioral geneticists... We are pretty much alike but we are not, of course, clones" (p. 142).

The question – as I mentioned above – indirectly bears a predisposition to negate the racist understanding that communities can be classified as superior or inferior. About hundred years ago this issue was a heated one. In our days, at least in the academic environment, it is settled. There is no proof that human societies can be "superior" or "with less capabilities".

MYTH AS A WORKING HYPOTHESIS

The word "myth" has many meanings and definitions. "Myth" may mean from a "false story" to a "philosophical metaphor" and form "a lie" to "unifying social story". It may mean the thinking of the primitive man, but also the thinking of human beings in general. It may mean an inadequacy of human thinking or simply human artistic imagination. It may mean primitive society or simple communal behavior. The historians, the anthropologists, the psychologists etc., approach the issue according to their preference.

My understanding (my tentative definition) of "myth" is associated with

---

[34] I think this is what Wittgenstein meant when he wrote in *Tractatus*: "Either a thing has properties that nothing else has, in which case we can immediately use a description to distinguish it from the others and refer to it; or, on the other hand, there are several things that have the whole set of their properties in common, in which case it is quite impossible to indicate one of them. For if there is nothing to distinguish a thing, I cannot distinguish it, since otherwise it would be distinguished after all" (Wittgenstein, 1922, 2.02331).

two concepts: The "Language-game" of L. Wittgenstein and the "Paradigm" of T. Kuhn. Both share the conviction that the meaning of a concept or of a word has a meaning within as system, in a "game" or in a "paradigm". There are studies that associate the two, e.i., Wittgenstein, Kuhn, Hassard. They definitely do not stick to a "universal" definition but they recognize that at times people, societies and academics resorted to various definitions within a "context" in order to explain some phenomena.

According to Wittgenstein this context operates as a language-game. In his *Philosophical Investigations* (1953) he wrote:

> "But how many kinds of sentences are there? ... There are countless kinds: countless different kinds of use of what we call "symbols", "words", "sentences". And this multiplicity is not something fixed, given once for all; but new types of language, new language-games, as we may say, come into existence, and other become obsolete and get forgotten" (Wittgenstein, 2001, No 23).

A central feature of language-games is that a language is used in a context and that languages cannot be understood out of their context. A word has a meaning only within the language-game, and based on the use of the word. Wittgenstein gives the example of "water", which can be used as an exclamation, an order, a request, or as an answer to a question. The meaning of the word depends on the language-game within which it is being used. This word has no meaning apart from its use within a language-game. It depends on what the user wanted it to mean.

Kuhn, a decade after Wittgenstein, defined scientific paradigms as models from which spring particular coherent traditions of scientific research:

> "Men whose research is based on shared paradigms are committed to the same rules and standards for scientific practice. That commitment and the apparent consensus it produces are prerequisites for normal science, i.e., for the genesis and continuation of a particular research tradition... No wonder, then, that in the early stages of the development of any science different men confronting the same range of phenomena, but not usually all the same particular phenomena, describe and interpret then in different ways...When the individual scientist can take a paradigm for granted, he needs no longer, in his major works, attempt to build his field anew, starting from first principles and justifying the use of each concept introduced." (Kuhn, pp. 11, 17, 19).

With reference to the above two approaches to the meanings of the words and of the sentences, the question "what is a myth?" becomes easy (or impossible) to answer: It depends on what one means! The obvious question that follows is "when is what one means true and when is it false?" This problematic opens another intricate philosophical chapter which I will not deal with here. I believe that both Wittgenstein and Kuhn believed that each researcher was confident of his scientific approach and of its truthfulness, but themselves had "doubts". Their entire endeavor was one of doubt. But with confidence to cope with the difficulties, too. Wittgenstein in his *On Certainty* (Wittgenstein, 1969) wrote: "But is there then no objective truth?" (108)... "If you are not certain of any fact, you cannot be certain of the meaning of your words either. If you tried to doubt everything you would not get as far as doubting anything. The game of doubting itself presupposes certainty" (114,115).

Eventually, I will venture *my* definition of "myth" or rather I will list the peculiarities and the characteristics of "myths", as *I* see them: Myths are beliefs. The believers naturally believe in them, as a reality (truth), or as a symbolic act of some social importance. Those who do not share the same belief see a "not-true" story. In short, one's absolute truth is a myth of the Other. The agreements are seen between those who share the same beliefs/understanding.

A corollary of the above is that when we have two sides, A and B, each has her own truth and not-truth. A third party, C, may agree with A or with B (and disagree with the other side). Or she may disagree with both. But she cannot agree with both, if she is sensible. In this study on the "modern Greek myths" I will be sometimes like, say A opposing the beliefs of B and some other times as C opposing both. And in a confrontation of this kind nobody is impartial, irrespective of intentions.

When one claims that an event or an interpretation is a myth, he means that it is also false/not-true. But a myth is something more than a mistaken belief. A mistaken belief may easily be abandoned or changed once new (correct) information is provided. A myth is a belief that operates as a basis for a set of conclusions. And a myth is not a personal or private matter, it is a social phenomenon; it is shared with others forming a community. In other words, a myth is an instrument for preserving an identity. That is why it is more resistant to change.

Yuval Noah Harari uses the concept of "imagined orders" to explain the shared myths. The Sapiens, he writes, invent myths that they are not related to an objective reality but they are still needed to be seen as basic principles? "[Humans] insist that the order sustaining society is an objective reality created by great gods or by the law of nature... [T]he imagined order is not a subjective order existing in my own imagination – it is rather an inter-subjective order, existing in the shared imagination of thousands and millions of people". (Harari, p. 131).

This approach to myths corresponds to what I named above "unifying social story". Harari's conclusion, however, is puzzling: "It follows that in order to change the existing imagined order, we must first believe in an alternative imagined order." This new imagined order is, according to Harari, "more powerful" than the previous one. So he suggests that "a more powerful imagined order, the state… will dismantle the less powerful imagined legal system". "There is no way out of an "imagined order" (p. 133). And as a consequence, no way out of the myths, where in this case myths mean stories that do not correspond to realities.

But what does Harari mean by a "more powerful" imagined order or myth? Is it the more convincing one? Is it the more realistic one? Is it the one that is closer to a reality? Or is it simply the more recent one, the one that is "en vogue" ? And don't we need to answer Wittgenstein who voices a claim in *On Certainty*: "But is there then no objective truth?" (108)… "If you are not certain of any fact, you cannot be certain of the meaning of your words either. If you tried to doubt everything you would not get as far as doubting anything. The game of doubting itself presupposes certainty" (114,115).

I will be given the opportunity to clarify my point (my definition of myth) further below, as my search will develop, as I will be explaining my "method" and again when I will be dealing with specific "myths". For now, I will only claim that I am justified to have my own definition of myth since up to now many others came up with so many.

MY METHOD / METHODOLOGY

The reader who read the above up to this point is probably able to predict with a fair accuracy my methodology. As I tried to explain, I am not inclined to proceed with a "method" that confines a research within the restrictions of a "discipline". A multi-disciplinary approach, on the other hand, even though sounds promising, it is not clearly defined as of its limits and priorities.

What I followed as a "method" to my satisfaction is to start with the questions that trigger a research and let the initial findings open all possible paths to further studies without presuming any preordained discipline and/or method as a guide. All possible knowledge, of any field of knowledge, will be utilized, to the best of the abilities of the researcher, and the outcome will determine the value of the study. Is my conviction that "the more one knows, the many more means one has and the better one thinks" a truism?

I tried to show that it is not the "academic discipline" or the "method" that leads a study, but the questions that initiate it.[35] The way the questions are put, on the other hand, is of foremost importance. Actually, the questions and the way they are put direct the whole endeavor. That is why, when a research is initiated "within" a discipline, the results are also limited by that discipline.[36]

To be honest, any questions put by anybody, and the way they are put, mean much more than what appears on the surface. They show the interest of the one asking, her queries, worries, anxieties, agonies to "find our", and why not, her beliefs and her ideology. Unless the questions are not pseudo-questions, in the sense that they do not correspond to a real need for a "truth" but they are only assigned – e.g., by a supervisor to satisfy a curriculum – to initiate a routine "research", the initial question(s) are the most important part of any study.

One has to consider, apart of course from the final findings, at the beginning and at the end of a study, how and why the whole effort started. Normally, questions are put to find the "truth" behind a phenomenon. But this infers that there is a reaction to the existing "knowledge" in the said field, and/or doubts as of the validity of the current "reality" associated with the questions. In other words, a study is not detached from the researcher. Understanding his work is closely connected in understanding him.

The present study, is *my* study that starts with *my* questions. This point of view should not trigger the problematic of "objectivity". The tens of studies that I referred to above, almost all of them contradicting each other, cannot be attributed to an assumed "objectivity" of the academic proceeds. Being conscious that human beings are often subjective increases the probability for a "more" objective approach. As for any study that is related to ethnic identities, two entities – as I mentioned above - should be kept in mind: the national feeling and empathy of the researcher.

My "methodology" will become clearer as the Greek "myths" will be presented and analyzed below. Actually, at present I do not have a clear idea of what I am going to face and to where I will be driven! That is why I call this work a "study" and a "research". In practice every researcher as she shapes her findings in a comprehensive way constructs her own branch of philosophy of science, of "truth" and her "own method", either by accepting

---

[35] A great part of the confusion as of what a "myth" is arises from the strict boundaries that are imagined in areas such as science, philosophy, various academic disciplines, etc. (See above: "The plethora of academic approaches") Once boundaries are set, then an unproductive effort is generated to integrate complex phenomena within the narrow limits of "disciplines" and "schools".

[36] If the questions differ, the same method and discipline may give different answers; or if the questions are of the same "understanding", then different disciplines will give similar results. We often see that not the disciplines (anthropology, sociology etc.) but the ideologies (Marxism, racism, etc), which ask similar questions give the similar results.

an existing model or by improvising.

I would still like to add few scattered notes that I think are somehow related to the methods and methodologies. I liked the remark by George Box, "all methods are wrong but some are useful". The different disciplines and the tested and currently known methods may prove useful. But this is different than "following" a method from the beginning. That kind of an academic routine will endanger the study, leading it to known paths that may stimulate repetitions, and worse, endangering new and fresh findings. In connection to that I would also like to remind a comment of a statistician: "In general, when building statistical models, we must not forget that the aim is to understand something about the real world. Or predict, choose an action, make a decision, summarize evidence, and so on, *but always about the real world* [my underlining], not an abstract mathematical world: our models are not the reality" (Hand).

***

CHAPTER 1

THREE MYTHS RELATED TO THE ORTHODOX CHURCH

Introduction - One's truth is a myth of the other

If one googles for "national myths", for example for British, American, German, Japanese, Chinese myths, she finds a special kind of stories. For example, in the British case, the legends of the origin of Scottish nation, King Lear, the life of Merlin, the story of Arthur, of Robin Hood, of Lady Godiva. In the American case one finds "folklore stories" on "founding myths", e.g., Columbus, the pilgrims, or the revolutionary war figures like George Washington and some legendary creatures like Pecos Bill (whom I read pathetically when I was about ten). In the German case we see Lorelei, a beauty, who "once" lived on a steep rock on the Rhine and who, like the sirens of Homer, attracted and terminated the sailors. For Bavaria we read that "once upon a time" there reigned a tyrannical king who eventually was turned to stone by a curse. We are all familiar with Pied Piper luring rats away from the city by his music. In the Japanese case we read again the creation myth of Izanagi and Izanami, gods and spirits (kami) and monsters. The Chinese, too, have stories of floods and river Gods, of snake spirits and of immortals.[37]

The Greeks, too, have comparable myths. They have the ancient mythology first and foremost. Let's call all these myths "classical myths". My interest, however, is not in *these* myths but in another kind. The above mentioned myths have some common characteristics: They are accepted as "traditional stories", as "legends", sometimes as "fairy tales", "epic stories", "folk tales", "fables", etc. In each case they are not treated as true stories, as "history", for example. They may be interpreted as "symbolic narratives", or as "parables" or as "allegories", and in this case, they may be somehow associated to a "true past", i.e., to real, actual events. But in this case, too, the story is not read literally.

On my part, I am interested in myths that are accepted as a reality, as true and they are read literally. I am interested in this kind of myths because this case bears ambivalence and is challenging. Most importantly, these "myths"

---

[37] See: Barber, Richard. British Myths and Legends, Edit., London: The Folio Society, 1998. https://en.wikipedia.org/wiki/Folklore_of_the_United_States
https://theculturetrip.com/europe/germany/articles/7-myths-and-legends-youll-only-hear-in-germany/Europe Flame Tree Studios, Japanese Myths & Tales: Epic Tales, Flame Tree Publishing, 2019.
Flame Tree Studios, Chinese Myths & Tales: Epic Tales, Flame Tree Publishing, 2019.

influence social life at a greater degree, since they are seen as actual situations. As Thomas Theorem goes (formulated in 1928 by William Isaac Thomas and Dorothy Swaine Thomas) "if men define situations as real, they are real in their consequences." Let's call these myths "national myths."

On the other hand, a "myth as a reality" seems as an oxymoron. If a story corresponds to a "reality" and is seen akin to a "fact" or to "history", why should one call it a "myth"? It should be seen as "history"! The answer is simple: The one that calls a story "myth" and the one that sees the same story as a true story are different persons. (By the way, it will be me here below who will name various situations as "myths".)

In other words, I am interested in the cases where I see myths where others see true stories. Why do people see different things when they look at the same event? This is another question that triggered this study. In ancient times or in the "old times" myths represented beliefs shared by the totality of a community, or at least by a great part of it. Different communities believed in different myths; but still these myths were shared myths/stories within each community. I am interested in myths that create a controversy, that are disputed and discussed; in other words, in modern myths, as *I* see them.

In short, in this study by "myth" I understand a "non-true" story, a "national myth". However, sometimes the situation becomes quite complex and blurred, bringing to fore an additional dimension. Not only are there cases where I see a (modern and national) myth which I understand as a non-true story when others see it as a reality, but some may see *my* reality as myth! We face a situation where one's truth is a myth of the Other. In this case the questions are not only "what a myth is?" and "what are the modern Greek myths?" but, also "why people interpret situations so differently?"

As a corollary of the above, one may say: For a "myth" to exist, i.e., to attribute the name "myth" to a phenomenon, two features are needed. First, it should be believed (or to have been believed in the past) by some people, and second, it should not be believed by others. If these two traits are not present a "myth" cannot exist. The name "myth", in the sense of "not exactly true", is given by those who do not believe in the particular phenomenon, but it is or it was believed by some.[38]

The relation of (Ancient) Mythology and the present-day Greeks is of this type: Modern Greeks understand Mythology as non-truth stories, as classical myths – they do not see gods on top of the Olympus - contrary to the ancients. If all (or almost all) believe in a phenomenon as true, i.e., if there is a consensus

---

[38] If "myth" is understood/defined as "what you consider a reality/truth, for me is not-true" than other concepts, too, fall under this category: Prejudice, stereotype, conspiracy theories; these are also "you believe in it, not me". This approach to these various concepts is an Occam's razor.

as of its truthfulness, we have a "reality" or "history" or a "religion", but not a "myth". In modern times the name "myth" appears when there is a discrepancy.[39]

Normally, to believe or not to believe in a phenomenon as "true" is associated with other tendencies, too. Once a phenomenon is seen as a reality, it is "accepted", it is even somehow "approved". It is usually seen also as "useful" and/or worth defending; it is "appreciated". The contrary happens with non-true stories: they are seen as false stories, lies and usually harmful. The demarcation line between the two cases are quite clear but, as explained above, in cases where the reading of a myth is seen as a symbolic, figurative or allegorical one, the "degree of its truthfulness" may be unsettled, undecided and debatable.

The modern Greek national myths will be presented and examined below with these questions in mind and within this framework. The "myths" will be related to the beliefs of real existing groups and personalities. Often two groups will appear, say A and B. A "believing" in a phenomenon as true and B not believing in it and seeing it as not-true:

Perception of phenomenon:	as true	as not-true
Group A	YES	NO
Group B	NO	YES

The classification, however, of the modern national Greek myths is not easy. A thematic classification is almost impossible to handle since each myth – as will be shown below – is interconnected with other various themes. A myth related to present-day cuisine recipes, for example, may be connected to Ottoman heritage – what to choose in this case as basis, the recipe or history? – or the myths on sports may be connected to nationalism. A chronological classification, on the other hand, presents problems, too: Is the date that the myth refers to or is its birth date of the myth to be taken as the guide? Eventually, I decided to present the modern national Greek myths according to their importance: First, the basic ones, i.e., the ones that somehow constitute the foundations upon which the less important ones are built. Then the secondary myths and/or the ones believed with a smaller number of Greeks follow.

I will begin, however, with an "exemplary myth", the Secret School, for two reasons. This myth encompasses almost all the characteristics of the national Greek myths: Firstly, it has its fans and its critics, it is quite modern/recent, but more importantly its creation is well documented and it

---

[39] This explains why Sir James Frazer (as explained above – Anthropologists) dedicated many pages to the "myth" of Attis who was born miraculously by a virgin who conceived by putting a pomegranate in her bosom and was resurrected as god, whereas Frazer does not include the story of Christ in his list of "myths", he prefers the word "religion" for Christianity.

has been extensively discussed; and secondly, it will serve to show what all the above discussed theoretical points actually mean. The exemplary myth will give an idea to the reader of what kind of myths will follow.

5- The Secret School: an exemplary myth

We bought a summer house in 1983in Dimitsana, a historical village in the center of the Peloponnesus, which we still have and often visit. There was an old man in the village who used to volunteer to guide the visitors. I heard him narrating the story of the Secret School pointing at a cave on the hill to the south of the village: "There was the Secret School!" In about ten years time the location of this school changed. The old man started mentioning a deserted and ruined monastery of the tenth century - the "Old Monastery of the Philosopher", as it is called. This new location is about eight kilometers from the original one. In the last few years new official traffic signs are placed in various roads showing the direction to the "Secret School". Also a path is paved to enable access because the monastery is in a very remote location. From the mayor of Dimitsana to the young students, almost all in the village "know" that this school once existed.[40]

A traveler in Greece will find many Secret Schools in various locations all around the country. Their numbers keep on increasing the last years, too.[41] Their existence is a "well-known fact" so its proof is not required. Especially history textbooks referred to these schools for decades in relation to the Turkish Rule – i.e., the Ottoman Rule from the 15th to 19th centuries which in Greece is known as Tourkokratia.

According to this myth which is widely known in Greece, during the Ottoman rule the Greek priests and monks used to educate young children in secret schools because the "Turks" had prohibited the teaching of Greek. It was in 1960ies when I first read in a history book by G. Kordatos that this story was a myth: "According to a tradition there were 'secret schools'. This tradition is made up by our teachers. Such schools did not exist anywhere. This is a historical lie... There was no need for secret schools since the Turkish state did not prohibit them." (Kordatos 1957, p. 552). He then enumerated tens of Greek schools of the Ottoman period, mostly started by the newly appearing middle classes, all around the geographic area that in our

---

[40] In the documentary *The Other Town* (2011) we see how the Secret School is discussed among the villagers of Dimitsana.
[41] According to historian Panayiotis Stathis in the decade of 1960 there were eight villages where the existence of a Secret School was claimed and in the 1970's this number increased to 102. These locations attract tourists (Stathis, 2001).

days comprises modern Greece.[42]

I later read that the first to state that the Secret Schools never existed were two Greek historians, Manuil Getheon in 1939 and Giannis Vlahogiannis in 1945 without elaborating, but stating that such schools were not documented and that there was not any relevant historical reference.[43] Much later, the Greek historian Alkis Aggelou, first in 1974 in short form and later in 1997 as a much detailed version published studies on the appearance of this myth (Aggelou 1974 and 1999).[44] According to him, too, there was not any prohibition by the Ottomans for establishing Greek schools and, on the contrary, during the period of the Ottoman rule the Christians had many schools. He then traced the origins of the myth.

According to Aggelou, the myth of the "secret school" started in the first quarter of the 19th century with reference to an anonymous poem – *My tiny moon / light my way / to go to school*, etc. The myth actually started getting its

---

[42] Yanis Kordatos (1891-1961), was a lawyer who dedicated his life to history writing. When he was young he was an active member of the Greek Communist Party. Starting from 1924 he challenged the Greek historiography vis-a-vis the Greek Revolution of 1821, stating that it was not a national uprising against the Turks, but a class struggle against oppressors who happened to be both Turkish and Greek dignitaries and landlords. He published his studies in a hostile social environment, facing fierce opposition and threats, but insisted on professing that modern Greeks were a new nation and not the "continuation" of ancient people. He was the first to use the term *ethnotita* ("ethnic group") to describe the Grecophone communities of the Middle Ages, distinguishing them qualitatively from the modern Greek "nation". The approach of Kordatos, who was apparently influenced by Marxist historiography, was a negation of traditional national paradigm. He published studies on ancient Greece, the Byzantine period and modern Greece, as well as works on such topics as the life of Christ, Greek philosophy and Greek literature. The role of Kordatos as a historian is underrated by the "academia" in Greece for two reasons: In general, because he has a lawyer by profession not affiliated to a university; and specifically by the "left" because he was not in good terms with the Greek Communist Party. For more information see: Millas, 2008, pp.496-498.
Actually Kordatos called the Secret Schools openly and clearly a "lie" in his book on language in 1943: "There were not any secret schools anywhere. This is a historical lie. In the big centers sometimes the priests that happened to be a little educated taught the children of the rich how to read and write and especially how to read. These lessons were given not in proper buildings – the rich people wouldn't spend money for them - but in the churches. There was no need for secret school since the Turkish state did not prohibit them. The 'privileges' of the Patriarchate were numerous since the 'Christian subjects' [ραγιάδες/flock] had full autonomy. Only the middle classes [later] felt the need for schools and then the Greek areas under the Turkish rule turned to a place full of schools." (Kordatos, 1973, first edition 1943).
[43] It is worth noting that the first three historians who opposed the myth of Secret School (Getheon, Vlahogiannis and Kordatos) followed "a lonely road" outside the established academic world (Stathis, 2007).
[44] In 1974 two more academicians, Linos Politis and Dimitrios Pallis, stated that the Secret School is not documented historically. The year 1974 is not a coincidence; it signals the end of the oppressive regime of the "colonels" (1967-1974). Similar views were not tolerated during this dictatorial period.

modern shape by a painting by N. Gyzis (1886), depicting an old monk teaching a number of children and a "kleft" (Greek fighter) looking out for a possible Turkish threat.[45] In 1900 I. Polemis, a well known Greek poet, was inspired by the painting and wrote a poem titled Secret School. The myth was in a sense documented.

The Secret School

Despair stood outside dressed in black

The evident darkness of bitter slavery

And inside, under the vault of the church

The church that every night

Is turned to a school

The scared candlelight

Trembling calls for dreams

Gathering the young slaves.

Dimitsana has been a religious educational center in the Middle Ages and it is famous for its school which operated in the Ottoman period.[46] In 2010 with N.Dinç we filmed in Dimitsana the documentary *The Other Town* that was related to national prejudices vis-à-vis the Other, the Turks. Among other questions, we asked old and young people what they believed about the Secret School. Interestingly, not only almost all of the Greeks that we asked seemed to believe in this myth as a historical reality, but many of them were not even aware that a different opinion in this matter existed and that this story might have been a fabrication. The mayor was unable to explain how Dimitsana could have had a secret school when the town is also famous for the recognized schools it had during the Ottoman rule.

It is an irony that one of the most important natives of Dimitsana, Michail Ikonomou (Kazis) (1798-1879) in his published memoirs refers to the schooling in his town during the Ottoman rule saying: "Education was protected and freely exercised." He mentioned by name eight graduates of the School of Dimitsana, all from different towns around Dimitsana who later obtained important positions as clerics in the Peloponnesus" (Ikonomou, p.

---

[45] Nikolaos Gyzis (1842 – 1901) is one of Greece's most important painters, representative of the Munich School.
[46] Actually there are two monasteries, the "Old" and the "New" Monastery of the Philosopher. The first dates from the 10th century and the second form the 17th century. During the Ottoman period the second was known as a religious educational center. Four Patriarchs of Jerusalem, two Ecumenical Patriarchs (of Istanbul) and many clerics studied in this school.

30).[47]

A visitor to the gunpowder museum of the village whom I asked during our filming if he believed in the story of the Secret School and if he would like to search and find out if it really existed, he gave the most interesting answer that I have ever heard, giving a reason why he did not want to probe into the matter farther: "*If we ever disputed the truth of secret schools wouldn't we also be denying the existence of Ancient Greece?*"

This surprising comment apparently shows how national myths may be part of national identities. Their dispute creates concerns. We will be given the opportunity to discuss national myths and Ancient Greece again. For the moment we may keep in mind that the facts about the past are not only simple matters of historical investigation and discovery. The denial of some historical events or of some myths is related to beliefs. Seen from this point of view, history becomes sacred, and its denial or its challenge may be perceived as blasphemy.

Indeed, the story of the Secret School which for decades was experienced as an "innocent" and pleasant legend associated to poems and folklore, related also to tourist attractions, as we will see below turned to an ideological fight the last 3-4 decades when it was challenged,. Two camps appeared, somehow identified as right and left and/or as for and against the Secret School: A great part of the academic world sees a myth, i.e., a made-up story; whereas some conservative groups, many intellectuals and the Greek Church are for the traditional story. In general, the academics represent a prestigious scientific community, but the conservatives are more numerous and they feel legitimized based on the populous support and the backing of the Church.

A crisis that started due to a school book in 2005-2006 demonstrates the extent of the controversy. A textbook for the 6th grade was prepared by a body of experts headed by Prof. Maria Repoussi. There was a fierce attack against the book mainly for the omission of the contribution of the Church during the last centuries in matters of education and in the Greek Revolution of 1821 against the Ottomans. In this book, apart from the absence of role of the Church in the "national cause", the Secret School was not mentioned, either. The official press release of Archbishop Christodoulos on 10 December 2006 was as follows:

"The Greeks face the danger of losing their national consciousness…
There is an effort to re-write our history in order to demolish the

---

[47] M. Ikonomou was born in Dimitsana, he took part in the Greek Revolution, he had been the secretary to Th. Kolokotronis, the most important military leader of the uprising, and later was active as a governmental dignitary. He published his 900 pages memoirs in 1893. The modern "Library of Dimitsana" published these memoirs anew in 1976.

foundations upon which we base our national consciousness… This book contains unacceptable passages… We yield and abolish everything due to political expediencies… No European power can force us to forget what we are. Why should we, the Greeks, not respect the richness of our history?"

The dean of Athens University Georgios Babiniotis, sided with the Church: "In the textbook of 6th grade of primary school the contribution of the Church in the Greek Revolution of 1821 is completely omitted. Thousand of priests that shed their blood are erased with a single move". The dean also praised the historical contribution of the Secret School.[48] On the 25th March, which is the anniversary of 1821 Revolution, the right-wing organization Chrysi Avgi (Golden Dawn) burned the book in public.

Even the official newspaper of the Greek Communist Paper "Rizospastis", attacked the book, but with "class character" arguments: "All these supposedly progressive efforts are supported by modern Euro-fans who also supported another four-volume book of History of the Balkans, which has been sponsored directly by the State Department of the USA, the foreign ministry of Germany, the foundation of Soros and other similar 'beneficiary' institutes."[49]

Many television and radio programs and many newspapers supported the Secret School block taking a position against the historians and the writers of the textbook. The Academy of Athens, too, upon a question put by the Minister of Education for their opinion, demanded extensive changes on the philosophy of the book. Before the general elections of September 2007, the Minister of Education M. Giannakou promised an improved version of the book. After the elections, however, the setting had changed. Giannakou was not reelected and the new leadership abolished the book.[50]

In summary, and limiting the issue to the secret school, the arguments of the two sides are as follows: First the exponents of the "myth", i.e., those who claim that the Secret Schools did not exist:

1- Historical records that document the school are not found; either of their existence, or of their prohibition.

2- There was no reason for the Ottoman State to prohibit the schools of the Greeks/Christians since they had allowed the existence of the Greeks as a "millet", i.e., as a distinct religious/ethnic group.

---

[48] (7 May 2006) http://www.ecclesia.gr/greek/holysynod.asp?archive=yes&what_sub=d_typou&etos= 2006& id=721
[49] Rizospastis 30 January 2007.
[50] For a detailed analysis of this "textbook crisis" see: Liakos, 2012, pp. 137-160; Millas, 2019b, pp. 269-278.

3- The existence of many Greek schools around the Ottoman Empire is well documented.[51]

The supporters of the Secret School thesis have a different approach to the matter:

1- Some prioritize the oral and popular tradition. For example the children's poem *"My tiny moon / light my way / to go to school"* is seen as a sign that prove the existence of a clandestine night education in the past.[52]

2- The testimony of the existence of legal schools and the related "freedom" rendered during the Ottoman period is disputed claiming that the witnesses were unreliable.[53]

3- The prohibition of the schools is seen as a normal and expected practice since the Ottomans are depicted as liable for similar acts. A different attitude by the Turks is seen as unexplainable.[54]

4- There is often a poetic rhetoric in favor of the existence of the Secret Schools that is difficult to follow. This emotional "argumentation" is, however, persuasive for many. Tasos Gritsopoulos (1911-2008), a native of Dimitsana and a widely read historian and philolog, is one example out of many.[55]

---

[51] See: Vakalopoulos, 1973, p. 306-345 for the rich educational activities of the Christian-Greek communities during the Ottoman period. The last years various historians explain why the Ottomans were not interested in prohibiting Greek schooling which was mostly religion oriented (Patrinelis, 2005, p. 321-336)

[52] See, for example the related evaluation about the Secret School: "The oral tradition very often has a sounder historical basis than written witnesses. Because the myth is the automatic creation of the psyche of the people and it is created without any prejudice." (Papadakis).

[53] For example, some tried to discredit the historian Manouil Getheon (Μανουὴλ Γεδεών 1851-1943) who had written that the Greeks during the Ottoman period had their own schools, by arguing that Getheon was living in Istanbul under the threat of the Turks and that is why he did not dare to write the actual situation. In a religious blog of the "Orthodox Group of Dogmatic Research" (Ορθόδοξη Ομάδα Δογματικής Έρευνας) we read: (https://www.oodegr.com/ oode/istoria/o8wmanoi/ kryfo_sxolio_gedewn.htm): "Those who opposed [the Secret School] based on the pretext rendered by Manuil Getheon and discrediting what they call the 'nationalist' historians', tried to beautify Tourkokratia [the Ottoman rule] in relation to many issues, included education. In this way they opposed the Secret School as "unnecessary" having first baptized Tourkokratia a regime of 'absolute freedom'".

[54] In a study on the Greek (and Turkish) textbooks (Millas, 1991) I showed how the Greek textbooks – which our sons studied at school - presented the Ottoman rule: "It is impossible to imagine a greater catastrophe for our nation than our enslavement to the Turks. The Turks being savages and without civilization were disastrous in their impact, and did not grant a single right to the enslaved nation. (Diamantopoulou, p. 8.) Then it is explained that the Greeks were forcibly converted to Islam, that the churches turned into mosques, that they had to pay heavy taxes 'to stay alive', that they faced 'disgraceful humiliations' and suffered denial of all justice. The last decades the textbooks have a more controlled approach and many stereotypes are superseded. However, the negative image of Tourkokratia in the Greek society is still valid (Millas, 2006). Also the teacher's book for the primary school suggest that the teachers in the primary schools should teach that "the Greeks all thought history favoured education and especially during the years of slavery their efforts were impressive" (Stathis, 2007, p.226).

[55] In an article we read these sentences: "Befittingly the existence of the Secret Schools is questioned. Because [it is claimed] there are not documented historically… We do not need to have evidence of the

5- It is claimed that the official line of the Ottoman state to allow some degree of self-governing to the "millets" varied from time to time and from place to place. So, the historical documents that confirm the existence of Greek schools do prove that in other occasions they were not prohibited.[56]

6- The secret schools sometimes were defined and interpreted in such vague and self-contradictory ways that their non-existence could not be defended: any schooling can be seen as "secret".[57]

7- The oppression of nationalist Turks, mostly the Young Turks, against non-Muslims in the 20th century is anachronistically ascribed to the Ottomans of the past centuries.[58]

Some say that all myths incorporate somehow a small part of a truth! On my part, I conceive as truth – whatever we mean with this word – an understanding not molested with lies; especially with lies that their existence are openly recognized. Truth and reality should be like the oath in courts: all of it and nothing but it. Once truth is mixed with fantasies, and if we are aware of it, it should be on probation.

The above mentioned arguments in favor of the Secret School are based mostly on an evaluation of the character and practice of the Ottoman state:

reason why these informal schools of the first period [of Tourkokratia] have been called Secret, because the People are not accountable, they are the creators of a toponym... Still, this psychological fear of the oppressed people after its subjugation to the barbarians creates its reason, and as a real situation against the terrorists and as a poetic expression, whenever this turned to an expression... There were as many orders of the Sultan to establish Secret Schools as official ones." (SIC). (Gritsopoulos).

These sentences in Greek: Ὀρθῶς ἀμφισβητεῖται ἡ λειτουργία Κρυφοῦ Σχολείου. Διότι δὲν μαρτυρεῖται στὶς πηγές,.. Τὸ γιατί αὐτὰ τὰ ἄτυπα σχολειὰ τῆς πρώτης περιόδου δουλείας ἀποκαλοῦνται Κρυφὰ δὲν ἔχει ἀνάγκην ἀποδείξεως, γιατὶ δὲν λογοδοτεῖ ὁ Λαός, δημιουργὸς ἑνὸς τοπωνυμίου. Ὡστόσο ὅμως αὐτὴ ἡ ψυχολογικὴ φοβία ἑνὸς καταποντισμένου λαοῦ μετὰ τὴν ὑποταγή του στοὺς βαρβάρους ἔχει τὸν λόγο της καὶ ὡς πραγματικὴ κατάστασις ἔναντι τρομοκρατῶν καὶ ὡς ποιητικὴ ἔκφρασις, ὁποτεδήποτε καὶ ἂν ἔγινε ἔκφρασις... Γιὰ τὴν ἵδρυση καὶ λειτουργία Κρυφῶν Σχολείων ἐξεδόθησαν τόσα σουλτανικὰ διατάγματα ὅσα ἐξεδόθησαν καὶ γιὰ τὰ φανερὰ Σχολεῖα.

[56] "During the Ottoman occupation there were officially operating Greek schools established by the private initiative of the Greeks and the Church and this education did not face the reactions of the central Ottoman government. It is, however, considered probable that in certain cases Turkish dignitaries in remote areas might have created difficulties or have forbidden the operation of some schools for various reasons and mostly because school paved the way to the upheaval that the liberation movements created." (https://el.wikipedia.org/wiki/Κρυφό_Σχολειό).

[57] Georgios Metallinos, a well known scholar and priest, in his book titled *Tourkokratia* (Turkish Rule) mentions the school: "[The Secret School], not documented, with respect to its legendary side, has no doubt prestige, in the sense that the organized education which was impossible at that time, is compensated by the humble care of the Church at the narthex of the churches and in the monasteries. Nothing, however, demonstrates officially a usual and systematic persecution of education by the Turks" (Metallinos, p.133). Or "Even though there are historical documents that confirm the existence of the secret schools at a local basis, there are not any related recording in the sources of that time about prohibiting the establishing of schools". (https://el.wikipedia.org/wiki/Κρυφό_Σχολειό).

[58] The mathematician and journalist Mihalis Stoukas (Μιχάλης Στούκας), in an article related to the Secret School reminded what the French journalist René Puaux in 1913 wrote having visited Argirokastro, a town still an Ottoman land at that time: "No book printed in Athens was allowed in the schools of Ipirous... The history of Greece was prohibited. In this case there were additional secret lessons." (https://www.protothema.gr/stories/article/675499/krufo-sholeio-muthos-i-pragmatikotita/)

This state is "negative", e.g., backward and barbaric, so the Greeks suffered, so the problems in education are unavoidable and explicable! This reasoning is not "a little bit" correct. It is simply wrong, or rather, irrelevant. The Ottoman Empire, like all empires of pre-nationalism eras, was not concerned with the languages used, simply because the languages, then, were not associated with nationalism, national demands, disobedience and uprisings.[59]

When the great threat of nationalism appeared and separatist movements made themselves felt with references to ethnic languages the empires reacted accordingly. In the case of the Ottomans these developments happened first in a limited scale when the Greeks appeared with national uprisings, i.e., in late 18th century. The Ottomans turned to full-scale nationalism and harsh measures much later, in the end of the 19th century and especially at turn of the 20th. It was only then that the Greek educational system was attacked by the Ottomans.

A rare, first hand information about the role of "education" in the case of the Greek Orthodox youth highlights the role of language and of education and explains the reaction of the Ottoman nationalists, too. An article titled "The Hellenization of consciousness" written as memoirs by Aggelos Ioanides, a lawyer and a teacher himself, first appeared in an almanac of the Greek School of Istanbul published in 1949-1950 in Athens. In this article Ioannides narrates what happened in the years 1877-1882 when he was in school. Ioannides shows how young boys, starting from "zero" turned into Greeks with national consciousness within a few years.[60] Some excerpts are as follows:

> "[My first day in school.] One would see all kind of boys. A fantastic variety of dresses, of faces and of speaking. Rough boys in coarse dresses (aba in Turkish), with fez on their heads, speaking mostly Turkish, young Anatolians from Kayseri [Turkish speaking Orthodox, HM], islanders from Chios and Mitilini, from Ioannina [Northwest Greece], Europeanized ones, deacons with beards, sons of expatriates from Russia, rich well dressed boys, phanariots with dreamy eyes of well educated families who spoke French. This was the group I met in my class... Anastasios Hourmouziades taught sophisticated Greek grammar the first year... The second year the mixed group became a bit more compact as Hourmouziades taught the 'Ancient Greeks, the Athenians and the battle of Marathon.' There were glimpses in the

---

[59] The empires were keen about other "dangers", such as foreign interventions, social uprisings due to religious affiliations, disobedient local dignitaries, etc., but I will not get in these issues and in the analyses of the empires.

[60] The article is retrieved and published again recently with notes and evaluations by Savvas Tsilenis. The referred school is "The Grand School of the Nation" (Μεγάλη του Γένους Σχολή), in Istanbul.

eyes of the Anatolians and of the bearded deacons… And when he explained why to die for the country (πατρίδα/patrie, HM) is of the same value as to die as a martyr for ones' religious belief, this caused a lot of fuss… On the subsequent years, we were not a group of a variety any more. We had heard [our teacher] Aristocles who explained why the ancient people of Anatolia had declined even though they had many capabilities; but not the virtues of our ancestors, nor their brave character with the spirit of freedom. We heard … Amaksopoulos who drew the parallelism between our folk songs with the epic stories of Homer… We heard our great teachers who taught and formed our characters and when we reached the end of the 8th class and received our diplomas, we were not a group of a variety [κάθε καρυδιάς καρύδι] any more, but we were all of the same kind, good, educated Greeks." (Ioannides).

This is the kind of education that the Young Turks fought: The nationalist education of the very late decades, not the religious education of the Middle Ages. The argument "the Turks prohibited the education of the Greeks because they were worried that once educated they would revolt and demand national rights" is not supported by historical facts. Such as reasoning could not have existed in the 15th -18th centuries. The Turkish oppression on education happened in the 20th century. To attribute the practices of a nation state to an empire is anachronism and means inability to understand both of them, neither the empire nor the nation state. Anachronism, on the other hand, is the essence of nationalism: The supposed 'uninterrupted national character' is not imagined only as a continuum from the past to the present (and to the future), but from the present to the past, too. Once one knows what the Turks have done recently, one can estimate what they ought to have done in the past, too! This sounds a bit racist; and indeed it is.

On the other hand, to concentrate on these arguments and on counter arguments – the Secret Schools existed/did not exist - may lead one to miss the background that augmented the issue and boosted the escalation. If the controversy were only these different "historical" evaluations vis-à-vis the schools' existence a solution or a compromise could be imagined. Or at least the dispute wouldn't be so fierce. But the aggressive and ferocious argumentations indicate that a special basic problematic fosters the controversy: On one hand, each side perceives a malign intention in the point of view of the other, and on the other hand, each side tries to impose a special understanding to the other – or to the third parties and/or to the wider community.

Above we saw the head of the Greek Church claiming that "there is an effort by some to re-write our history in order to demolish the foundations upon which we base our national consciousness." What does this mean? *Who* tries to re-write *our* history? *Why* do they want to do that? *How* can this be attained by disproving the Secret School? *How come* some Greeks participate in this malignant crusade against "our history and national consciousness"? The answers of these questions lead to the basis of the controversy and to the understanding the Secret School issue.

Actually the controversy of the Secret School takes place at three levels. One has to go from the highest, the most apparent one, to the lowest, the most secluded one, to see the whole picture. Then the myth of the Secret School may be utilized as an exemplary case enabling the understanding of the other national myths, too.

The first level, the elementary apparent one is presented above. It is a disagreement on a historical, almost on an academic issue: Secret schools existed/did not exist. The second level is expressed indirectly or it is inferred: There is a fight going on between social forces. It may be seen as conservatives versus progressive (modern) intellectuals; or the Church versus representatives of the Enlightenment; or East versus West; or the old versus the new; or the religious groups versus the secularists; or the average citizen versus the academics; or the traditionalists versus the scientists. It is mostly an ideological and political fight – not a case of historiography. History is in the agenda in the first level. In the second, the arguments are ideologically politicized.

In the second level the two groups are involved in a discrepancy. Some feel challenged due to the new interpretations of the past and the present. They feel that what is at stake is "our history", the reputation of "our heroes", the heroic past of "our nation", of "our Church", etc.[61] The challenges are mutual: First the "academics" influenced by the worldwide academic developments dared to introduce a new interpretation of the past; then the conservative forces saw a threat, an attack on their reputation and even on their rights and their existence and defended their historically gained advantages, their positive image as educators of the nation by insisting on the old story of the Secret Schools; then the academics felt disregarded and even dishonored. Thus we have the two opposing groups. The "second level" of

---

[61] P. Stahis in his convincing presentation demonstrated how the myth of the Secret School survived criticism and kept its popularity. The myth has these characteristics: a) It sounds familiar and persuasive (indeed, the priests once acted as teachers in churches and monasteries, the Church organized teaching, education is "imagined" as a constituent of the Greek national identity); b) It is in tune with the official national ideology (the "barbarian" Turks should be against education), the backwardness of the nation relative to the ancient ancestors is explained by the presence of the oppressive Other, the Church is seen as a protector of Hellenism and the myth is seen as a creation of the "people" and this seems enough for its legitimacy; c) It is accepted by many because it has various readings and its vagueness helps its being adapted to all situations; it helps tourism, too; d) It is repeated by many sections of the community, schooling, media, etc., and these repetitions operate as conviction. (Stathis, 2007).

controversy expresses the fears, agonies and convictions of the parties involved. But, how and why do these feelings occur?

THE SECRET SCHOOL: AN EXPRESSION OF NATIONAL NARRATIVE[62]

The driving force behind the conflict about the Secret School, the "third level", is related to the grand national myth. I already defined my terms above: 3. The Meaning of Words: Nation/myth. I mentioned, too, the definition of B. Anderson, that a nation is "an imagined political community, both inherently 'limited' and 'sovereign'". Both these terms indirectly assumes the existence of the Other. A) The notion of "limited" infers the line where our society ends and some other society starts and B) the term "sovereignty" voices "our" determination for the non-interference the other societies in our affairs. I then presented how the Greek myth – the grand national narrative – incorporates two key concepts: A) our greatness as a nation, B) the Other as the enemy, the problem.

The myth of the Secret School, is an indirect expression of this national narrative. More importantly, I suspect, most (maybe all) national myths are in a similar relation to the grand national narrative. They repeat the national imaginary: "us" as superior and the Other as a scapegoat for our ills or a threat that necessitates (secures?) the union of the nation. Once national myths are viewed under this perspective the myth is read anew, simplified and decoded. The basic constituents of the national self-perception are all present in the myth:

a) We survived as a nation because we were for education, knowledge and culture; we acted as an organized society establishing schools, simple people together with the cultured higher classes and the Church, securing the national union,

b) and all these in spite of the Other (in this case the Turks), the enemy that is a national danger and that renders our unity necessary.

There is logic behind the attachment to this myth. To challenge the myth means to jeopardize the national unity. Who would dare such an endeavor but the enemy of our nation? Why do "they" attack our "history"? "History" in this case refers to the myth. The word "They" refers to our enemies: they may

---

[62] National narrative, grand narrative, grand national narrative, grand national myth or official historiography are expressions that sometimes are used alternatively. Generally, they express the dominant belief about the history of the nation. Naturally, there is not a text that may be presented as such; the national narrative, etc., is an abstraction. The closest text of such a narrative is possibly the history textbooks of the primary schools: they are simplistic and in broad lines they express the superiority of "our nation", its heroic past and the Other, i.e., the enemies that are the prerequisites for a heroic past. It is a summary of what the nation is expected to believe about itself.

be the Turks or the Westerners (the old rivals the Catholics, for example) or the imperialists or the Big Powers or those who are jealous of us. There are some Greeks that join the enemies due to ignorance, but worse, sometimes because of self-interest. This makes them traitors. And then the discussion of similar myths acquires a very serious tone: The issue becomes one of our survival as the nation.

Many national myths, mostly looking disconnected from each other, repeat and reproduce the grand national narrative: "we are superior and there are national enemies around." However, if this is the case, if all or almost all national myths are related to a grand national narrative, then as a hypothesis the possibility that this narrative itself is also a myth, and especially the basic myth that feeds all the others comes to the agenda. This hypothesis operates as a challenge that motivates one to look up for more similar national myths.

6- A Patriarch as a national-martyr

When the Greek Revolution for Independence started in 1821 in the Peloponnesus the Sultan hanged the Greek Orthodox Patriarch Grigorios V (1746-1821) in Istanbul considering him responsible for his rebellious flock. The Church of Greece in 1921 considered him a "national-martyr" and proclaimed him a saint. A national-martyr (εθνομάρτυρας in Greek) is the person who suffered and died for his country.[63]

On the other hand, a small number of Greeks have a different opinion on this matter: They claim that Grigorios was against the Revolution, reminding that the Patriarchate anathematized the revolutionaries. The Greeks who are in favor of Grigorios recognize the existence of this condemnation but counter argue that the act was forced by the Ottoman authorities and/or it was seen necessary to save the lives of the Christians who lived in the Ottoman lands and were under the risk of a pogrom. In an internet site we read (I summarize):

> "There are four different views on this topic. First, some - for example Marxist G. Kordatos, but some conservative politicians like P. Pipinelis, too - claim that Grigorios and the Church were consciously against the Revolution because they opposed the "atheist

---

[63] This Patriarch was born and had his first education in Dimitsana. He did not attend any secret school but the regular religious Greek schools of his time. Sometimes the term "nationalholymartyr" (εθνοϊερομάρτυρας) is also used in Greek.

Hercules Millas | **69**

beliefs of the French revolutionaries." Second, some believe that the excommunication was real but forced by the Sultan, not being a result of free will – therefore void. Third is the view that the anathema against the Revolution was annulled almost immediately and secretly by the Church. The fourth view is that the anathema was a phony one to fool the Sultan. Various historians share these various views." [64]

As it happens with national myths – which are called urban myths, too - the opposed views are defended vigorously. This approach cannot produce a conclusive result, however, since most of these views are hypothetical and speculative. They can neither be falsified and negated, nor proved. How can one decide what the Patriarch thought and how he felt as he signed a decree two centuries ago? One can study all available historical documents and reach an interpretation inferring and/or evaluating but there will always be some margin for refutations.

The present-day thinking behind the arguments for or against the role of a "national-martyr" is of a greater interest and use. The controversy may shed light not so much to what happened two hundred years ago, but rather on how some Greeks think today. When the "sacrifice for the country" of Gregorios is deciphered, the agenda becomes clearer. Moreover, looking at the greater picture may be a more productive approach in understanding the historical role of the Church and the ideological issue of "martyrdom". The almost two millennium long history of the Greek-Orthodox Patriarchate of Constantinople (the Church, from now on) cannot be presented here its history being very rich and complex: religiously, politically, ideologically, but also when seen from the point of view of the individuals involved. I will venture only an outline.

The Church all through the ages faced various enemies but it enjoyed alliances, too. The first clash was with Rome, about who was going to be at the top of Christianity. "Finally in 595, provoked by the claims of Rome, the Patriarch John the Faster took the title of Ecumenical, world-wide. The Pope, Gregory the Great, was naturally indignant and cried that Antichrist must be at hand… In May 1054 once again… the two great pontiffs of Christendom place each other under the ban" (Runciman, 1956, p. 97, 100).[65]

---

[64] https://el.wikipedia.org/wiki/Πατριάρχης_Γρηγόριος_Ε

[65] The present Ecumenical Patriarch Bartholomeos signals two events as the reason of "estrangement" of the East from the West: The mutual anathematizing of 1054 and the Fourth Crusade of 1204 (Clement, p. 27). When the Western Crusaders captured Constantinople, according to the memoirs of Villehardouin terrible things happened: "Then followed a scene of massacre and pillage: the Greeks were cut down, their horses, palfreys, mules, and other possessions snatched as booty. So many was the number of killed and wounded that no man could count them… But by this time it was past six o'clock, and our men had grown weary of fighting and slaughtering… So much booty had never been gained in any city since the creation of the world" (Joinville, p, 91, 92).

In 1453, after the capture of the capital of the Byzantine Empire , the Eastern Church lived in Istanbul for about four centuries under the protective umbrella of the Ottoman State. During these years the Church experienced a number of ambivalent relations.

A) With the "West", the Catholic Rome, the basic controversy continued but there were also efforts by religious figures to reach to an agreement on theological issues that caused the controversy and the big schism. Especially in the 16th century, when the Venetians and the Spaniards were fighting the Ottomans for supremacy in the Aegean area and in the Peloponnesus, the Church hoped, expected and looked for the political support by these forces against the Ottomans.[66]

B) The Church occasionally "flirted" with the Lutheran, the Calvinist and the Anglican movements, as a counterbalance to Catholicism. In these fights the consulates of European states in Istanbul such as England, Belgium, Austria etc., took part in all kinds of intrigues, for or against the Patriarchate. (Runciman, 1968, p. 238-319.)

C) Russia was a different case. Mostly in a military contention with the Ottoman Empire and being religiously Orthodox Christian, Russia was perceived as a natural ally of the Church and the Greeks.

D) On the other hand, the Church lived under the Ottomans, not having an alternative: "[For the Greek speaking Orthodox people] the Sultan's turban was slightly less objectionable that the Cardinal's hat... And, anyhow, would the Sultan allow his Greek subjects to ally themselves so intimately with the West?... The Muslim conquest had not resulted in the disestablishment of the Church. On the contrary, it was firmly established with new powers of jurisdiction that it had never enjoyed in Byzantine times" (Runciman, 1968, p. 237,181).

Under these complex and difficult political conditions, mostly in isolation from the rest of the Christian World and without the protection of a state with which a common religion was shared, the Church of Constantinople – as it was "normal" in those pre Renaissance eras and geographies– was tied to its religious tradition. In the 17th century, when there had not yet appeared the notion of "nationhood" and nationalism, neither the Greeks had "national claims", nor the Ottomans national worries. The Church, naturally, did not call for resistance against the newly formed political situation; on the contrary

---

[66] Some Patriarchs hoped, mostly in the 16th century, for the help from and an alliance with the Venetians and the Spaniards that were in war with the Ottomans: Mitrophanis III (1565-1580, twice patriarch) even met the Pope before becoming Patriarch; Ieremias II (1572-1595, twice patriarch) corresponded with the Pope; Neofitos II, (twice patriarch in the years 1602-1612), wrote a letter to the Pope recognizing his superiority creating the reaction of many Orthodox Greeks; Timotheos II (1612-1621), too, by a letter accepted Pope as the head in Christian hierarchy. (Patrinelis, 1974, p. 94-98).

it saw the Ottomans as a guarantee for the Church. (Patrinelis, 1974, p. 94-96).

The Church of Constantinople during all those long centuries and in spite of some wavering retained its Eastern identity and resisted efforts of conversion to Catholicism or to any other dogma. It preserved also its main policy which was the coexistence with the Ottoman State. The reason was realism and the balance of powers, expressed as "Ἀπόδοτε οὖν τὰ τοῦ Καίσαρος Καίσαρι καὶ τὰ τοῦ Θεοῦ τῷ Θεῷ" (Render unto Caesar the things that are Caesar's, and unto God the things that are God's); the justification was "all were the will of God".

The internally expressed sporadic "deviations" were in each case subdued harshly. The Church showed that it was not willing to tolerate Renaissance-like movements: The Patriarch Gennadios Scholarios burnt the book of Plython Gemistos (1360-1453) which was not in line with the religious dogma but with the "humanist" Antique Greece. In 1572 the Holy Synod excommunicated the Patriarch Mitrophanis III because he made approaches to Rome. Cyrilos Lukaris (1572-1638), one of the best educated Patriarch, was perceived as "too westerner" and suspected of being a "Calvinist"; he had a tragic end, being humiliated and eventually strangled.

Lukaris was from Kriti. He studied in Venice and Padova, visited various European countries like Holland, Germany and Poland, he had close relations with the Protestants, Anglicans as well as the Pope and he corresponded with the Tsar, with various diplomats and scientists of Sweden, England, etc. He was the first to establish a printing press in Istanbul (1626) which was eventually ransacked. He authorized the translation of the New Testament in vernacular. (Patrinelis 1974, p. 129-131; Vakalopoulos 1974, p. 380-381). His close aide Theofilos Korythalefs [Θεόφιλος Κορυδαλεὺς] (1570-1645), a cleric with studies in philosophy and medicine in Padova and who helped in the creation of an educational institution in Istanbul had to leave office, too. (Tsolias, p. 27).

This conservatism of the Church changed substantially when a new philosophy appeared in Europe with the Enlightenment and the French Revolution. The hitherto defensive fights of the Church were against the threats of proselytism, abandonment of the paternal heritage and/or losing prestige; the French Revolution was the turning point for the anxiety of existence. The new philosophy was against religion and especially against religious institutions. The republican revolutionaries clearly declared and put in practice political changes that resulted in confiscating church property and ending the social role of religion.

The Ottoman state, which was in the beginning indifferent when the

French Revolution occurred, was alarmed when Napoleon moved his armies to Egypt and Eastward towards Greece. This conjecture expedited the alliance of the Ottoman State with the Orthodox Church against a common enemy (Patrinelis, 1974b, p. 125). The Patriarchate and its environment published and circulated declarations against the new "atheist" movement, e.g., "The Christian Confession" [Χριστιανική Απολογία], "The Paternal Teaching" [Διδασκαλία Πατρική] and "The Confession of Christianity" [Απολογία Χριστιανική]. The first two were circulated in 1798 and the third one in 1800, twenty years before the Geek Revolution. (Apostolopoulos, Kitromilidis, 1990).

The basic ideas and arguments in these declarations were clearly anti-Enlightenment: The new ideas were against the Christian religion, the revolutionaries were atheists, the idea of freedom was not realistic and the true liberty was attained through the Church, the reign of the Ottomans is God's will and it was this State that secured our existence (Patrinelis, 1974b, p.125 and Dimaras, 1985, p. 97).

However, the actual big fight – the "cold war" or the "World War" of that time - was taken place in Europe between the Republicans on one side and the Royalists in alliance with the Church, on the other. It was the middle classes that opposed the nobility, the *Ancien Régime*. The term "Holy Alliance" was also used for the alliance of the monarchist great powers, Austria, Prussia and Russia that was established in 1815 with the purpose to restrain liberalism and secularism in Europe after the defeat of Napoleon. The role of the Patriarch vis-à-vis the Greek Revolution can be best evaluated having this general picture in mind.

The conflict of the Church of Constantinople with the ideas of the Enlightenment had started earlier than the French Revolution. In the 18th century and as a religious establishment it was natural for the Church to be against the Greek clerics and laymen who were educated in the "west" and were influenced by the "new" ideas of the late 18th century. Some cases show the understanding and practices of the Church vis-à-vis the ideas and the political developments that appeared in the "west" with the movement of the Enlightenment.

- Methodios Anthrakitis [Μεθόδιος Ανθρακίτης] (1660 -1736), a cleric who taught physics, mathematics and philosophy in Western Greece (Ioannina) was forced in 1723 by the Church to appear in Istanbul to explain his position. He later wrote "I am persecuted because I teach philosophy, not because I belong to a heresy as the Church claims." The Church condemned all his work and burned all the copies of his physics and philosophy books. At the end he was obliged to "repent" and condemn all his work and burn his own notes.

He was allowed to teach only the holy texts. Two of his sins were to use the vernacular and to criticize the clergy. (Tsolias p. 31-36)

- Hristothoulos Pamblekis [Χριστόδουλος Παμπλέκης] (1733-1793) who had studied sciences and philosophy in Germany and was a follower of the French "Encyclopédistes" was excommunicated in 1793 (Tsolias, p. 55-77). The Church anathematized his readers and even the priest who buried him, too. Pamblekis might have been a Deist, but he called himself a Christian believer.

- In 1806 the Sultan's order for the extermination of the klefts (Greek bandits) and Kolokotronis, the later commander of the Greek Revolution, was accompanied with the anathema of the Patriarch Kallinikos IV (Kolokotronis, p. 45).

- Rigas Velestinlis [Ρήγας Βελεστινλής] (1757-1798), was a Greek intellectual who tried to organize a (French type) revolution against the Sultan (not against the Turks). He was a follower of the Enlightenment with rich publication activities. Patriarch Grigorios IV, condemns his declaration for uprising in 1798, sending letters to all parishes asking, if seen, to confiscate the declarations of Rigas – characterized "full of rotten ideas" – and be burned (Vranousis, 1963. & Kitromilidis, 1990, p.61).

- Stefanos Doungas [Στέφανος Δούγκας] (1767(?)-1830) was forced by the Church to stop teaching mathematics and philosophy in 1817 and to denounce all his hitherto teachings and what "in his writings was against the Holy Scriptures". He said that all was like experiencing the Inquisition (Karas 1993, p. 76, 82).

- Theophilos Kairis [Θεόφιλος Καΐρης] (1784-1853) a fighter in the Greek Revolution, a professor of mathematics and philosophy, probably a Deist, was seen as a dangerous person by the Church of Greece. He was expelled from the country for his "antichrist teaching" and later was imprisoned. He died in prison. It was not allowed to be buried in proper cemetery. Even his grave was opened and his corpse decimated by unknown people! (Karas, 1977).

One can mention many cases where the Church acted against "the ideas of Enlightenment". For example, Panayiotis Kothrikas [Παναγιώτης Κοθρικάς] (1762-1827) was forced to denounce and stop teaching the System of Copernicus about 160 years after Galileo who in 1633 was forced to do the same and 50 years after the Pope allowed Galileo's books to be published.[67]

---

[67] (Stolias, p. 42). The Inquisition's ban on reprinting Galileo's works was lifted in 1718. In 1741, Pope Benedict XIV authorized the publication of an edition of Galileo's complete scientific works. All traces of official opposition to heliocentrism by the church disappeared in 1835. In 1939, Pope Pius XII, described Galileo as being among the "most audacious heroes of research". On 31 October 1992, Pope John Paul II

Athanasios Psalidas [Αθανάσιος Ψαλίδας] (1767-1829] was accused by the Church for atheism because he taught the views of Voltaire and Rousseau. Panayiotis Sofianopoulos [Παναγιώτης Σοφιανόπουλος] (1786-1856), a doctor and a fighter of the Greek Revolution, was excommunicated by the Church of Greece for his modernist ideas.[68]

It also becomes apparent that the anti-western and anti-Enlightenment position of the Church continued after the establishing of the modern Greek State, both by the Patriarchate of Istanbul and the Autocephal Church of Greece. The anti-Enlightenment policy was not the result of the Ottoman enforcement but an ideological choice. I will come to this issue later, for the moment, it should be noticed that the Church could not have acted differently for an additional reason, too: The proponents of the Revolution were against the Church, in the first place. The controversy was not one-sided.

The books and the leaflets that were circulated by the "modern" Greeks in the beginning of the 19th century and before the Greek Revolution portrayed the Church as corrupt, as backward, in the service of the "barbarous" Ottomans, as enemies and as exploiters of the Greek people and hypocrites in religious belief.[69] These views were in line with the perceptions of the followers of the Enlightenment. Actually the Greek revolutionaries interpreted the eastern Greek political scenery as a replica of the western French society: They assigned to the Orthodox Church the role of the Church played in France and they saw the Ottoman Sultan and the State as "nobility". The Church, after a point, felt the need to defend itself by a counter attack.

The conflicts related to the "new ideas" of the movement of Enlightenment were not limited with the Church. Laymen were criticized, too. Some accused the "Phanariots", the Greek dignitaries of Istanbul and who were in the service of the Port, as being against the idea of a revolution for independence. Korthikas was one example of a Phanariot (Aggelou, 1991). Markos Zallonis attacked the Phanariots in his book published in1824 in

---

acknowledged that the Church had erred in condemning Galileo for asserting that the Earth revolves around the Sun. John Paul said the theologians who condemned Galileo did not recognize the formal distinction between the Bible and its interpretation. (https://en.wikipedia.org/wiki/Galileo_Galilei)

[68] The anathema/excommunication is practiced by the Church of Greece until today. The days I write these lines, May 2020, the retired bishop Ambrosios declared that he anathematized the Prime Minister of the Country, K. Mitsotakis, the minister of education and the deputy minister of interior because they closed down the Churches for a number of days due to the pandemic of Coronavirus. The official Church stated that the anathema is void since this can be done only through the Synod. And they did that in 1987 anathematizing the committee that was assigned by the government to check and tax the Church property. There are many cases of anathematizing the last decades – Roidis, Laskaratos, Venizelos, Aggelopoulos, etc - but these will not be part of our endeavor because here I am interested only in myths, i.e., in cases whose validity is disputed; whereas the cases of anathema are all hard facts, not disputed by anybody, even though criticized by some.

[69] Well known publications are the following: The Anonymous of 1789 [Ο Ανώνυμος του 1789], The Brotherly Teaching [Η Αδελφική Διδασκαλία, in 1798], The Russian-French-English [Ο Ρωσσαγγλογάλλος in 1805], The Greek Law-State [Ελληνική Νομαρχία in 1806].

French: "The Phanariots saw Greece as part of the Phanar [the district where the Phanatiots lived in Istanbul]. There was no home country for them outside this place… As the Greek nation was suffering under the Sultan's humiliation, they turned themselves to the Sultans" (Zallonis, p. 141, 143).[70]

Leaving aside the "personal responsibilities of the historical developments" it becomes highly probable that the anti-revolutionary policy of the so-called "national-martyr" Patriarch is a myth. On one hand, there is a continuous and persistent policy on the part of the Patriarchate (the Church) against the French Revolution and the related ideas, and on the other hand, there is no historical documentation of the Patriarchs' sympathy for the revolutionaries. On the contrary there are documents that point towards the contrary. Apart from the official declarations of the Patriarchate and his letters, we have the official representative of the Austrian diplomacy praising in the years 1797-1799 Grigorios as "a logical clergyman, a fighter against the French ideas and interested in preservation of the order" (Iliou, p. 25)

Why then the myth of martyrdom is reproduced? The short answer is that the issue is not one of historiography, but of ideology. It is also an issue of interest: When the Church feels presently being attacked due to past incidents, automatically it resorts to protect that past. But the policy of the Church will be handled as a whole after we see some more myths related to its "national" role.

7- What happened on the 25th of March 1821 in Agia Lavra Monastery?

Nothing special happened even though people felt very tense in those days. This monastery is in Kalavrita, in a central part of the Peloponnesus. This southern part of Greece was to be the theater of the Greek Revolution. The "Turks" had sensed that the Greeks were

---

[70] The mutual accusations that originated from the parties in conflict, naturally, did not always depict a true picture. Some were one sided or exaggerated the ills or were outright unjust. There are different and positive evaluations of the Phanariots, too (Fokas). What is important is how the parties in conflict saw the roles of the other side and of themselves.

making preparations for an uprising and they were seeking safety in castles.[71] There were some acts of violence the previous days in the southwest and northwest of the Peloponnesus, in Kalamata and Patras, as well as in Kalavrita. Some "Turks" were killed and armed Greeks had appeared in the streets.

Actually the Greeks Revolution was first attempted in February 1821, far from today's Greece, at the boarders of Ottoman-Russian states by Alexandros Ypsilantis. The purpose was to initiate a general uprising against the Ottomans. This effort failed. The second wave of the uprising started in March 1821 in Peloponnesus in an anarchic way and by sporadic attacks in various areas, Kalavrita included. However, the official and well-known story is different. The narration goes as follows:

On the 25th of March, the day of the Annunciation of Virgin Mary, Bishop Germanos raised the "Holly Banner of the Revolution" in the Agia Lavra Monastery, blessed the arms and the revolutionaries took an oath for "liberty or death". This is the official day of the beginning of the Greek Revolution which is celebrated each year. There are various gravures depicting the event that decorate schools and other buildings.

According to Ioannis Grigoriadis in the Greek case there are two events of "inventing tradition" which have a special significance. The first is the Secret School and the second the Agia Lavra ceremony. Both of them "distinguish themselves in terms of fussing the religious and the national and putting a nationalized version of Orthodoxy in the very heart of the Hellenic nation-building project" (Grigoriadis, p. 31).

There is ample evidence that nothing special happened in that monastery that specific day. Germanos himself who later wrote his memoirs does not mention the event. On the 25th he was in Patras, in a city far away (Germanos, p. 14). Other fighters of the Revolution who wrote memoirs did not mention the event of Agia Lavra, either (Kolokotronis, p. 72-73; Makriyannis, p. 22; Trikoupis, p. 74-76). Ikonomou mentions that there was a decision to start the revolution on that day (Ikonomou, p. 88). Westerners that took part in the Revolution, too, testify that the revolution had started earlier than the 25th (Gordon, p. 78 and Finlay, p. 211).

Some western historians who had first hand information having participated in the events do not mention the ceremony at the Monastery

---

[71] I use the term "Turk" in parenthesis because there is a problem with the identities. The Greeks and the "Western" historians and politicians used this term for the Ottomans. The Turkish speaking Muslims of the Ottoman period, however, identified themselves as "Turks" much later, as late as the beginning of the 20th century. The word "Turk", when in parenthesis, points to this anachronism. There is a similar situation with the word Greek, precisely the word "Hellen", to which I will refer further down and in relation to a national myth. "Hellen", too, is used anachronistically for older times.

(Gordon, p. 78; Finlay), as it is the case with various Greek historians, too (Paparrigopoulos, p. 768; Vakalopoulos 1980, p. 328-330; Vournas, p. 84-85). Especially Vakalopoulos gives a very detailed account of the events, making clear how, when and by whom the first steps of the Revolution were taken.

One can imagine why the story of Agia Lavra with a Bishop blessing the arms and starting the Revolution was appropriated and it is still recreated. The story (the myth) of Agia Lavra is popular because:

1- It is appropriated by the Church since in this way the Church is presented as a vital force in the Revolution and in the creation of the new nation state.

2- The people of Kalavrita – who are the ones that are very "sensitive" to any kind of doubt about this story – take a special pride being the "first" among the revolutionaries and they endorse the story.

3- The story presents an event – the Revolution – as an organized process and not as a chaotic series of uprisings.

4- The revolution and the fate of the Greeks and, as a consequence, of the Greek nation is shown as a religious process: A bishop is at the top, the flag carries a cross, the background is a monastery, the oath is religious, and most importantly, the day is 25th of March, the day of the Annunciation of Virgin Mary. On that day Mary received the good news of the son she was going to give birth to; in the case of the Greeks, the good news is the new nation-state to be born.

5- The story was also endorsed by the Greek State and reproduced through the schooling process.

I once tried to show how the story of the Greek nation-building was constructed as a narration similar to the familiar story of Jesus Christ:

There was darkness before Christ and hope after Him, as is the case with the Greek nation: Darkness before the Revolution, i.e., Turkish domination and slavery, but hope for the future. The word Resurrection, *Anastasi* in Greek, is used for the rebirth of the Greek state as well as in the case of Christ. There is a similar cyclical story plot: first a fulfilled life in Heaven (as in glorious ancient Greece), followed by the sin and the punishment (the Ottoman domination), all as a result of divine will due to the sins of the community.[72] Then we have the suffering (of Christ and of the subjugated Greeks) and afterwards the sacrifices (of Christ and of the Greek nation-martyrs). This is followed by the Resurrection, of Christ and of the nation.

---

[72] See for example *Patriki Didaskalia* of 1798, mentioned above, which originated from the Orthodox Church, and the way the Ottoman domination was explained: it was the consequence of not following the orders of Christianity.

Life after death is secured, both for the Christians and for the Greeks (through the "eternal" nature of the nation).[73]

The grand narrative of the Greeks is based on the old religious motif of Christ and therefore it is easily understood by the greater community. The martyrs and the heroes of the nation have suffered for the sake of the continuing existence of the nation, and are thus, like the saints, respected on similar grounds. The national heroes, as we saw above, are called *ethnomartyres*, nation-martyrs. Greek metaphors that describe national sacrifices borrow themes from religious imagery. Heroes die "on the altar of the home country" (*sto vomo tis patrithas*), and historical developments are often presented as predestined.[74] Those who do not agree with the general ideology of the state are treated as traitors, who just like Judas, the student of Christ, have betrayed their benefactor. And all start anew on the 25th of March, on the day of the Annunciation of Virgin Mary (Millas, 2006).

All these are encompassed in the modern history of Greece as a process of "invention of tradition". What is more difficult to understand is how the believers of the official national narrative (a myth, according to me) cope with the arguments of the skeptics. To get acquainted with the counter arguments of the believers that oppose the "historical evidence" of the non-believers may give a clue as what are the dynamics that create and preserve the myths. I will present some arguments that protect and preserve the myths here below. However, before doing that, I think it would be useful to deal a little with the dynamics that enables the preservation of the myths even when they prove not reliable and reasonable.

8- The testimony of the myths.

THE DEFENCE OF A MYTH: CONFIRMATION BIAS

I had the opportunity to teach Greek and Turkish history in various Turkish and Greek universities respectively for about fifteen years and mostly in a context of bilateral relations. The main difficulty in dealing with nationalist prejudices and myths was the resistance of my students to a new and "different" interpretation of the past. When they sensed that what they had already learned as history and on which they had based their national identity was disputed they felt challenged and threatened. History for them was not a story of the past; it was *the* story on which they constructed their

---

[73] According to Hugh Seaton-Watson, "nationalism has become an *ersatz* religion. The nation, as understood by the nationalists, is a substitute of god; nationalism of this sort might be called *ethnolatry*" (Seton-Watson 1977, p. 465). The idea that eternal life is secured for all those who have suffered and persevered (following the example of Christ's sacrifice) is in harmony with the sufferings and sacrifices of the Greek nation.

[74] The verse "it was the will of God that Constantinople should fall into the hands of the Turks" (*Itan thelima Theou i Poli na tourkepsi*) is well known among the Greeks.

being. They either voiced their objection - "what you say makes no sense!" – or stopped communicating in class.

Both Greek and Turkish history education is characterized with some principles and beliefs which are sometimes plainly stated but often inferred, too. The uniqueness of "our nation", its centuries-long existence, its superiority, its past grandeur, as well as its enemies, the "other", are some points of a black and white narration. I knew from the outset that unless I coped with this national "philosophy of history" the best that I could manage was to enforce my students to memorize and repeat what I taught as curriculum but not being able to secure a change in their deeply believed myths.

I tried the following approach with good results:[75] In class there was not the slightest effort or intention of avoiding crucial and sensitive topics of the past since self-censorship may provoke the national sentiments of people who feel proud of the deeds, sacrifices and sufferings of their ancestors and who have been victims of the "other side". Furthermore, the effort of voluntary "forgetting" in order not to aggravate interethnic hate, infers a past that cannot be rationally explained or justified; it is as if one confesses that one is unable to deal with the past of his ancestors or cope with the deeds of his neighbors. Escaping to oblivion may give also the impression of a guilt of the "other" which is pardoned in a hurry and prior to an apology.

Whenever history was in the agenda "change" was the key word. It was always reminded that people, nations and their worldviews, national ideals and targets, ideologies, attitudes, understandings, interpretations, daily life and social values and even racial compositions of ethnic groups change continuously. We tried to talk about the Turks and the Greeks of a specific time and geography. Presenting the other nation as "always positive" is as bothering as condemning it in general. We tried to look at people through other perspectives than their ethnicity. These other perspectives presented striking similarities among members of different ethnic groups.

The relativity and subjectivity of our own personal judgments and values and the influence of prejudices on our actions were discussed. Subjectivity was not conceived as a weakness and a source of doubt and skepticism which could cause reluctance when action was needed. On the contrary, it was presented as a mechanism of an extra check on our values and feelings before an act is taken and which renders confidence and greater assurance. Prejudice is as harmful as ignorance; ignoring the existence of probable prejudice is worst of all.

---

[75] This is a summary of my unpublished presentation in the conference "Cyprus in Textbooks – Textbooks in Cyprus", organized by Georg-Eckert Institut in Braunschweig, 28-30 April 1994. See also: Millas, 2017.

We tried to understand the motives of the people in the past. We mostly agreed that we in our times - with our present values - would have acted differently. We praised tolerance which was defined as respect to others, to their ideals, needs, fears, sensitivities, dreams, aspirations, weaknesses; respect to all these, especially if they do not directly harm us. We made some jokes with some national "sensitivities" but we were not ironical or cynical about them. We learned – in class - to feel even more proud and superior, personally and as a nation, having been able to accept some of "our" faults and deficiencies. Self criticism was turned to a means for self-esteem. I spent more time discussing all these matters than speaking about what happened in the past.

The most useful approach in dealing with myths, however, was the use of the "other" as a historical example. I explained the nation-building of the Greeks to the Turks and the nation-building of the Turks to the Greeks. After a while some students in class would comment: "Doesn't this resemble to our case, sir?" I did not show them their myths, they discovered them themselves! My students were not "challenged" vis-à-vis their beliefs. There were no attempts to demonstrate how one's identity was a historical construction: this would have been perceived as an offense and would have triggered reactions. They believed that they found out this by themselves by studying the "other". This heuristic approach proved very efficient. I did not feel any opposition from my students.

When I experienced this teaching (in the years 1990-2010) I was not aware of the terms "confirmation bias" and "boomerang effect". These theoretical formulations are related to some human traits. Indeed, this tendency of ours (of sapiens), was even noticed by Thucydides (460-400 BC) 24 centuries ago: "They thought that there was no danger, for they had under-estimated the Athenian power, which afterwards proved its greatness and the magnitude of their mistake; they judged rather by their own illusive wishes than by the safe rule of prudence. *For such is the manner of men; what they like is always seen by them in the light of unreflecting hope, what they dislike they peremptorily set aside by an arbitrary conclusion"* (Thucydides).

Human beings are less "rational" than what they think they are. Especially when emotionally charged issues such as religious or national beliefs and myths are to be confronted, "confirmation bias" is introduced as a "method" of reasoning: This tendency is to search for, interpret and remember information in a way that confirms one's prior beliefs and values.[76] Since all human conditions and experiences are complex and rich in variations one easily can choose the data that suits one's thesis, discarding or omitting or

---

[76] I dealt with the emotional side of sapiens above in another context, too : 4- A tentative assessment. TO BE "SIMILAR"/ "DIFFERENT" AND STATISTICAL THINKING.

"forgetting" or considering secondary all date and facts that are contrary to one's beliefs and convictions. Thus, this biased approach, confirmation bias, is used to defend, reproduce and conserve any preferred belief and myth.

Individuals are inclined to search for information that is consistent, rather than inconsistent, with their personal beliefs. Experts claim that people who are more confident in themselves seek out contradictory information to their personal position to check an argument. Individuals with low confidence levels are happy with "confirming" information. Therefore, two individuals may have the same information but they may interpret it differently and in accord to their bias. Another way of "defending" a belief is to demand higher standards of evidence for hypotheses that go against their current expectations ("disconfirmation bias"), whereas they are satisfied with a "simple" and doubtful data when the case is to confirm one's own belief.

These mechanisms are quite complex, still not clearly understood and they are related to human feelings rather to calm conscious approaches. Various tests and investigations show that confirmation bias is not directly related to errors of reasoning or to levels of intelligence or to hypocritical behavior. The phenomenon may even appear in the field of science, for example, in a "peer review" phase which can have a mitigating effect on innovators being accused for their opposing evidence if judged "too weak" by a scientific group. Absence of open-mindedness, i.e., of not searching the reason "why an initial idea may be wrong" may be the result of the kind of education and of a cultural trend. People in general prefer positive thoughts over negative ones ("Pollyanna principle") and desired arguments are more likely to be believed true. Sometimes, as a safer choice, they prefer to accept a probable false hypothesis instead of rejecting a probable true hypothesis. All these work in the same direction: in safeguarding a belief or a myth.

Is confirmation bias, this human tendency, a new discovery? No, even Thucydides had sensed it centuries ago. But confirmation bias and this shortcoming of "ours" were ignored all through history. "We" preferred to believe that we are objective actors in a rational environment. I was impressed that Francis Bacon (1561–1626) who in his *Novum Organum* (in 1620) wrote almost all about confirmation bias:

> XLVI. The human understanding, *when any proposition has been once laid down* (either from general admission and belief, or from the pleasure it affords*), forces everything else to add fresh support and confirmation; and although most cogent and abundant instances may exist to the contrary,* yet either does not observe or *despises them, or gets rid of and rejects them* by some distinction, with violent and injurious prejudice, rather than sacrifice the authority of its first conclusions. It was well answered by him who

was shown in a temple the votive tablets suspended by such as had escaped the peril of shipwreck, and was pressed as to whether he would then recognize the power of the gods, by an inquiry. 'But where are the portraits of those who have perished in spite of their vows?' *All superstition is much the same,* whether it be that of astrology, dreams, omens, retributive judgment, or the like, in all of which the deluded *believers observe events which are fulfilled, but neglect and pass over their failure,* though it be much more common. But this evil insinuates itself still more craftily in philosophy and the sciences, in which a settled maxim vitiates and governs every other circumstance, though the latter be much more worthy of confidence. Besides, even in the absence of that eagerness and want of thought (which we have mentioned), *it is the peculiar and perpetual error of the human understanding to be more moved and excited by affirmatives than negatives, whereas it ought duly and regularly to be impartial; nay, in establishing any true axiom the negative instance is the most powerful.* [My underlining, HM] (Bacon)[77]

Another human tendency related to confirmation bias is the "boomerang effect" which is also called "backfire effect". This is the case when people, who believe in something, reject the evidence that clearly show that their belief is wrong and, on top, start believing even more strongly. This "effect" is a relatively recent discovery, it was first discussed in the 1950s. Boomerang effect is not the rule and it is a rather exceptional case – whereas confirmation bias is very common. The study of L. Festinger, published as *When Prophecy Fails* (1955) which can be read as a tragic-comic novel, too, is worth to be mentioned here.

The study and the story are about a group of psychologists who spent time in a cult society whose members were convinced that the world would end on December 21, 1954. Some aliens from outer space were to come in a flying saucer and the "chosen ones", i.e., the cult members, were to be saved. As you know, the prediction failed. However, after the shocking disillusion the "believers" instead of accepting their mistake they increased their activity in propagating their beliefs.

"But man's resourcefulness goes beyond simply protecting a belief. Suppose an individual believes something with his whole heart; suppose further that he has a commitment to this belief, that he has

---

[77] Not to forget our main topic which is Greek myths: In our days the myth of the miracles of Virgin Mary who is believed that responds to requests, attracts thousands of visitors to the island of Tinos (Greece) every year on the 15th of August. The believers marvel in the Church of Virgin Mary the hundreds of votive gifts that show the innumerable pilgrims who have profited by the miracles. However, the number of those who requested a favor but were ignored is never discussed. Had Francis Bacon visited the island - four centuries ago - he would have asked "where are the names of those who have been denied in spite of their requests?"

taken irrevocable actions because of it; finally, suppose that he is presented with evidence, unequivocal and undeniable evidence, that his belief is wrong: what will happen? The individual will frequently emerge, not only unshaken, but even more convinced of the truth of his beliefs than ever before. Indeed, he may even show a new fervor about convincing and converting other people to his view." (Festinger, p.3).

Leon Festinger, sets the conditions under which this effect occurs:

1. A belief must be held with deep conviction and must have some relevance to action.

2- The person holding the belief must have committed himself to it; that is, for the sake of his belief, he must have taken some important action that is difficult to undo.

3. The belief must be sufficiently specific and sufficiently concerned with the real world so that events may unequivocally refute the belief.

4- Such undeniable disconfirmatory evidence must occur and must be recognized by the individual holding the belief.

5- The individual believer must have social support. (Festinger, p. 4)

The crucial point seems to be the fifth condition. The members who showed a greater tendency to accept their "mistake" and stop believing in the myth of the "end of the world" and in the paraphernalia, were those who were not in close connection with the group. When the group members reinforced each other with various "new interpretations" their beliefs did not only fade, but on the contrary obtained even new dynamics. For example, the believers attempted to proselyte or to persuade nonmembers reassuring that their beliefs were correct.[78]

Festinger and his associates present similar cases of "boomerang effect" from history, too. For example, the Sabbatai Zevi (or Sevi) case of the 17th century, the Millerites of mid 19th century and the case of Christ and his Apostles. In these three cases "unequivocally refutation" of a belief did increase the zeal of the believers. The 1954 case, however, was the only one that was investigated "alive". I will complete this "confirmation bias and boomerang effect" issue with some observations by Festinger:

"Two opinions, or beliefs, or items of knowledge are *dissonant* with each other if considering only the particular two items, one does not

---

[78] This finding is in line with my definition above: "A myth is a belief that operates as a basis for a set of conclusions. And a myth is not a personal or private matter, it is a social phenomenon; it is shared with others forming a community." (4- A tentative assessment – MYTH AS A WORKING HYPOTHESIS.

follow from the other... Dissonance produces discomfort and, correspondingly, there will arise pressures to reduce or eliminate the dissonance. [Either] The person may try to change one or more of the beliefs, opinions, or behaviors involved in the dissonance; [or] to acquire new information or beliefs that will increase the existing consonance and thus cause the total dissonance to be reduced; or to forget or reduce the importance of these cognitions that are in a dissonant relationship... The dissonance would be largely eliminated if they discarded the belief that had been disconfirmed... It may be less painful to tolerate the dissonance than to discard the belief and admit one had been wrong... Rationalization can reduce dissonance somewhat. For rationalization to be fully effective, support from others is needed to make the explanation of the revision seem correct... But there is a way in which the remaining dissonance can be reduced. If more and more people can be persuaded that the system of belief is correct, than clearly it must, after all, be correct... Consider the extreme case: if everyone in the whole world believed something there would be no question at all as to the validity of this belief. It is this reason that we observe the increase in proselytizing following disconfirmation." (p. 25-28).

The embarrassing question that arises is if this study of mine which is critical to myths will cause an impetus, that is, a new enthusiasm in favor of myths! Having this problematic and all that was said about confirmation bias in mind, we may now see how some myths are defended and explained as a reality in Greece.

THE ARGUMENTS OF THE "OFFICIAL VIEWS"

I found the following arguments in favor of the Agia Lavra story:

"There is no doubt that the most valuable treasure that is kept in the monastery [of Agia Lavra] is the Holy Banner of the Revolution on which the fighters of 1821 took their oath. Actually this is the first flag of the Greek nation and was raised by Bishop Germanos for the oath. The Banner is horizontally rectangular and the Assumption of Virgin Mary is depicted on it. In spite of all the fires and the looting that the monastery suffered the Banner was not damaged at all. Today it is kept in a case in the monastery as the most valuable National treasure."[79]

This paragraph is from a tourist guide on the internet. I translated the whole paragraph to point the patriotic tone and the hint that there may have

---

[79] https://exploringgreece.tv/destinations/agia-layra-to-monastiri-orosimo-tis-epanastasis-toy-1821/ z134 52/#.Xs6N_m5uLIU (Γ)

been even a miracle that saved the Banner from all ills. The guide further on explains that "original historical sources" show that this is the place where the Revolution was declared on the 25th. "Other sources", it is added, confirm the same but they show the date as the 23rd of March. Some historians, however, "claim that this is a legend since Germanos did not mention the event in his memoirs. But other historians that searched the matter state that the memoirs are not complete since they have mistreated before their publication."

Nikos Kiriazis [Νίκος Κυριαζής] is a publisher of the internet newspaper Kalabryta-News. In his article he explains that the rich archives of the Monastery of Agia Lavra leave no doubt about what happened in 1821. He refers by name to fourteen eye witnesses of the events who have testified for what happened. Most of the names are not identified as persons who left any other written documents behind except the mentioned archives.[80] One eyewitness is Alexandros Despotopoulos (1803-1895) who published in 1861 a short leaflet of eleven pages, i.e., forty years after the event and 23 years after the official date of the Revolution was decided. This leaflet is his speech in the historical meeting of the 25th of March. He was 18 years old at that time (Despotopoulos).

But the writer of Kalavrita-News gives another evidence: "It is the Holy Banner itself that secures the best evidence and this is done by the Turkish bullet that hit the Banner during the attack in Kalavrita on 21/3/1821, as it is clearly seen exactly on the head of the Angel that is on the left of the picture" (SIC). There is a contradiction in the two dates: The Holy Banner attacked on the 21st of March and Despotopoulos witnessed the declaration of the Revolution on the 25th. I presume all these can be clarified once one reaches the rich archive of the Monastery.

The historian Vasilis Kremmidas mentions another eyewitness, the high priest Filaretos Dimitriou, but he also ironically expresses his concern about the validity of this testimony. The high priest in 1889 testified in writing that Bishop Germanos blesses the arms under the Holly Banner in Agia Lavra Monastery, also exposing the detailed history of the Banner. The historian commented: "A 92-year old monk, was mobilized to testify officially the validity of events that he remembered in all details after almost 70 years, at a time when all involved had died and in spite of the fact that the main hero of the story Germanos had rejected the role he was assigned to" (Kremmidas,

---

[80] https://www.kalavrytanews.com/2011/02/blog-post_2557.html (E)
The eyewitnesses in Greek are: Αντιστράτηγος Β.Πετιμεζάς, Σπύρος Καρασπύρος, Μπολιαρίτης, Σταμάτης Μποτιώνης, Καλλιμάνης εκ Σαββανών, Θεοδ. Ανδρικόπουλος, Π. Κασκανδράμης, Π. Θεοδωρόπουλος, Πρόκριτος Κ. Παπαδαίος από Μαζέικα, Γιαννάκης Λαμπρόπουλος εκ Παγκρατίου, Αν. Παπανικολάου, Απ. Παναγόπουλος εκ Βυσωκάς, ο τότε (1821) διάκονος του Π.Π.Γερμανού και μετέπειτα Αρχιεπίσκοπος Αθηνών Θεόφιλος Βλαχοπαπαδόπουλος, ο Αλεξ. Δεσποτόπουλος. The date they testified is not mentioned.

2007, p. 18).

It is of interest to see how Wikipedia refers to the issue. There are two different references. The first is titled "The Legend of Agia Lavra" and is more "neutral". The ideological controversy for and against the "legend' is explained in some details, stating that some call the story a myth and some a fact. The arguments of both sides are listed. The absence of the event in the memoirs of Germanos is explained – by the reference to proponents of the "legend" - by his humbleness. Various eyewitnesses are mentioned, some of them being westerners like François Pouqueville.[81] The textbooks, in which the "legend" was first included (in one case in spite of the will of the author), and that in later years was excluded are also explained in details.

The second Wikipedia article titled "Agia Lavra of Kalavrita" is more inclined to the "legend". It is mentioned that "according to some original sources" the story of the 25th of March is valid. Some other sources, it is added, refer to the date as the 23rd of March and some others show Patras as the place the event took place. As for the absence of the event in the memoirs of the top actor, Germanos, this is explained by the bad handling of the manuscript before its publication. Many eyewitnesses are mentioned too.

***

Until now three myths – to be exact, what mostly academics call "myths" - have been presented: The Secret School, the national-martyr Patriarch and the Holy Banner of Agia Lavra Monastery with which the Greek Revolution started on the 25th of March 1821. All three share the following:

A) They present the positive role of the Church: The Church and the priests decisively contributed in the education of the Greeks for ages when the Greeks were enslaved. The Church contributed in the preservation of the Greek language, of the Christian Orthodox religion and in consequence, of the Greek national identity. The tragic end of the national-martyr Patriarch is an additional example of the positive role of the Church. His sacrifice influenced positively the Revolution of 1821 since it sent a message worldwide of the suffering of the Greeks thus securing help of the third parties. The Holy Banner, used on a Holy Christian day on the 25th of March, is a symbol of the involvement of the Church in the national cause of 1821: It started it.

B) The three myths express the merits of the Greeks and of the Greek nation: The Greeks are lovers of knowledge, taking even great risks in order to go to secret schools. They do not hesitate to risk their lives and die heroically as martyrs for the home country when needed. They act in unity

---

[81] Historian V.Kremmidas in his study demonstrated that this information about the eye witness was made up (Kremmidas, 1996).

under a banner and take an oath in the name of liberty and of national sovereignty.

C) All three stories include the Other, the "Turk": The merits of the Greeks are presented in contrast and as a consequence of the deeds of the Ottomans – who are in all cases called Turks. The Turks as enemies enslaved the Greeks, prohibited their education, hanged the Patriarch and fought the Greeks.

These stories are seen as real historical events by a great number of Greeks.[82] A wide consent in favor of these stories is normal considering the secular educational system as well as the teaching of the Church throughout the last decades. The Greek State propagates these beliefs by various means: in addition to the textbooks, by assigning commemoration days, setting symbolic representation of the events (museums, statues, paintings), enabling researches in this particular line, etc.

The skeptics cause the discrepancy. As mentioned above, to have a myth there should be a belief or conviction in one group of people and a disbelief in another. It is the second group that uses the word "myth" to define the thinking of the first group: One's belief is a myth for the other. Naturally, as a corollary, one's myth is a reality for the other.

As a compromise or a sign of "reconciliation" sometimes the word "legend" is used by the defenders of these "myths", especially when they face facts that contradict their convictions, but also by those who do not want to embarrass the believers of the myths. A politician, for example, would utter the word legend more often trying to satisfy his voters who may belong to either side. This situation leads to the issue of "sensitivities". Believing or disbelieving in a myth is "sensitive" and even a taboo for various reasons. The local people are keen in preserving the myths (or stories) that are linked to their villages or towns as it is prestigious to belong to a place that is associated with a heroic past and/or a rich history. National pride is a taboo case worldwide. These stories and the related activities – museums, commemoration days, etc. - attract tourists, too.

The days I was writing these lines the ex-President of Greece Prokopis Pavlopoulos in his very last day in his post issued two Presidential decrees (No. 35 and 36, 2020) with which he established the 17th of March as the day of "Declaration of the Greek Revolution" in both the Eastern Mani, as well as in the Western Mani, in two distinct areas in the Southern Peloponnesus.

---

[82] An opinion poll showed that 71.7% of the Greeks believe that the Secret School is a reality (23.9% said it is a myth) and 42.7% believe that the Greek Revolution started in Agia Lavra on the 25th of March (42.1% called that date and place a myth). *Ελεύθερος Τύπος*, 9 July 2020, according to ΚΕΦΙΜ (Κέντρο Φιλελεύθερων Μελετών).

By coincidence, West Mani is the hometown of Pavlopoulos. Both districts hereon will have a holiday to celebrate the event on the 17th of March; meanwhile the 25th of March remains the official day of the "Declaration", too.[83] One would expect that this politician will use the word "legend" to be on the safe side, not offending his potential voters unnecessarily; or he may silence similar issues whenever possible.

The argumentations of the parties in discrepancy seem to be using the same methodological approach. Both sides argue that there are historical facts proved by documents and eyewitnesses or disproved due to their absence. History is the discipline mostly mentioned. Often a lot of psychoanalysis is attempted to explain why the "other side has such a bias and unacceptable views".

A more careful approach, however, will show that the parties have different methodologies, references and intentions. Both sides have "historical proofs" that demonstrate their theses but these are of a different kind. More importantly, the discrepancy transcends the issues that are supposed to be the reasons of their disagreement. Sometimes the problematic of national identity is being inferred by references to the past. Some other times today's politics and interests are defended with references to some historic conflicts. Actually, what happened in the past is not the main issue; it is today's conflicts that are fought through the arguments of the real or invented events of the past. Some arguments of today will be helpful to see why the controversies on "myths" are so widespread and enduring.

I will first use the argumentation of Vasilios Haralambopoulos [Βασίλειος Χαραλαμπόπουλος] (born 1927) to make my point. He is a philologist, historian and ex-head master of senior high school, he has many publications on issues of history and mostly on Greek Revolution. According to his biography he has been connected with institutions that are identified with "Christianity" and "patriotism" (Haralambopoulos, p. 188). Due to these affiliations one would expect that he would support the view that what some historians (and me) call "myths" are historical realities. Indeed, he does. Here is his approach in defense of his views.

With respect to the Secret School he criticizes those who, with the argument that there are no documents in this direction, do not believe in its existence. He counter argues that "instead we have the oral tradition which is a "common consciousness and belief" and the poem *My tiny moon / light my way / to go to school*. (p. 43). The oral tradition mentions secret schools in many places. "Those who deny the existence of Secret School … also claim that the Turks did not prohibit the establishment of schools, that there is not such a

---

[83] *To Vima*, 7 June 2020.

prohibition". The counter argument of Haralambopoulos is that the Turks ignored even the written rules and in many cases violated the rights of the Greeks. "There was no law that imposed forced islamization, but this still happened. There was no order that prohibited the restoration of the Churches, but still they did not allow the basic repairs". In the same token, he infers that even though there are no Ottoman documents of prohibition of the Greek schools, still they were not allowed, making the secret ones necessary.

He then reminds a letter sent to a German by a Greek (in 1822, during the Revolution) saying that the Turks prohibited the schooling of the Greeks. "Therefore, there was no full liberty to establish schools, nor the teachers could teach in freedom our national history. These things happened in secret. This is the way the legend of the Secret School was created" (p.44). He then continues explaining how in the 18ᵗʰ century the Greeks established many (non-secret) schools all around. "But the honor to preserve the education and the spiritual tradition belongs to the Secret Schools... Because in those years of slavery, when the darkness of slavery was very deep the Secret School preserved the light of education. This is a beautiful historical legend, *probably with many imagined parts*, but definitely with a historical basis" [My underlining] (p. 44).

For the national-martyr Patriarch, Haralambopoulos expresses the following thinking:

> "Lately, some, not specialized historians but journalists, artists and individuals who are involved in history as amateurs, doubt the patriotism of the Patriarch, they call him conservative and a friend of the Turks. Some even accuse him of treachery because he anathematized the Revolution that was started by Ipsilantis. Some teachers endorsed these ideas as supposedly new scientific views. In this way many wrong ideas spread among students and teachers. The critics of the Patriarch have political motives or an enmity against the Church and the clergy. Irrespective of the motives, the worse is that in this way our national history is systematically distorted, the national symbols that have inspired the older generations are denied and the reality is deformed. These critics disregard the general contribution of the Patriarch. [His input in organizing the Church, in education and in philanthropy are mentioned, HM] They isolate an event, the anathema. They present it with exaggerations and by silencing other sides of the issue, so that the meaning of his sacrifice is not seen... What they do is not objective history writing but propaganda or a misinterpretation of the events. Real history writing does not operate in this way. The real historians do not examine the events and the

actions of the human beings as isolated happenings, but they also examine the reasons that caused those actions, the situation and the condition of the time, the drives, the purposes and the motives of the actors... The historian should not limit himself in expressing views based on ethical values and criticism which show ideological prejudices and even bias. [The Greeks in 1821 were not influenced by the anathema because] they knew that the Patriarch was forced by the Turks to take that decision. Neither did a serious historian accuse him for doing that... The Church decided to obey to the orders of the Sultan in order to avoid a mass massacre of the Christians... It is also apparent that the anathema did not include harsh wording and curses which are normally included in anathemas... and does not show any enmity against the revolutionaries" (p. 83-85).

Haralambopoulos also adds that the tragic death of the Patriarch helped the Revolution because the Western public opinion was shocked with his hanging and eventually backed up the Greeks. But what is important is the end of the story of the Patriarch:

"His canonization [declared a saint] was confirmed by some miraculous happenings after his death. The first miracle, which is God's Grace, was the miraculous saving of his body that the Jews threw into the sea having tied a heavy stone on him. But the stone slipped and the body appeared... The other miracle is that the body stayed sound and without any smell for one month until it was taken to Odessa... In 1871, 50 years after the Revolution, the Greek government asked and received his body from Russia. When they opened the coffin in the presence of the prime minister A. Koumounthouros and many other dignitaries, his body again appeared 'preserved to a great extent', as the written protocol of that day shows. According to the Orthodox belief, this preservation of the body was a sign of his being a Saint (p. 108).[84]

Methodologically, the above understanding differs from the understanding of a modern historian who normally: 1) is cautious about "oral tradition" that refers to hundreds of years old stories; 2) by "absence of documents" about the prohibition of Greek schools understands not only the Ottoman ones but also the absence of Greek documents, too; 3) sees a letter written to ensure political help as highly doubtful in reflecting the real situation; 4) rejects as irrelevant the use of argument such as "absence of full liberty and of freedom to teach our national history", since to expect "liberty, freedom and national

---

[84] These lines are published in 2007. In a book of 1988, it is mentioned that "the *bones* of the Patriarch" were brought to Greece form Russia (Kardasis, p. 64, 65). Patriarch Grigorios V was proclaimed a Saint by the Church of Greece in 1921.

history" in the Middle Ages is anachronism ; 5) and uses the term "serfdom" instead of "slavery" to define the status of people of that time.

Haralambopoulos correctly claims that a historian should not only narrate the events but he/she should look for the motives and general situations of that time. He then proceeds in explaining the historical "framework" by references to the motives of the "Turks", the national aspiration of the Greeks and the role of the other states. He is not aware, however, that it is exactly this framework – the national paradigm - which is rejected by the critics of the myths. The critics do not perceive a world where nations are in continuous conflict. They distance themselves from nationalism and they perceive different "general situation and motives" and a different "framework". Their approach is critical vis-à-vis nationalism, its assumptions and references. The discrepancy is not one of "what is right or wrong" but of which *framework* is to be taken as a starting point. (I will come to this issue below.)

Another important difference between the believers and nonbelievers of the above myths lies elsewhere: In the political, ideological and identity domain. The above argument, that the critics of the myths have "political motives or an enmity against the Church and the clergy", is correct. But the "framework" of the "enmity" is not explained. The point is that the three myths have been instrumentalised and they can be understood only if "the conditions of the time, the drives, the purposes and the motives of the actors" are understood.

The real issue is not the existence or not of the Secret School, the role of a patriarch or the exact date of a revolution. It is the role of the Church that is jeopardized. That was a struggle as old as the time of the Enlightenment and it was between the parties of the traditional section of the society and the more modern social forces. In fact, the Church is in defense, feeling that some new ideas challenged it and whatever it represents. On the other hand, the "critics" feel the need to show that the traditional centers of powers do not deserve to enjoy the prestige that they claim and that they actually have. The whole controversy is an issue of who will have the right to determine what is right or wrong. To prove that the stories and the "legends" that render prestige to the Church are "myths" is an act of dethronement.

And these three myths are directly and/or indirectly related to religion: The priests teach Greek in the churches and the monasteries, the most important national-martyr is the Patriarch, the Greek Revolution is blessed by a priest in a monastery by blessing a Holy Banner… To doubt these is to doubt the authority and legitimacy of a centuries old authority.

It is interesting that the defenders of these myths quite often use phrases such as "there is no doubt that", "leaves no doubt that", whereas the critics of the myths basically express doubts on what is being believed until recently. Doubt versus belief is a very old controversy, but it culminated with the Enlightenment. The mottos, *de omnibus dubitandum* (doubt everything)[85] versus *credo* make themselves felt behind the supposedly historical arguments. How else can one explain the miracles related to the Patriarch? How else can one explain the integration of a miracle and the canonization of the Patriarch which can be accepted only as a "belief", into a historical event which can be approached only on "documentation"?

At this point it should also be reminded that the above three myths are directly supported by the Greek State. The State and the Church have created a much wider myth, an ideology, known as Helleno-Christianity, which will be one of the modern Greek myths to be examined below.[86] At this point an event may prove a useful example to see how the above myths can be used as materials to defend political and ideological positions.

On the 21st of June 2000 the Archbishop Hristodoulos (deceased in 2008) who opposed the government's decision not to include the item of "religion" in the planned new identity cards in Greece, organized a campaign calling a mass demonstration. He put in practice his threat: He made use of the Holy Banner of the Lavra Monastery. He waved the banner as a flag in demonstrations. This act symbolized a new (holy) Liberation War. The myth of the Banner was instrumentalized in an ideological fight. Thousands took part in these demonstrations. It seems very logical that the Church would not like to lose such an effective weapon as the sacred story (myth) (Vasilakis, p.403).[87]

However, a book titled *Secret School* circulated in 2012 to prove the existence of this school refuting the arguments of the "revisionists", as the skeptics are named. The very first sentence signals the role of the Church in this historical debate and the ill intentions of its enemies: "It is well known that the revisionist historians want to completely disconnect the Church from the Revolution of 1821 and from all the other historical events to which the modern Greek state owes its existence" (Kekavmenos, p. 19).

---

[85] A motto attributed to René Descartes. It was also Karl Marx's favourite motto.

[86] There are many supporters of the above three myths that are not directly connected to the Church and to religious beliefs. This case will be dealt with below.

[87] Historian Vasilis Kremmidas, too, criticized in 2005 the said Archbishop for the same reason: "Today's Archbishop uses the historical myths that have been constructed by the Church in the mid 19th century … presenting the Church – and himself – as the only defender of the nation, of the tradition and the authenticity of the people" (Kremmidas, 2021, p. 214).

The structure of the book shows how a "proof" can be inferred by highlighting irrelevant events. The first 24 pages are about the revisionists and their arguments (very informative); the next 108 pages are about the Turks and their persecution of the Greek education; the next 28 are about the hindering of religious freedom by the Turks; 20 pages are allocated to the schools that the Turks closed down; and only 8 pages are used to provide the documentation prior to 1821 of the existence of the Secret School. There are 12 more pages of "proofs" that originated after 1821. But this is the period in which the national myths had already flourished and all the stories about the secret school are suspected of fabrication. As it is well known, when a war starts the first victim is the truth!

According to Kekavmenos the oldest document about the Secret Schools dates to 1743. A preacher in a book addressed to children: "You receive neither a Greek nor a Latin education; you learned to read freely, perhaps not even freely, by the simple books of our Church." The "not even freely" is considered the "highly valued" and oldest evidence of Secret School: if not freely... it should be through secret schools! (p. 154).[88] The next oldest document is from 1771. E. Voulgaris (Ε. Βούλγαρης) published a brochure addressed to the western world to show the dramatic situation that the Greeks faced with the intention to secure help. At some point after referring to the Turkish "barbarisms", the "dangers" faced in education are mentioned. Dangers? Then it means there were secret schools! The third old document is from 1855; but it is about of what happened in 1785. Therefore, it is considered a document of 1785! These are the old documents of the period before 1821 that prove that during the 15th, 16th, 17th and 18th centuries there were secret schools.

The basic reasoning is indirect: Since the Turks were oppressive, barbarians and enemies of the Christians and the Greeks, and since they had the power to do it, why shouldn't they prohibit the education of the Greeks? This is the reason that led the author to allocate so many pages about the oppressive and barbaric Turks. And the Greeks who were so willing to study shouldn't they resort to illegal education, i.e., secret schools?

A recent book by G. Karabelias is about myths, too, and in favor of their reality. The first impression one gets is that the author tries to reconcile the opposing views about the existence of the Secret School. "Nobody ever claimed that the prohibition of education [of the Greek schools] was general, constant and systematic. Even the most passionate defenders of the Secret School knew that there were proper schools during the Ottoman period in

---

[88] "Μήτε ελληνικήν, μήτε λατινικήν έλαβες μάθησιν. Έμαθες, ναι, να διαβάζεις ελευθέρως, ίσως μήτε ελευθέρως, εις τα απλά της εκκλησίας μας βιβλία". I read that some children learned to read *fluently* and some *not so fluently*!

many places. They also knew, however, that the Turks after the conquest of Constantinople for decades they closed down the Greek schools… Therefore, the reference to the Secret School has a form of exemplary symbol (SIC, μορφή παραδειγματικού συμβόλου) of the difficulties and the persecutions that the education faced in Greece under the Turks, and this is the way the Greek people perceived this case" (Karabelias, p. 214, 215).

He then goes on criticizing the "revisionist" historians for trying to deny the oppressive character of the Ottoman State. It is interesting to see that he accuses the historians, who see the Secret School as a myth, for creating themselves a myth about a "tolerant Ottoman State". He also blames the "revisionists" for ignoring the "thousands years old inclination of the Greeks towards education" and the "liberating role of the Orthodox Church".[89] It becomes clear again that the main issue is not the status of the schools but the role of the Church, the greatness of the Greek nation and the character of the Turks.

This book also brings to light anew some rather forgotten – or suppressed - controversies about the East-West relations, the Greek identity and the movement of the Enlightenment. "The Greek Enlightenment movement was only a *reflection* of the western one and it came to send away (να εξοβελίσει) the traditional "eastern spirit" (ανατολίτικο πνεύμα) (p. 275).[90] About the Greek national identity - if it is an "old" or a "new" phenomenon - and about what the "revisionists" are trying to do we read [All italics and parentheses below are in the original]:

> The national and social-class controversies that existed in relation to the Turkish rule were *replaced* [by the "revisionist" historians, HM] completely with the *real* but *secondary* controversy between "Enlightenment-Church". But this attack is not the result of a simple ideological whim of the author [Kremmidas is menat, HM], but he sees it indispensable in order to construct the shape of the Greek national consciousness as if it was formed supposedly *after* the French Revolution. And he does that, because if the Greek national consciousness was really formed after the clash with the Orthodox

---

[89] Karabelias also notes an interesting contradiction in the approach of the "revisionists" who naturally side with the Enlightenment: It was the intellectuals of this movement that at the end of the 17th century criticized the Ottoman Rule as oppressive and not the Church, whereas today's intellectuals who claim an affiliation with the Enlightenment consider the Ottoman rule tolerant. What Karabelias missed, however, is that the contradiction works both ways. Today's Church and its allies present the Ottomans as "barbarians" whereas at the beginning of the 19th century they praised it as tolerant! These "contradictions" can be explained. The Greek nationalists that tried to start a revolution presented a negative Ottoman State, whereas the Church that was for the ancient regime and against the revolution did the opposite. After two hundred years the perceptions changed. The Church and the Greek nationalists of today present a negative Other, and the modern historians try to distance themselves from nationalist stereotypes.

[90] *Πνεύμα* in Greek means spirit, soul, mind. In all cases it is something beyond "material body" and more enduring. Sometimes the word *ψυχή* (psyche) is used instead.

Church, there would neither be a continuum of Hellenism, nor any relation with the Byzantine Empire and Ancient Greece. This view is a Western construction,[91] in the realm of a middle class and cultural development and of a revolution that is a continuation of the French Revolution. But if on the contrary, the continuous national character, its close relation with the modern national consciousness, with Christian Orthodoxy and the Byzantine Empire is a fact, as it is confirmed by historical reality, then also the general continuous existence of the [Greek] consciousness will also be real and not a simple imitation of the West." (Karabelias, p. 287).

This is a very rare case where the controversy about the myths mentioned above is so clearly explained. For their believers, the acceptance of the myths as realities means the acceptance that the Greek national consciousness is as old as the Byzantine Empire and Ancient Greece. If they are proved wrong, the Greeks are downgraded to a new nation without history. In other words, the discussion of the myths is not about some "historical" events. It is about the role of the Church, but even more importantly about the identity of each Greek who is indirectly associated with this discussion. Also the perception of the "West" is critical: The West by its influence harmed the "traditional Eastern/Greek spirit". Behind these perceptions lies a very critical period of the history of the Greeks which will be our next topic.

HOW SOME GREEKS PERCEIVE THE "WEST" – IN 1800 AND TODAY

Karabelias, as mentioned above, sees a *basic* controversy that is national and of a social-class nature and a *secondary* one which is between the Enlightenment and the Church. The criteria of ranking social phenomena as *basic/secondary* are not explained, nor why the two areas of conflict are separated and not seen as one: as a social controversy where the followers of the Enlightenment confront the Ottoman State and the Church.

This confrontation was not special to Greece but was experienced in many countries around the world. Some called it a fight of republicans versus royalists or liberals versus conservatives or left versus right. (I will be using the term "East-West" to denote the Greek case.) Ethnocentric reading of history misses the general picture. Naturally, similar social movements do have their ethnic and geographic peculiarities, too.

---

[91] The "Western construction" should be read here twofold. A) It is a reference to the modern understanding of the nations and the related national identity. But this is a recent development that appeared in the mid 20th century. The irony is that according to the second reading B) it is the West that perceived the reborn of the Greek nation and in consequence the "continuation" of this nation from antiquity to the present. This will be discussed in the following chapter.

Calling *secondary* a historical phenomenon amounts to refusal of paying due attention to it, and/or trying simply to silence it. Even if the conflict between the "westerners" and the "Greek spirit/the Church" were *secondary*, doesn't it deserve to be studied and explained? This is an important phase of Greek history especially because it is still not finalized.

I discussed in length the conflict of Enlightenment-Church above (11- A Patriarch as a national-martyr). Now I want to present and compare two books of the first decade of 1800 and a third one of 2016 which analyze the old conflict. The three together give a clear idea of what the argument of the parties was, but more importantly, they show how this old issue is perceived by some Greeks today.

The first book, *Hellenic Nomarchy, that is On Liberty* [Ελληνική Νομαρχία, ήτοι λόγος περί ελευθερίας] was published anonymously ("Anonymous Greek") in 1806 in Italy. (Nomarchy was in the sense of "reign of law"). It was "salvaged" and became known to the Greek public anew after 142 years, in 1948. Its radical anticlericalism may be one reason of its being silenced for so long. I will translate some pages, partly summarizing and without comments.[92]

> 1. On liberty: "You, the eternal souls of my free ancestors … and you, my holy homeland … our happiness depends on our government provided it is approved by the majority … then we will know what liberty means … in the State of Law freedom is for all, having dedicated it to the laws which they are formed by the people freely … the laws take care of the needy, too … if a human being is not free he will not understand his difference from a slave … the Greeks [the Hellens] should know that slavery is the reason for their unhappiness … the fights of the Souliots against the tyrant of Ipiros show that Greece [Hellas] still gives birth to Leonidases and Themistocleses … Rigas helped us to get rid of the barbarous tyrants[93] … by home country [patrie] the Greeks mean the place they are born, the slaves are indifferent to this word … one loves his home country more that his own life … the free man dies in war for his love for the homeland and the honor of his nation" (Anonymous, p. 11-65).
>
> 2. On tyrants and slaves: "The people of our times are so much used to be slaves … that they praise those tyrants … O! Greeks, these tyrants are made of theocracy and oligarchy … and theocracy is the body of the clerics … they always tried by using the name of god to rule the citizens and they succeeded in this due to the general

---

[92] Some of the books and pamphlets that expressed the ideas of the "westerners" in those years are the following: *The Anonymous of 1789*, *The trumpet of truth* (1792), *Answers of an anonymous to mad accusers* (1793), *Brotherly Teaching* (1798), *Russianenglishfrench* (1805), *The Greek State of Law* (1806), *The thoughts of Kriton* (1819).
[93] I will discuss the case of Rigas further down.

ignorance ... These tyrants own all the richness of the country, they rent the land in such a way that the people are turned to slaves ... From the time that Christianity was established until 1453 [he means the Byzantine Empire, HM] freedom continuously diminished ... superstition, the lies and the vain life of the priests and of the patriarchs corrupted the hearts of the kings ... the three powers appeared in Greece: tyranny, the religious body and the nobility which for almost eleven centuries molested the Greeks and destroyed Greece ... The vanity of the popes and of the patriarchs produces the schism between us and the Latins ... and today Greece is under the hateful thrones of the Ottomans" (p. 66-84).

3. Greece and its chains: "The Ottoman state is tyrannical ... their religion is full of superstitions and they believe in silly things. Their customs are barbaric, their character haughty and proud. Ignorance is deep and general ... The Ottomans are ruthless, Tyrant Ali Pasha hanged, beheaded, strangled, impaled, buried or skinned alive the Greeks ... they exploited economically the Greeks ... in the European part of the Ottoman state the proportion of the Christians to the Ottomans is 80 to 20 ... On top, the Greeks have to satisfy their lust and hunger so that they can barely live, except those who collaborate with the tyrants" (p. 85-107).

4. The collaborators of the tyrants: "Two are the reasons of the tyranny that the Greeks face: the ignorant clergy and the absence of cultured citizens ... You vile Sinod of Constantinople, you have nothing in common with the teachings of Christ, you think only of money that you steal daily from the poor Christians ... the priest in Ioannina is known as adulterer and being gay ... your lust for money is enormous ... you are like wolfs that eat the innocent sheep of the Orthodox Church ... today we have two more genders apart from man and woman, we have the rich and the poor ... why should one man control the fate of many ... the Sinod buys the throne of the patriarchate from the Ottoman Vezir paying a great amount of money and then they sell it again making profit and they call the buyer 'Patriarch', who in order to get his money back he sells the right to collect money to archbishops who in turn sell this right to priests of lower ranks, and these get their money back by rubbing the poor people ... to be able to read a little is enough for somebody to qualify for patriarch, to be able to write is not a prerequisite ... pride and corrupt soul of the twelve idiots of the Sinod do not allow them to see the harm that is caused to the people ... in getting money from the people the clergy does not differ from the Ottomans ... the

ignorance of the people enable the clergy to use the weapon of excommunication and usually they forgive the ones anathematized so that they can be threatened anew ... the archbishops eat and drink like pigs ...Damn you with the consolation that you supposedly give, saying that the Ottoman tyranny is the will of God ... [and a story among many] There was a young nun who was visited at nights by the archangel Gabriel and all the other nuns envied her. But when after nine months she gave birth to a baby-archangel the other nuns hated her. But the mother nun believed that she was a saint" (p. 108-158).

5. The resurrection of the nation [γένος][94]: "There are some dirty people who say that we cannot fight and win against the big Ottoman kingdom, we are not able to govern ourselves, that 'freedom' does not mean anything, we should not shed our blood, they may kill us all if we revolt ... dirty [Greek] lords of Constantinople, you are cowards that see the fleas as giants ... But the situation has changed, Apollo has appeared in his ancient place ... in all our cities today we have one or two schools, Logic and Physics have awaken so many people ... our students read about Xenophon and Plutarch ... the Greek children will be enlightened faster and easier if, the language of the people, vernacular is used instead of today's practice ... Some people are afraid of using the word 'liberty' because they are afraid that our [Greek] dignitaries and the clergy would declare them atheist ... You Greeks! Do not forget that the weapons of justice are invincible and the Ottomans will run away when they face the armed Greeks ... it is better we are all dead than to surrender to foreign powers ... Greeks, the time to liberate our home country has come ... our character, our traditions, the weakened tyrant, the participation of so many and the new educational efforts support this convention of mine (p. 159-181).[95]

I preferred to translate these sentences instead of summarizing the text in my own words so that the national sentiment and the climate of the time are better seen. This is a discourse of a rising nationalism. The choice of words is characteristic of the new ideology: Liberty, freedom, homeland/home country

---

[94] In the first years if the 19th century the terms of nationalist ideology had not yet developed fully among the Greeks. The word γένος ("gene" etymologically is related to this word) was used instead of ἔθνος (ethnos, the word used for "nation" in present-day Greek). In Greek the distinction between nation and ethnie does not exist, "ethnos" is used for both. Some academics use the word "ethnotita", too, the last decades. I will refer to this issue down below.

[95] The same anticlericalism in encountered 190 years after the publication of *The Hellenic Nomarchy*. Konstantine the Great who is proclaimed Saint by the Orthodox Church is called "murderer who killed thousand innocent people, his own son included, a corrupt personality who orchestrated miracles, who destroyed Ancient Greek monuments, etc. Similar characteristics are attributed for "Great Thodosios", too (Simopoulos, 2010, pp. 223-358).

(in Greek πατρίδα/patrie), nation, tyrants, theocracy, oligarchy. We see new enemies that are not related to religion but to social status and ethnic differences: the ignorant, hypocritical and dishonest clergy, the villain Sinod of the Patriarchate and the Patriarch himself, who all together exploit the people, the Ottomans who are corrupt and barbarians and torture the people. Then, there are "our ancestors" who were cultured, free, brave etc: Leonidas, Themistocles, Plutarch, Xenophon. We see the use of "Hellens" (Έλληνες) and not even once the word "Romios"; the Byzantine Empire that is presented as a (foreign) state that deprived the Greeks of their liberty.[96]

We also see a new understanding or rather a set of new values: to respect the majority, to take care of the needy as a society, the lack of liberty that means slavery, to die for the honor of the nation and for the homeland, to make fun with the clergy and the nuns…

In 1798 the Patriarchate of Constantinople published a declaration, titled *Fatherly Teaching* (Διδασκαλία Πατρική) against the Greeks who expressed ideas in favor of the French Revolution and the Enlightenment. Athamantios Korais, probably the best known Greek proponent of the "new ideas", answered the same year publishing the *Brotherly Teaching* (Η Αδελφική Διδασκαλία). These two texts summarize the basic theses of the two groups: The "easterners" and "westerners".[97] The polemic continued for about a decade with related publications and subsided when the (national) Greek State was founded. But actually only the *publications* stopped, the controversy continued, even until today; only the counter arguments are supported in a roundabout way. The myths that are being discussed here are related to this context.

The best way to show the arguments of the two sides is to resort to their texts. Here I already presented a well known book that voices the views of a "westerner". A book of an "easterner" will follow. The first book just presented dates from 1806 and the one to be presented from 1800. The reverse of the order makes sense, however. The debate was triggered by the "westerners", who under the spell of the Enlightenment and the French revolution started influencing the Greeks. So the *Fatherly Teaching* of 1798 was an "answer"; actually the "westerners" preceded so I chose to show their

---

[96] I will refer again to the issue of Hellens/Romios and the evaluation of the Byzantine Empire below.

[97] The role of the Phanariots/Patriarchate of Constantinople/Istanbul and their fight against the Greek revolutionary forces of 1821 is described by the Scottish historian George Finlay who was an eye witness of those years (Finlay). According to him, the Patriarchate and the Greek aristocracy were used by the Sultan to enslave the Greeks (p. 343); the Patriarch and the Holy Synod as well as the Greek dignitaries of Istanbul were always ready to serve the Sultan as his agents (p. 349). One should be cautious about these evaluations, however, since they appear in a book of 1856, i.e., at a time when the official historical interpretation of Greece had been formed and the tension between the Patriarchate and the Church of Greece had just ended. In 1850, the Patriarchate recognized the Church of Greece that was established in 1833.

arguments first. The two books presented here are matured products of the debate. An evaluation of 2016 by an "easterner" will follow to show how the old debate is still alive and related to the myths discussed above.

The author of *Christian apologia* [Ἀπολογία Χριστιανική] is Athanasios Parios (1721-1813) who was declared as saint by the Patriarchate in 1995. He is known for his ardent opposition to Korais, the best known "westerner" of his time, as well as for his monastic life.[98] In the first page of his 130 page book (the new edition) makes it clear that he wrote these lines to oppose the blasphemy against the Christian Belief that shook the Church of God and that originated, not from individuals but from a nation of the West. He means the French who "refused the Holy Gospels and the belief in Christ." They destroyed monasteries, the churches, etc. (Parios, p. 80). He added: "Since I address to Christians and since it is of no use to talk to the libertines it is self understood that for my proofs I will make use of principles that you accept as Christians" (p. 84).

Indeed he exposed his views with references to the Bible and to the text of the Fathers of Christianity. First he tried to show that liberty/freedom (in Greek there is one word ελευθερία) is a chimera. Only the atheists believe in it. In many pages he explained that freedom can be of the soul and of the body. The soul is taken care by Christianity; once one believes, he is free. The body by creation is a "slave": We are all slaves of God, at home there is a superior, at work there is somebody who asks you what to do, so we are always restricted somehow (p. 87-92).[99]

As for the political systems, "the best is the monarchy". This system is "perfect and more just when the monarch is not a tyrant." It is "an imitation of divine rule, where God is at the top of all kings" (p. 93). The "libertines" are against all political and spiritual power so that they can freely do terrible things: "They become insolent, rude, they commit murders, adultery, incest and other similar things that I am unable to describe. This is what the 'illuminated ones' are. Of course, the truth is that the Franks were always of that sort, but now this 'liberta' finished them completely, ... they turned to animals that are without the ability to think" (p. 99). In connection with these Parios explains that philosophy cannot do what belief can provide and as a proof of that he reminds The Bible, Romans 1:22 "Although they claimed to

---

[98] I will be referring to the second edition of 1800 and to its new publication of 2016, which is presented with an introduction by G. Metallinos. I will continue commenting on this introduction.

[99] It is of interest how G. Metallinos, who wrote the introduction to this book, justifies the thesis of Parios in a footnote (p. 87): "The term freedom does not so much mean political freedom but autonomy from any center of reference... In this sense, the theses of Saint Parios are absolutely correct since man is a being that is determined by others [forces]» (ετεροκαθοριζόμενος). However, considering that the French Revolution and the political uprising were about "political freedom" all the arguments of Parios against *other kind* freedom/liberty become irrelevant. Furthermore, even if the arguments of Parios are "absolutely correct" they still are against a movement that seeks political freedom.

be wise, they became fools" (p. 100).

"We owe obedience to the archons ... because they are the organs of God ... Render unto Caesar the things that are Caesar's, and unto God the things that are God's ... The Church with this kind of teachings controlled the wrath of the people so that they do not try to revolt" (p. 109-110). Parios then explains how those "enlightened" persons rejected the Apostoles, the Scriptures, the Gospel, the prophets, Christ and God and replaced them with Voltaire and Rousseau in order to establish "liberta" (p. 111). Even the devil did not do that, since he at least accepted the existence of God. "They call Christ imposter and holy Gospels myths and nonsense" (p. 114).

As for "equality" which is mentioned on the banners of the rebels, Parios makes it clear that such a condition is not possible: "How can ever the one that cleans the excrements be equal to the nobles and to the distinguished? ... How can human beings be equal when one is very rich and the other suffers of hunger?" (p.101).[100]

A long chapter follows (p, 117-159) where he explains that, in spite of what the atheists say, Christ is the true God. Then Parios reminds his readers that the "outer wisdom" which is also called "philosophy" is considered "slavery" by the Fathers of Christianity. One should be a slave of the "higher wisdom" of God. Therefore, all "outer wisdom" should be subjected to and not against the "higher one". "Let's stay away from Geometry with its complicated shapes and from the chatterbox Algebra and from any human knowledge and science. What is needed is belief, not proofs. Belief and proof are two different things" (168). The next eight pages are about how corrupt Voltaire was.

People like Voltaire try to show that the Holy Scriptures are myths and lies. These kind of books "should be condemned, criticized and burned, as it is also required by the Holy Sinod" (p. 179,180). "The Christians who go to Europe and especially the students should be very careful because ... most of them come back as atheists" (p. 183). In the epilogue as last advice we read that atheism is the result when there is no fear of God and exists a corrupt and dirty life. He mentions "comfortable life, unending dances, the mania for theaters, sexual anomalies that start from childhood, satanic fantasies, haughtiness and similar dirty and dark drives" as acts of corrupt behaviors. In the next page he added "egoism, jealousy, prostitution, adultery, gluttony and festivities spree" (p. 190, 192).

The Ancient Greeks pose a danger, too, apparently because they were not Christians: "Many well educated people acquainted with the texts of the pagan

---

[100] At this point Metallinos intervenes with a long footnote to justify this argument of "inequality" which cannot be easily accepted by the Greek readers. His argument resembles a Marxian approach claiming that economic inequality is a basic problem (p. 102).

Greeks, especially with spiteful and dirty Loukianos, they do not want to read religious books. This carried them away from what is holy and drives then towards atheism … They hear and think only numbers, lines, shapes, cones, cylinders, pyramids, planets, bodies, matter, nature. They do not mention God. And at puberty they join the school of dirty Aphrodite"(SIC) (p. 194). "Close your ears with hate and disgust and do not listen to the atheist blasphemies that these animals vomit from their dirty mouths" (p. 195).

I wouldn't be writing about *The Greek State of Law* of Anonymous Greek and *Christian apologia* of Parios, both published more than 200 years ago if I believed that their dispute is by now superseded. However, these ideas are still haunting over Greece today, mostly discussed indirectly and through the controversies about some myths. The two writers are diametrically opposed to each other. They belong to two different worlds. Normally, they should have been by now only of a historical interest. However, their ideas and their arguments are still somehow present within the Greek society. First I will compare the two texts summarizing the main ideas presented in them, then I will refer to G. Metallinos who evaluated anew *Christian apologia* in order to show how up to date these issues are. It should be kept in mind that the comparison is not about how the "West" or the "East" are but on how the Other side and "the self" are being understood; it is a comparison of perceptions.

Four areas of dispute seem to compose the main discrepancy: A. The role of the Church versus the ideas of Enlightenment (and the West); B. The ancient Greeks and "our" relations with them; C. The character of the "Turks" and D; The need or not of a (national) revolution. Lets see these in more details (first the "westerners" then the "easterners"):

THE WESTERNERS	THE EASTERNERS
1. Their references are the ideas of Enlightenment and thinkers like Voltaire and Rousseau.	1. References are from the Bible and the Fathers of the Church.
2. Each side demonizes the symbols (books, thinkers and ideas) of the Other side.	2. Each side demonizes the symbols (books, thinkers and ideas) of the Other side.
3. Claim: The East has been left retarded, undeveloped etc. because of the tyrants	3. Claim: The West is corrupt and problematic because of the new ideas of the atheists.
4, The clergy, the Church and the patriarchs are ignorant and tyrants.	4. The "libertins" are atheists and corrupt who deny Christ.
5. Freedom/liberty is basic for the happiness and the welfare of the people.	5. Freedom is a chimera and what is important is the salvation of the soul.
6. If we are not free we are slaves and unequal.	6. We are slaves of God and of our superiors and equality is not possible.
7. A state of law and laws prepared by the "majority" are needed.	7. The best state is monarchy.
8. A revolution is needed against the tyrants.	8. Christ teaches that archons should be obeyed since they are God's choice.
9. Ancient Greeks are our glorious ancestors and we should study them.	9. We should be very cautious when we read the works of the ancient Greeks especially their philosophy.
10. Physics, math and geometry are useful.	10. Math, physics, etc. are not of importance, religion is.
11. Homeland is important and we may die for it if it is for liberty.	11. (These notions are absent)
12. In the time of the Byzantine Empire freedom diminished.	12. The Byzantine Empire is "our" basic heritage.
13. The vanity of the Church caused the schism with the Latins.	13. The westerners were against us.
14. The Ottomans are tyrants and they must be fought.	14. The existence of the Ottomans is God's will and they secure our existence.

Georgios Metallinos (1940-2019) wrote a long introduction and many footnotes for the recent publication of the *Christian apologia* of Parios. The highly respected reverend G. Metallinos studied theology and literature in Athens and continued his studies in Germany and England and he published more than forty books, mostly on ecclesiastic issues. He was a professor at Athens University. His position on the above mentioned issues shows how contemporary some old beliefs may still be.

"From the Romaic (Greek Orthodox)[101] perspective the French

---

[101] A Greek of today calls himself Hellen (Έλληνας) but also Romios (Ρωμιός). (The feminine case fallows

Revolution (F.R.) is a continuation of a long revolutionary process in West Europe which caused gradually the subjugation of Western Romania/the Byzantine Empire to the Frankish tribes and the final cultural and social enslavement of the first Patriarchate of the Romania/Byzantine Empire, enabling the enthronement of the first Frankish Pope" (Parios, p. 15) This appears in the first page of Metallinos' introduction in the book by Parios. He then mentions the other revolutions: *Renaissance, Reform* and *Enlightenment* which culminated in 1789. The F.R. is characterized as a threat for the Ottoman Empire and for the Romaic Patriarchate, mainly because of its anti-Christian character (p. 18).

The F.R. is defined as an anti-religious movement and not as a social one from the outset. All criticism that folllows is based on this criterion. Vis-à-vis these developments "The Romaic Patriarchate as a guarantor of the Romaic tradition could not keep silent unless it accepted its self-abolition" (p. 20).[102] Many Greek texts appeared at that time that reflected the Frankish-French ideology (p. 23). These texts, always according to Metallinos, reflected a "slave like ... mania for Europeanization" and were against the Christian Byzantine Empire . The end result was "the common worries of existence of the Ottoman Empire and the Greek-Orthodox Church" (p. 22-23).

When the Bonapartian French powers reached the islands of the Ionian Sea (Western Greece) they tried "to give an end to Christianity and to revive the ancient Greek paganism". Therefore, when the joint powers of the Ottomans and (Christian) Russia fought against these French the Patriarchate was on their side (p. 25). "The circulars of Patriarch Georgios 5th are logical and they do not need to be explained by the presumed Ottoman pressure", they are the result of the Patriarch's free decision. In the circular of 1798, which Metallinos attributes a great historical value we read:

> "The cunning snake deceives the human kind ... is spreading atheism with the pretext of freedom and revolting against God ... In Egypt they [the French] loooted the country and killed the innocent Christians ... Their satanic intentions are seen ... So God established the present kingdoms to keep people in the right route and in order ... The kings are assigned to teach people to obey and control their excesses and bad actions ... The sneaky demon creates a chaos with the pretext of liberty and equality ... these are rebels against God and enemies of peace" (p. 26-27).

---

the same understanding but the endings change in compliance with the Greek grammar.) Etymologically "Romios" comes from Roman and the word was used instead of Hellen to stress the religious difference from the ancients. So "Romaic" is a way of reminding that a religious and Byzantine identity is in the agenda.

[102] It is not clarified who asked for this guarantee of preserving the "tradition"?

According to Metallinos "The Patriarchate had to react as a constituent of the Ottoman State and its zeal originates from the permanent suspicion that the ethnic Romaic section and the whole Orthodoxy feel against the Frankish West" (p. 30).

"The reason that the Ottoman State and the Greek-Orthodox Church moved together was that at that moment they had common interests in fighting against the French danger" (p. 34). "One should not read the acts of that time anachronistically with today's criteria... The nation faced a direct danger ... to change master and to have a "French-type" one, was equal to becoming a French type nation, in other words the disappearance of the [Greek] nation. *The same thing* is *happening today in another context*" [my underlining, HM] (p. 35). "The destruction of the Ottoman State in favor of atheist France meant the domination of the '*Franks' (Φραγκιά) and the realization of its permanent goal which is the extinction of the Byzantine Empire* " (p. 35). [My underlining, HM].[103] It is great naivety to believe that Napoleon was acting in favor of the Greeks ... But this applies also today and this is the weak point of Greek foreign policy, that is, believing in imaginary 'philhellenes'" (p. 37).

The rest of the Introduction is a eulogy on the ideas of Parios and justifications of some of his extreme theses. Parios is presented as a defender of the Greek-Orthodox belief in "the conflicting East-West meeting" (p. 43); as an "ardent fighter against European Enlightenment" (p. 47); and as a saint after the decision of the Patriarchate in 1995. He then summarized the main ideas of the book by Parios ending with the main idea: "Let us not be afraid of slavery, but of sin. This is the real slavery. And this is what the French liberty proclaims." (p. 56).

9- Summary and Assessment

In Chapter 1, the most widely discussed three modern Greek myths, the Secret School, the role of the Patriarch in 1821 and the role of Agia Lavra Monastery are presented. The arguments of both sides, i.e., those who perceive these stories as presenting real events or at least a symbolic expression of a reality and, on the other hand, those who see myths that are detached from reality are presented in detail. This endeavor gives an idea of how myths are defended or rejected, as well as of some dynamics that are related to myths.

For a myth to exist two components are necessary: Some that believe in a story (as true) and some others that call the same story a myth, disbelieving. The three myths in this chapter are directly related to the Greek-Orthodox

---

[103] Apparently Metallinos believes that in the 1790ies the Byzantine Empire existed basically because the Church existed.

Church, more precisely, about the role of the Church in some events that are crucial for the "nation".

All the pros and cons arguments about these stories incorporate issues about the (positive) character of the Greek nation as well as the enemies of the nation, (the Other). For the "believers" challenging the validity of these stories is perceived as disputing the identity of the nation but also the positive role of the Church.

The controversy between the "two parties" shows that there is a demarcation on the ground of East/West, or conservatism/modernism or right/left that sometimes go back to a few centuries. The perception of the "West" is also discussed in connection to this dichotomy. Behind the controversy on the "historical verification" or "refutation" of these stories/myths there exists a fight for the recognition of the positive role of the Church and of its followers. The strife is about the role that the conservative forces played in the years 1789-1821; but it is also related to the "character of the nation" even though this is indirectly inferred.

There is an effort on the part of the state to bring peace between past rivals. For example the statue of the Patriarch Gregorios was placed in front of the University of Athens in 1881, at the same place where in 1871 the statue of Rigas was placed before. In 1875 the statue of Korais joined them (Koulouri, 203). The last two were the declared enemies by the Patriarchate prior to the Revolution (by the Patriarchate), but of course the Patriarch could not react to this gathering in the 1870s.

Another contradiction is the legitimacy of a Saint, Athanasios Parios. The main values of the modern Greek state at present are "independence, liberty and freedom, equality and a common fate with the European Community, i.e., the West. However Parios in 1800 but also G. Metallinos in our days clearly stated that the West "always" undermined Greek-Orthodoxy and Greek national identity: *"The same thing is happening today in another context"*. And again *"The destruction of the Ottoman State in favor of atheist France meant the domination of the 'Franks' and the realization of its permanent goal which is the extinction of the Byzantine Empire ".* So, some Greeks are left in between the official and the existing reality, on one hand, and the traditional view– still supported by some with references to a Saint – of the negative/enemy West, on the other.

At the end of the 18th century the revolutionaries saw a negative Ottoman/Turk and supported the idea of an uprising. At that time the Church was for obedience and even for support towards the Port against the Westerners: The Ottomans were the will of God. In our, days as we saw above and in connection to the Secret School, this position changed completely, it was reversed. The conservative Easterners of today, who are in defense of the

Church, claim that the "oppressive barbaric "Turks" prohibited the education of the Greeks" and that the Church tried to counterbalance the situation.

In connection with these some human psychological tendencies – "confirmation bias" i.e., to use only evidence that suits ones beliefs, and "boomerang effect", i.e., to believe even more in a myth when evidence proves it wrong – are discussed, too. The role of the State as well as the Church is being also discussed showing the forces that create and/or preserve some myths. The instrumentalization of these myths with political or power gaining motives is another aspect discussed above.

The three myths are still being discussed in Greece, but not clearly expounding the historical and social setting in which the controversy is experienced. The discussion is restricted in a narrow problematic of "historical documentation" or of one being patriotic and religious or not! In the beginning of the 20th century a new interpretation of the Greek Revolution appeared which claims that "mythical and symbolic meanings attributed to reality and distorted reality"; that was the Marxist/communist ideology (Repoussi, 176). Was this movement against myths or was it a new myth? A final evaluation of this situation will be tried after some more "myths" are being discussed.

***

CHAPTER 2

MYTHS RELATED TO ANCIENT GREECE

10- How old can a nation be?

The above three myths are related to the Orthodox Church and to national ideals. There are several national myths related to Ancient Greece, too, that are (presumably) secular. However, these are of a different kind. The three myths above (the secret school, the Patriarch and the Lavra story) are being discussed in Greece widely as "myths". One can find various books and hundreds of articles that are in opposition on these issues. As we have seen above, there are supporters, on both sides, for and against them. The references to the Ancient Greece, on the other hand, are not perceived and approached as "myths", at least, not as widely as it is done with the above three "classical" myths. The "beliefs" about the Ancients are more widely internalized.

The Ancient Greeks, in general, are seen as "our ancestors" and especially their language as "our language". The modern Greeks see themselves as the heirs of the ancient glory.[104] The basic understanding behind these beliefs is the "uninterrupted existence of the nation" for the last three millenniums. On the other hand, the thousand years of uninterrupted "national" continuum is disputed, not so much in Greece but worldwide in the academic milieu and in the context of the modern understanding of the "nation". The related controversy is introduced in Greece by the academics that came in contact with the world academic developments.

The turning point was the decade of the 1980s when, in the "West", the "nation" was defined anew as a relatively new construct and even as an "imagined" society.[105] Benedict Anderson defined the nation as "an imagined political community – and imagined as both inherently limited and sovereign... Nationalism is not the awakening of nations to self-consciousness; it invents nations where they do not exist" (Anderson, p. 15). He reminded that Seaton-Watson also inferred this "imagining" when he wrote "All that I can find to say is that a nation exists when a significant number of people in a community consider themselves to form a nation, or

---

[104] Among 34 countries of Europe the Greeks rank first in having a glorious self-appreciation. When asked, they answered that "we may not be perfect but we have a superior culture compared to other nations" by 89%. See: Eastern and Western Europeans Differ on Importance of Religion, Views of Minorities, and Key Social Issues | Pew Research Center (pewforum.org)

[105] See, for example the input of Benedict Anderson, Hugh Seaton-Watson, Ernest Gellner, Ernest Hobsbawm.

behave as if they formed one" (Seaton-Watson, p. 5). According to Ernest Gellner "It is nationalism which engenders nations, not the other way round... Dead languages can be revived, traditions invented, quite fictitious pristine purities restored... The cultural shreds and patches used by nationalists are often arbitrary historical inventions... Society no longer worships itself through religious symbols; a modern, streamlined, high culture celebrates itself in song and dance, which it borrows (stylizing it in the process) from a folk culture which it fondly believes itself to be perpetuating, defending, and reaffirming" (Gellner, p. 55-58).

Hobsbawm, too, gives the same message in his book titled *The Invention of Tradition*. But don't all these - the insistence in the "imagined" character of the nations, the people who "consider themselves" a nation, the "arbitrary historical traditions" that are invented to justify the existence of the nation - point to a mythical aspect of the nation? Isn't this belief in a nation a truth and an objective reality for many, but which at the same time is contested by some others as an "imagined construct"? Is it possible that the national paradigm is only a myth? With these questions in mind I wrote the following paragraphs.

Anthony Smith who put forward the ethnic origin of the nations ("ethnic cores, ethnie") stressed the mythical side of the human communities. "At the centre of every ethnie ... stands a distinctive complex of myths, memories, and symbols (or myth-symbol complex) with peculiar claims about the group's origins and lines of descent. These claims and this complex provide the focus of a community's identity and its *myhthomoteur*, or constitutive political myth" (Smith, 1989 (1986), p. 57-58). A. Smith proposed the following "ideal-typical definition" of the "nation":

> "[A] named and self-defined human community whose members cultivate shared myths, memories, symbols, values, and traditions, reside in and identify with a historic homeland, create and disseminate a distinctive public culture, and observe shared customs, and common laws. In similar vein, we may also define "national identity" as the continuous reproduction and reinterpretation of the pattern of values, symbols, myths, and traditions that compose the distinctive heritage of nations, and the identification of individuals with that pattern and heritage" (Smith, 2008, p.19).

The nature of the Greek nation is being discussed among the Greeks but especially among the academics. According to a Greek sociologist, the controversy tends to develop to one where "whilst the state-centric modernist theories regard nation as developed *from above,* a modern creation *ex nihilo* enforced by state elites on a *tabula rasa,* the ethno-symbolist approaches tend to privilege the community based, the horizontal, the *from below-popular* constituents of modern nations."[106]

The popular belief, however, is that the Greek nation is as old as the Ancient Greeks. This is what is taught in primary and intermediary schools. Even the prestigious 17 volume publication, in which about 300 Greek academicians in most cases expressed the "modern understanding of the nation" and narrated the story of the Greeks from antiquity to today, is titled *History of the Greek Nation* (Η ιστορία του ελληνικού έθνους) and this title is seen a natural one.

The believers of the primordial Greek nation do not normally discuss this issue since they consider it self-evident. It is the modernists who are more inclined to discuss the phenomenon of the "Greek nation", even though they do not necessarily share identical ideas. For example, in 2008 there was a conflict between the historian Antonis Liakos and the poet and critic Nasos Vayenas where both accused the other of constructing myths in this topic. The dispute was on how old the Greek nation and the "national consciousness" were. The first saw the beginning of Greek national identity to appear at the end of the 18th century and the second as early as the 13th. Still, both did not go as back as the Ancients. Liakos used the title "mythologies" to characterize the views of his opponent and Vayenas in his article used the words "creating of myths" as a characteristic of Liakos.[107]

This choice and use of the word "myth", interestingly, is in harmony with the basic characteristic of the "myth" that I pointed out above: One's truth is the myth of the other! In this case, of course, the problematic transcends the Greek case. As I pointed above, the time-depth of the nations is an academic worldwide issue and it is being actually discussed as such. I leave this international side of the dispute for a later opportunity and I turn to the Greek case and on how and when the myths that are related to the Ancient Greeks were developed.

11 – Ancient Greece and the creation of a nation

When Christianity started to spread among the Greek speaking populations in the first centuries of CE it had to face the legacy of the Ancient Greek beliefs and philosophy. The clash was a decisive one and it was fought both in the domain of ideas and of the symbols: Turning temples to churches, destroying "pagan" statues and manuscripts, prohibiting Olympic athletic

---

[106] Eleni Andriakaina, http://www.open.ac.uk/arts/research/finance-crisis-protest/comment-and-debate /dispute-between-anti-nationalist-modernism-and-primordialism
[107] "Μυθολογίες" and "μυθοπλασία" respectively. See: 1) https://www.tovima.gr/2008/11/24/ opinions/ mythologies-kai-agiografies/ and 2) http://geromorias.blogspot.com/2019/04/blog-post_83. html

meetings, etc. One of the greatest "rivals" of the New Testament was the Greek philosophy. Saint Paul was adamant: "See to it that no one takes you captive through hollow and deceptive philosophy, which depends on human tradition and the elemental spiritual forces of this world rather than on Christ."[108]

This enmity against the "pagan ideas" lasted for centuries. Even today the Greek Church uses the writings of The Fathers of the Church who condemned Ancient Greek philosophy, literature and social practices. For example, the "Anathema" that the Second Council of Nicea established and mostly is against the Ancient teachings, is read in the churches every year during the Feast of Orthodoxy.[109]

In present day Greece there are some small groups that criticize the Greek Church. Among other accusations that are directly related to daily politics, one allegation is that the Church was always against Ancient Greek philosophy, culture and heritage, inferring an anti-Greek attitude, too.[110] The defense of the Church - that is developed against what they call "New-paganist mythology" - can be found in internet blogs close to the Church. The main ideas of the 27-thousand word text are the following:[111]

> The ancient Greek philosophers and poets (from Plato to Homer, all of them) in their texts exhibit many contradictions and mistakes. Each one of them says something different, too, so one cannot reach a final truth - contrary to the consistent preaching of the Church. These ancient thinkers also defended harmful practices such as lechery, prostitution, adultery, cannibalism, atheism (ασέλγειες, πορνείες,

---

[108] Letter of Paul to Colossians 2/8, according to the *Holy Bible, New International Version*, Biblica Inc., 2011. Also see: *The Holy Bible*, by the American Revision Committee, New York: Thomas Nelson and Sons, 1901: "Take heed lest there shall be any one that maketh spoil of you through his philosophy and vain deceit, after the tradition of men, after the rudiments of the world, and not after Christ." There are other translations, however, that skip the word philosophy! "Be on your guard; do not let your mind be captured by hollow and delusive speculations, based on the traditions of man-made teaching and centred on the elemental spirit of the world and not on Christ". *The New English Bible, New Testament*, Oxford & Cambridge Un. Press, 1961. The Greek text is clear about "philosophy": "Βλέπετε μή τις ὑμᾶς ἔσται ὁ συλαγωγῶν διὰ τῆς φιλοσοφίας καὶ κενῆς ἀπάτης, κατὰ τὴν παράδοσιν τῶν ἀνθρώπων, κατὰ τὰ στοιχεῖα τοῦ κόσμου καὶ οὐ κατὰ Χριστόν".

[109] The Fathers of the Church were ancient and influential Christian theologians who established the intellectual and doctrinal foundations of Christianity. The historical period during which they flourished ends approximately around 700 CE. Anathema means: 1) something or someone that one vehemently dislikes. 2) A formal curse by a council of the Church, excommunicating a person or denouncing a doctrine. The Second Council of Nicaea (787) is recognized as the last of the first seven ecumenical councils by the Eastern Orthodox Church and the Catholic Church. In addition, it is also recognized as such by the Old Catholics and others. Protestant opinions on it are varied. The Feast of Orthodoxy is celebrated on the first Sunday of Great Lent (six Sundays before Eastern) The feast is kept in memory of the final defeat of iconoclasm and the restoration of the icons to the churches.

[110] See for example: Maravelias; Simopoulos, 2010.

[111] See: http://www.apologitis.com/gr/ancient/anathemata.htm. Interestingly, the Church accuses its opponents as creating a "New-paganist mythology" while others accuse the church as perpetuating myths.

μοιχεία, ανθρωποφαγίες, αθεΐα). The Church has to protect its followers. This is the purpose of the "anathemata". The anathema is not directed against the person or the "nation" (γένος) of the Hellens but only against the ideas of the individuals. Anathema is not a "curse" (κατάρα) but a means to keep somebody outside the Church community. Actually, the practice of anathema helped in preserving the nation. Besides, the person who behaves so badly puts himself outside the Church by his own will and the consequences are his responsibility. The Greek Christians did read the ancient texts but only for didactic purposes (για διδασκαλία), not believing in their mistakes.

It is clear that the Church is on the defense since old discourses and views need to be adjusted to the era of nation-states. It tries to affirm that it is not against the nation which is supposed to include the ancient Greeks, too: So the Greeks of today may read the "anathematized" ancient texts – for didactic purposes though. The Church only tries to protect its flock from mistakes and does not anathematize individuals but only "ideas". However, for the meaning of "anathema" (ανάθεμα) two prestigious Greek dictionaries give "curse" (κατάρα) as a synonym (See: Academy; Babiniotis).

For many centuries the word "Greek" (Έλλην) meant "pagan" and anti-Christian. For example, in the English translation of the New Testament the Greek word Έλλην (Greek) is correctly translated as "pagan". The Grecophones Byzantines called themselves "Romios (Ρωμιός), a word derived from "Roman" and the East Roman Empire's legacy. It is almost impossible to find a "Greek" baptized with an ancient Greek name until the end of the 18th century. All the Greeks until that time were using "Christian" names. But with the rise of the Greek nationalism and later the Greek nation-state, historiography recreated the past. This time the Christian past became a "national past".

12- Greek historiography and the perception of the nation (ethnos)

During the age of revolutions and on the eve of the Greek war of independence, that is, in the years 1780-1830, some Grecophone intellectuals of the Diaspora who lived in various cities of Western Europe and who were influenced by the French Revolution and the ideological controversies of the time spread republican ideas within their ethnic communities and proposed radical actions against "the tyrant", the Ottoman ruler. Others, such as those close to the conservative patriarchate of Constantinople, who lived within the boundaries of the Ottoman Empire anathematized them as "atheists" and advised prudence and adherence to "paternal ideals". For the latter, as we saw above, the Ottoman rule was God's will, rather a punishment for not being pious enough. It was during this period that questions related to national/ethnic identity were posed for the first time: are we *Romeoi* (Ρωμιοί/Romans, in the sense of Byzantines), *Grekoi* (Γρεκοί/Greeks, "the way the westerners call us"), *Hellens* (Έλληνες as the Ancients) or *Orthodox Christians*? There were serious political, ideological and identity disagreements among the Grecophone intellectuals of that time, but still all shared a sense of belonging to a common *genos* (γένος), in the sense of a community/race (Millas, 1994).

NAMING A NATION AND BUILDING ITS IMAGE

The mythical side of the nation is obscured when the nation is taken for granted. Some situations are perceived as given, as self-understood, as normal, as natural; and not as historical, made up, contingent, and/or as results of controversies that reached to an end sometimes even by coincidental events. In the first case the need in investigating the national discourse does not arise. One may get involved, for example, in writing a voluminous study on the Greeks not questioning even the basic terms: What does one mean by "Greek"?

The Grecophone Orthodox Christian community living in the Ottoman Empire under the official status of a *millet* (religious community), and which in our modern times could be identified as an "ethnic group", perceived itself as a *genos*. *Genos* is a Greek word etymologically originating from Sanskrit, meaning a group of the same origin (*genus* in Latin, *gen/gene* in English, but meaning something different). During the years of nation-building the word *genos* was gradually replaced by *ethnos*, and the latter was and is still used in Greek in the sense of "nation". There is no other word for "nation" and the ethnic/national distinction does not exist among the Greeks in general, but only among a small group of historians who are aware of the latest trends in historiography.[112] "Ethnic" (*ethnicos*) is used for "national". In other words, in the Greek historiography "Greekness" and Greek nationhood are heavily loaded with a sense of "ethnicity" and not with citizenship and/or loyalty to a state. This may be due to the historical fact that the Grecophones did not directly associate "identity" and "state", since a communal identity (as *genos*, characterized by a consciousness of a religious difference *vis- a-vis* the Muslim Ottoman state) was widespread and established among them long before the existence of a state with which the community identified itself.

---

[112] The Babiniotis dictionary defines "ethnic/ethnos" the same way as one would define "nation"; it adds that the "foreigners use the Greek word 'ethnic' to denote national groups and minorities." The last decades academics use the "ethnotita" in the sense of ethnic.

However, until the end of the 18th century the name of this "nation" was not self-evident. Greek intellectuals were in doubt and shared different opinions. Georgios Gemistos (Γεώργιος Γεμιστός, 1355-1452) was a "Greek" who very early stated that "we are Hellens, like the ancients as it is apparent from our genos and our language". But this utterance was silenced and soon forgotten. There were a few more utterances of "Greekness" in the next three centuries but this opinion never became popular among the people. In 1768 Evgenios Boulgaris (Ευγένιος Βούλγαρης, 1716-1806) suggested the name Grekos (the Greek version of "Greek") and objecting the use both of Romios and Hellen because they reminded the Romans and paganism respectively, and especially "because in our days all the nations of Europe know us as Greeks". Apparently the most important ideologist of Greek nationhood Adamantios Korais (Αδαμάντιος Κοραής, 1748-1833), too, was for the use of Grekos and adamantly against the name Romios because that was the name of the Romans who actually enslaved "us". (Dimaras 1974, p. 349-350).

Eventually the word Hellen was preferred. It is of interest that the Greek-speaking intellectuals at the eve of the Greek Revolution missed the important point that when the Westerners used the word "Greeks" they used it for both the ancient Greeks and the modern Greeks. Whereas the Greeks at the end of the 18th century tried to choose a name for the new nation and for themselves that differentiated the modern Greeks from the ancient Greeks (the Hellens). The unity of the ancients and the modern Greeks was a conviction of the Western intellectuals, not of the Grecophones of that time. And this approach of most modern Greek intellectuals originated basically from their conviction that the Ancient Greeks were of a "pagan" character, and therefore different from "us", a view that originated from the Church and from the Christian belief. In other words, the continuity of the Greek nation from antiquity to the 19th century was a Western concept.

This uninterrupted existence of the "Greeks" for a few millenniums is noticed in the Western discourse from very old times. For example, the Byzantines were seen and referred as "Greeks" by the Crusaders of the Fourth Crusade of 1204, too (Joinville). The term "Greek-Orthodox" was not used by the Greeks and the Orthodox Church, simply because they would not identify themselves with "pagans". As its name, the Eastern Church used titles as Eastern Orthodox Church (Ανατολική Ορθόδοξη Εκκλησία) and/or Orthodox Catholic[113] and Apostolic Church (Ορθόδοξη, Καθολική και Αποστολική Εκκλησία). The prefix "Greek" originated in the West and in the Modern times of Nation-States.

Quite naturally, the western historiography perceived and presented the

---

[113] Catholic here does not mean the historic doctrine and practice of the Western Church, but "universal". It is a Greek word used from the early years of Christianity until today by the Greek Orthodox Church.

Greeks as a continuum from ancient times to the modern times. For example, *The History of Modern Greece – From Its Conquest by the Romans, B.C. 146, to the Present Time*, by James Emerson (Tennent) published in 1830 narrates the story of the "Greeks" as expressed in the title of his study, as an uninterrupted existence from the past to the present (Emerson).[114]

The Romantic Movement as well as the Enlightenment was enthusiastic with the "reborn" of the Greeks. Keats, Byron, Chateaubriand and so many others saw the "rebirth" of the "Greeks". Shelley wrote:

> The world's great age begins anew,
>
> The golden years return,
>
> The earth doth like a snake renew
>
> Her winter weeds outworn.
>
> Another Athens shall arise,
>
> And to remoter time
>
> Bequeath, like sunset to the skies,
>
> The splendour of its prime

As early as the 17th century the "Westerners" were already interested in Greeks, both in ancient Greeks and in their "grandchildren". That Racine in 1677 wrote and presented in Paris a play titled Phèdre (Phedra) was seen as a normal initiative. The western travelers that reached "Greek lands" were expecting to meet people that were related to the glorious past. They usually experienced dissolution; they could not meet people that resembled Homer and Plato. But they did two things. First they noticed "some traits" that were interpreted as characteristics of the ancients Greeks and that they reached our times, and second, they "explained" why the modern Greeks were not up to the standards of the ancient ones: It was due to the slavery incurred by the Turks.

Mirabal, for example, in the end of the 17th century met Greeks in Peloponnesus who were ignorant, short of education and even cowards, but they had a "vivacity" special to them that showed who their ancestors were. As for the shortcomings, those were explained by their centuries-long slavery

---

[114] "Although Romanticism did not produce any monumental historical masterpiece on Byzantium, it created the conceptual framework in which the connection of Modern Greece to its historical predecessor, Byzantium, appeared natural, logical, historically justified. See: also (Saradi, p. 12); (Yakovaki, 2015) for a detailed account of how Europeans discovered and reconstructed Ancient and Middle Age Greece.

(Mirabal, p. 51-52 and Simopoulos, 1984, p. 482 and 1985).[115]

Philosophers, too, perceived Ancient Greece as a model in the 18th century. To be a Greek/Hellen in the 17th and 18th century looked prestigious. Hume, for example praises and sees ancient Greeks as a model for progress in art and sciences:

"Greece was a cluster of little principalities, which soon became republics; and being united both by their near neighborhood, and by the ties of the same language and interest, they entered into the closest intercourse of commerce and learning… *[E]very circumstance among that people seemed to favour the rise of the arts and sciences.* Each city produced its several artists and philosophers, who refused to yield the preference to those of the neighboring republics: Their contention and debates sharpened the wits of men… After the Roman Christian, or Catholic church had spread itself over the civilized world, and had engrossed all the learning of the times; being really one large state within itself, and united under one head; this variety of sects immediately disappeared … But mankind, having at length thrown off this yoke, affairs are now returned nearly to the same situation as before, and *Europe is at present a copy at large, of what Greece was formerly a pattern in miniature.*[My underling, HM] (Hume).

The "modern Greeks" who initiated the Greek Revolution and envisaged a new state for the nation, shared this enthusiasm. Maybe it would be more precise to say that they were influenced by and *followed* this enthusiasm. In the subsequent years the modern Greeks adjusted themselves to the Western understanding: Today in Greek language there is a single word, Hellen (Ελλην), for "all Greeks", ancient, Byzantines and modern. This course of events shows the heavy and decisive influence of the "West" in the developing of the Greek identity or at least the name of the nation.

---

[115] The image of the modern Greeks in the "West" is still romantic. The days I was writing these lines I read in a Greek newspaper (December 5, 2020, Ta Nea) the reminiscence of P.K. Ioakeimidis of his meeting with Valéry Giscard d'Estaing in 2003 - and who had just died on December, 2. The writer was accompanying the Greek Prime Minister K. Simitis as an advisor on matters of European Union and they were visiting the President of France G. d'Estaing in his house. Ioakeimidis was given an opportunity to ask him why he had shown such a fervent support for Greece's joining the EU. G. d'Estaing reminded his close friendship with the old Greek Prime Minister K. Karamanlis and then added that he always felt as if he owed to pay back a kind of a credit note. "I owed something to Plato, I thought that Europe's integration wouldn't be fulfilled without the country of Plato and Aristotle. But I was somehow naïve and maybe romantic thinking that with Greece joining the EU, Plato, Aristotle and Pericles and the other wise Greeks, or at least some variations of those would be part of Europe. Unfortunately instead of Plato and Aristotle, most of the time, we met strange situations. We met people who were short of the wisdom and of the rationality of the Greek thought. And the most important, they did not want to see how EU operated. Now I am glad that with Kostas Simitis Greek rationalism comes back. Kostas is a great Greek."

It was not, however, only the name of the (Greek) nation that was indirectly guided by the western intellectuals. The *positive* image of the ancient Greeks was a Western discovery (or invention), too. It was first in the "west" that the taboo of the "pagan Greeks" that initially was introduced by Christianity was gradually abandoned, as the case of Hume shows. And this was done much earlier than the 18th century, i,e., the time that the Greek speaking Orthodox people in the East had experienced their "Greek Enlightenment".

When ancient Greeks were "anathematized" as pagans in the "East", in the "West" cultural developments such Classicism, Humanism, Renaissance and later Romanticism promoted an image of a positive Greece with exemplary heroes. To make the long story short, the ancient Greeks were first discovered by the Muslim Arabs when they conquered Syria and Asia Minor and met the Greek texts that had reached these places with Alexander the Great, i.e., during the Hellenistic years. When the Arabs reached Toledo having in their possession the translations of the ancient Greek texts, Spain in the 13th century turned to a contact place of Western culture and the Arabic one. Those years the Byzantines were not very interested in these ancient texts (Gutas).

The "West" came to know Aristotle through Avicenna (1120-1198) who appreciated the Ancient Greeks and had become a name of reference.[116] Soon Dante (1265-1321) in his *Divine Comedy* exalted Homer, Socrates and Plato even though they "were not baptized". Petrarch (1304-1374) tried to secure the translation of Homer. Boccaccio (1313-1375) sets for the translations of Euripides and Aristotle. The West by the 14th century was in a happy mood of enjoying the classical Greece.[117] Naturally this was a sign of a positive and

---

[116] Avicenna must be seen in context with his Islamic colleagues, for example with Ibn Rushd (Averroes) and others, who, during the Islamic golden age, served as invaluable conduits of textual transmission and interpretation of Hellenistic learning for an amnesic Europe.

[117] See for example how ancient Greece was an issue of interest as early as the 15th century in the German speaking geographies (Graecogermania).

highly esteemed Ancient Greece.

Romantic movement, much later, together with the Philhellenic Movement – was ready the see the "rebirth of the Greeks" without the need to make a distinction between the Ancient and the Modern Greeks – contrary to what the modern Greeks tried to do by drawing a demarcation line between the Hellens and the Grekoi or Romioi.[118] Eventually the modern Greeks jointed the Westerners and they accepted the unity and the continuity of the Greeks: Ancient, Byzantines and Modern.

Modern Greeks felt proud reading how the "westerners" perceived them; and they accepted the role assigned to them: to be the heirs of the ancient Greeks. In the introduction of the translation in English of Guys' *A Sentiment Journal through Greece in a series of letters*, we read the traveler's experience from "Greece". Is it ancient or modern? The question is not one of significance.

> "The glorious heights the Greeks arrived at, in every branch of science, and in the fine arts, have very justly rendered them a model for all other nations. The philosophers, and artists of succeeding ages, have invariably looked up to them for their fist principles.
>
> The Romans, their immediate successors, copied them in almost every particular; they adopted their virtues, they practiced their vices. Remotest nations, thru their means, felt the impression. Even Britain, situated at such a distance from the seat of the Roman empire, after falling a prey to her arms, became the imitators of her glories. It is therefore not surprising, that the civilized countries of Europe should early embrace every opportunity of information, with respect to *a people to whom they owe so many obligations. We hereby trace, as it were, our origin*; at least, we may say, the source of our manners, and the fountain of our knowledge." [My underlining, HM] (Guys, p III-IV).

Richard Clogg concludes:

> "During the centuries of the Tourkokratia [Ottoman rule over the Greeks, HM] knowledge of the ancient Greek world had all but died out, but, under the stimulus of western classical scholarship, the budding intelligentsia developed an awareness that were the heirs to an heritage that was universally revered throughout the civilized

---

[118] The picture is from a book of 1782 where Greece is presented as a woman in the form of a chained slave: Choiseul Gouffier, Marie Gabriel Florent Auguste de, French diplomat (1752-1817), Voyage pittoresque de la Grèce, Paris. A. Liakos comments on the imaging of the ancient ruins that are central in the Western cultures but not in the Eastern. "Neither the Chinese nor the Japanese culture possesses this culture… This picturing belongs to the Renaissance, it was experienced as extremely attractive in the time of Romanticism and it was related to nostalgia" (Liakos, 2007, p. 192).

world. By the eve of the war of independence the *progonoplexia* (ancestor obsession) and *arkhaiolatria* (worship of antiquity), to use the expressive Greek terms, had reached almost obsessive proportions. It was precisely during the first decade of the nineteenth century that nationalists, much to the consternation of the Church authorities, began to baptise their children with the names of (and to call their ships after) the worthiest of ancient Greece rather than the Christian saints" (Clogg, p. 27-28).

Whereas for a while, during the years just before and after the Greek Revolution the Byzantine Empire was presented as an anti-Greek hostile power by some Greeks who were in contrast with conservative Church circles. The Byzantine Empire for them was an oppressive regime against the Greeks, close to an invading Roman state. The understanding behind this view was a dichotomy of pairs such as the people versus the oppressor aristocracy (Muslim and/or Christian), the glorious ancient Greeks versus the Christian Patriarchate in alliance with the Ottomans and "us" the revolutionaries versus the "others", those who fight against "us".

The ideals of these Greek intellectuals who were for an ethnically/nationally independent state can be traced in the historical analysis entitled *Hellenic Nomarchy* (which was discussed in some detail above). Similar texts, which were shown and analysed above were clearly anticlerical, even sceptical on issues of religion, and they were attacked by the Greek Orthodox patriarchate of Istanbul as anti-religious. Their discourse was ethnic/national, in the sense of an identity that was defined as a historical continuum based on language and culture. A class controversy was indirectly voiced, too, since it was pointed out that some (e.g. religious dignitaries and wealthy farmers) lived in luxury, whereas the laymen suffered. In fact, during this pre-revolutionary period a contention prevailed between middle-class/secular intellectuals on one hand and the religious/conservative groups on the other, even though both sides tried to prove that their visions were not in opposition to communal traditions and values.

There were contrasting views about the period of the Byzantine Empire, too. According to *Hellenic Nomarchy* the story of the Greeks in the Byzantine Empire is as follows:

"[From the time of Roman conquest] until the year 368 when the Roman Empire was divided as East and West the Greeks suffered a terrible tyranny and sufferings due to the various harsh emperors. They could not free themselves from this subjugation ... since the country was very wide and they could not unite to cope with the tyrant. Therefore, from the time Christianity was founded until 1453 [the date signals the end of the Byzantine Empire, HM] instead of having an increase in the means of liberation, unfortunately they were curtailed. The superstitions, the lies and the corrupt lives of the priests and of the patriarchs dominated the soul of the kings, who instead of working for the benefit of the people they fought among themselves and they only built churches… They turned Greece to a waste land." (Anonymous p.81)

Even after the liberation and the founding of the Greek State the image of the Byzantine Empire among some intellectuals was negative. There were cases that this empire was perceived as a foreign and hostile regime. In a Greek novel of 1834, which for some constitutes the first Greek novel, published right after the founding of the new Greek state, one reads that the Ottoman fleet is called "Byzantine fleet", in the sense that both empires, the Byzantine and the Ottoman, were the same or of the same sort. During the 1820's the Ottomans asked the involvement of Egypt in subduing the Greek revolutionaries. This is expressed as follows:

"These naval battles were fought against the Byzantine, Egyptian and African fleets; these were battles which saved Greece" (Soutsos, p. 136 and Millas 2001, p. 330).

In the same novel we read how the author perceives the image that the Western world has vis-à-vis the modern Greeks and Greece: The West recognizes Greece as "giving life anew to the first born people of the world [αναγεννητὴν του πρωτότοκου λαού της γης]. We have to remind you the great shadow of the past which surrounds you here, and the great expectations of the century, which you have been the representative of the enlightened West against the East (p. 130) … the Holly Greece which I marveled as the victor of Asia in the old and new centuries" (p. 141).

THE FALLMERAYER EVENT

There were, however, Europeans who reacted and objected to the scheme of "the uninterrupted millenniums long existence of Greeks." The German-language scholar Jacob Philipp Fallmerayer (1790-1861), the author of *The Empire of Trapezunt*, for example, who had travelled extensively in the Ottoman lands, defended the thesis that Slav and later Albanian immigration virtually had swamped the Greek population of medieval Greece. It was therefore meaningless to claim that the Greeks were descendents of the Greeks of antiquity (Fallmerayer; Skopetea 1997; Millas 2000, p. 340; 2003, p. 166;). Of course, Fallmerayer's claims, whatever their historical accuracy, are important only if national or racial "purity" are important considerations. This seems to apply to certain authors of Turkish textbooks, too, who, in a derogatory sense, call the Greeks "half-cast" or "cross-bread" (*melez*) (Millas, 1991).

Some other researchers referred to the Byzantines who migrated to the West and identified themselves as Greeks (Hellens) inferring that *that* was their identity in the 15th century (Steiris). There may be two reservations on this view. First, in the 15th century the West had already formed and imposed the positive image of the Ancients and one may imagine the Orthodox Grecophones to follow the accepted western imagery. Second, the Byzantines knew that a declared "Hellenic identity" on their part would secure prestige. In other words, the existence of Grecophones who called themselves Hellens in the 15th century's West does not contradict with what is said above about the role of the West in the formation of the modern Greek identity.

The claim of a Greek historian who published one of the most detailed story of the Fallmerayer event is of a paramount importance: "The books that may compose a bibliography that appeared from the mid 18th century [on Greek history and until the time of Fallmerayer, i.e., mid 19th century, HM], are almost all with no exception, either simple translations or in the best case ... variations of foreign, French, Italian and especially German historical texts" (Veloudis, 1970, p. 9).

During the decade 1830-1840, the new state in the domain of historiography published some textbooks which were again translations of western historians and which were used as propaganda to promote the "nationalized ancient Greek history" (p. 16). Among the historians who followed were Oliver Goldsmith (1730-1774) and Edward Gibbon (1737-1794). The first really Greek effort to recount the story of the Greeks is Yorgos Kozakis-Tipaldos (1790-1867) who in 1839 published his *Philosophical Essay* with which he started what came to be known as "national" historiography.

Fallmerayer was not the first and only "mis-Hellen" [μισέλληνας/hater of Greeks, the opposite of philhellene]. According to Veloudis, Cornelius de Paus (1739-1799), Jakob Bartholdy (1779-1825), Alphonse de Lamartine (1790-1869) and Edmond About (1828-1885) did not see a birth of the Antique Greeks in the 18th century, either. But it was Fallmerayer, the historian who, after the failure of the 1848 revolution which he endorsed and his following turbulent personal life, the one that systematically combated the western romantic view of the rebirth of the ancient Greeks.

At the basis of his arguments there was a racist reasoning. He disputed the racist legacy of modern Greeks seeing somehow a Slavic and Albanian "blood". His view caused uproar in Greece. The rejection of the antique roots of the Greeks could not be accepted. Konstatinos Paparrigopoulos appeared as the most prominent historian who undertook the defying of Fallmerayer.

He did that by criticizing the used historical sources as well as their interpretation. He dedicated all his work to the "roots of the Hellens". According to Veloudis, Paparrigopoulos (1815-1891) made use of the works of western historians to do that, namely the J. W. Zinkeisen and Bartholomaus Kopitar, but he operated as a genuine and able historian writing his 12 volume work, too.[119]

My intention here is not to judge the two opponents but to show the course that produced the official Greek thesis about the origin and the roots of modern Greeks. Paparrigopoulos laid the foundation (or one of the foundations!) of the modern Greek identity: The Greeks compose a nation, the Greek nation, which is thousand years old and the binding force of this nation is the Greek language (p. 71). He exalted the "Greek" Byzantine period and he thus secured the uninterrupted continuum of the state. Fallmerayer thus triggered the creation of the grand national narrative of modern Greece.

13- Helleno-Christianity – the maturing of the national discourse

The Jacobin, revolutionary and republican discourse was silenced before the termination of the Greek uprising for independence and even forgotten after the founding of the new Greek nation-state. The founding of the Holy Alliance (of throne and altar) in 1815 and Metternich's determination to discourage popular class and anti-royalist revolutions should have played a decisive role in this.[120] Instead, a simple national myth dominated historiography during the 19th century:

---

[119] His main contribution was to produce the voluminous *Istoria tou Ellinikou ethnous*, [*The History of the Hellenic Nation*], (Athens, 1865-1874).

[120] It was as early as 1824 that Marc-Philippe Zallony (a Catholic Greek, fervent of the Greek revolution) wrote that he "wants a monarchy because he does not see as feasible a republican regime" and that "in our days it is doubtful if the kings will show sympathy to a national liberation war" (Zallony; Millas 1994, p. 194-199).

The Greeks, the descendants of the glorious ancient Greeks, after many centuries under the tyrannical "Turkish yoke" staged a national revolt and won their independence anew.[121] Greek-Orthodox Christianity, that constituted the basic belief of most of the Grecophones for centuries, was dexterously integrated into the ancient heritage. According to this ideological construction, the ancient Greeks were somehow the heralds of the new "light", of Christianity. The term "Helleno-Christianity" was invented (by S. Zambelios in the mid-nineteenth century) to express this national harmony, and religion was thus "ethniced" during this nation-building phase.[122] Greekness was closely associated with a religion, and even with a part of it: with the Greek Orthodox Church and its legacy (Grigoriadis). The class dimension of the Greek revolution was silenced in the nineteenth century. "Not only was the religion nationalized and turned to a crutch of nationalism, but nationalism itself also turned to a religion and Orthodoxy became a way of perceiving ourselves and the Church as a partner of the state" (Liakos, 2005, p. 143).

As was shown above, the sense of "being the offspring of a glorious past" was initiated and encouraged to a great extent by the European republican and romantic intellectuals. The Greeks themselves, on the other hand, promoted the idea of their "resurrection" because it was to their political advantage to appear as a nation that was the heir of a glorious past but which had suffered and had been unfairly treated by the (Muslim) Other. In fact, the national enterprise was presented basically as "religious liberation". In the Greek national iconography Greece was represented as a suffering woman mostly dressed in a torn ancient Greek robe. This image accorded with the grammatically feminine "definite article" that defines in Greek the word "Greece" (η Ελλάς).

It was during the nineteenth century that the Other – the Ottoman Turk

---

[121] See, for example S. Trikoupis (1788-1873), I istoria tis Ellinikis Epanastaseos [The History of the Greek Revolution], vols. 1-4 (London, 1853-1957); I. Philimon (1798-1873), Dokimion istorikon peri tis Ellinikis epanastaseos [Historical Essay on the Greek Revolution], vols. 1-4 (Athens, 1859-61); A. Frantzis (1778-1851), Istoria tis anagenithisis Ellados [The History of the Greek Rebirth], vols. 1-4 (Athens, 1839-1841).
[122] S. Zambelios, Asmata dimotika tis Ellados [Folk Songs of Greece], Athens, 1852.

who was benevolent and positive according to the messages of the Patriarchate on the eve of the Greek Revolution - was constructed anew in Greek historiography as the absolute negative Other: despotic, barbaric, backward, uncivilized, cruel, corrupt, perverted, exploitative, and so on. This image of the Turk in general was not different from the one prevalent in the West. And the more the Other was negative, the more the Greek revolution and the new state were justified and legitimised. The Ottoman period thereon was described in almost all historical texts of the nineteenth century as a period of darkness, of the death of the nation; on the other hand, the successful Greek revolution was named – and it is still known as – the "Resurrection of the Nation". The story of the nation is narrated in terms of the familiar story of Jesus Christ: death, resurrection and eternal life thereafter. The fighters of the revolution and of the subsequent wars are called "ethno-martyrs". The losses in this war are "sacrifices made on the altar of the homeland". Even the patriarch of Constantinople, who opposed and condemned the Greek revolutionaries of 1821 - but who was still hanged by the Sultan for his inability to control his "flock" - is metamorphosed into a "martyr of the Greek nation". This grand narrative presents all Greeks, the nation, being united and in harmony, and consistently against the Other. Class differences and skirmishes are redundant in this narration, as the Orthodox affiliation was considered the pillar of the nation (Millas, 2006).

The two pictures above show the changes in the image of Greece. The first (a copper engraving) appeared in 1801 in a book by A. Korais (Σάλπισμα Πολεμιστήριον/ War trumpet). There are various symbols of ancient Greek and the name of Homer is clearly seen. There are no symbols of Christianity. The negative "Turk" is present as the oppressor, even though in those years the Patriarchate had a different opinion about the Ottomans. A few decades later in a painting by Peter von Hess (1792-1871) about the capture of Tripolis (1821) the cross has a dominant place as well as the priest next to the warrior shows the new role of the Church. The Church has no reservation in joining the anti-Turkish imagery.

In the second half of the nineteenth century Greek historiography turned to the study of the Greeks of the Byzantine Empire, as well as of the Greeks living outside the national boarders of Greece and especially in Anatolia (Asia Minor).[123] The prominent historian Pavlos Karolidis (1849-1930) is

---

[123] Today we are in a position to suspect that there were also political considerations behind this thesis of "the Greek Byzantine Empire": it legitimised the Greek claims on the Ottoman lands. The decades 1850-1920 became the years of a national ideal known as the Megali Idea ("Great Idea"), according to which the Greeks could and should "liberate" all of their lost and enslaved lands and populations. Greek historiography was marked for a few decades by this irredentist historical interpretation. This idea, that was first voiced in the Greek parliament in 1844, proved unrealistic and was finally abandoned when the Greek armies were decidedly defeated in Anatolia in 1922.

remembered mainly for this enterprise.[124] The general tendency was to portray the Greeks as a great nation that created superior civilisations but had to face the menace of the Turks, who dominated "our" lands and who retained them, enslaving part of "our nation". The "Greek lands" were perceived to extend beyond the boarders of the new state. What legitimized the unity of the nation (the *ethnos*) was not the state but a historical "essence" or "Greek culture", defined by an enduring language and a religious affiliation expressed as Christian Orthodoxy. The synthesis was and it is still called Helleno-Christianity.

Kirtatas expounds how Western intellectuals starting from the 18th century "discovered" a glorious ancient Greece and how later the modern Greeks internalized this heritage by presenting various "paradoxical historiographical information". First, the Greek intellectuals noticed that they were somehow related to the ancient Greeks linguistically. Then it became apparent to them that this language survived due to the "Church" and its adherence to the grecophone "Christian Fathers". But, and this is the third "information", there was a gap of many centuries between the ancient and the modern Greeks; and, fourth, the westerners who were enthusiastic about their discovery were not historians but people of arts and poetry. Then, paradoxically, the ancient language was not actually promoted by the supporters of the revolution because they were against the conservative Church of Constantinople. The sixth step was the "discovery" of the "Greek" Byzantium in the mid 19th century which until then it was "not noticed" but – seventh - also the Macedonians were promoted to "Greeks". The eighth paradox is that periods that were seen as Greek – Roman, Venetian, Ottoman - were left for the Western historians to study. But also, ninth, the modern Greeks did not really study the Ancient Greeks either, this domain was left to the Westerners. And tenth, in the 19th century there was a revival of Byzantine studies and a preference to archaic Greek language. (Kirtatas, p. 151-266).[125]

14- Basic and secondary National Myths

The national discourse on the Ancient Greeks is a basic myth which operates as a source for tens and even hundreds auxiliary myths.[126] The main myth of "Ancient Greeks" set the foundation of the following assumptions: The ancient Greeks are the ancestors of the modern ones; since ancient and modern Greeks together form one nation they share the same characteristics; which are positive since ancient people were unique: creative, civilized, brave

---

[124] P. Karolidis, Σύγχρονος ιστορία των Ελλήνων και λιπών της Ανατολής από το 1821 μέχρι το 1921 [Modern History of Greeks and Other Nations of Anatolia from 1821 to 1921], vol. 1-7 (Athens, 1922-6).

[125] The issue of the Greek language and the related myths is discussed below in the chapter allocated to language.

[126] The term "core myth" is also used instead "basic myth".

etc.; the positive characteristics are shared by the whole nation since a nation is composed (supposedly) of people who share common characteristics; it follows that each individual Greek has these positive traits; the superiority of the nation is relative to other nations, which means that the "others" are inferior in comparison to "us"; and finally, this national belief /identity/myth infers the immortality of the self since one's lasting existence is secured through the immortality of the nation.

In the era of nation-states such a belief is the expected one. The national myths may differ but all somehow exalt the nation and its members. There are not, I presume, nations that do not have a very positive self-image. The superiority of "our nation" may be claimed on various grounds: past grandeur, present achievements, some special characteristics (e.g., bravery, good character), having established strong states or many states, having subjugated other people, endurance to suffering, having some distinguished co-patriots, achievements in specific areas (art, literature, sports, etc.). Even if there is nothing positive to present there is still a negative Other who plays the role of the scapegoat or of a justification: "We would have been great if it were not for the Other who hindered our successes."

Such a story, i.e., a national interpretation of "our" past and present, is satisfying and probably necessary to secure the coherence of the nation. First of all, it affirms the common origin of the group/nation. The nation is perceived as something like a family whose members are in a very close biological-like relationship. Each member of the nation has his/her share in the national grandeur: If in our nation we have Homer, Plato, Archimedes and Alexander the Great, we modern Greeks as the heirs of the ancient ones, should somehow possess similar characteristics!

Such an understanding has a racist tone. Racism claims permanent positive characteristics for us and relatively negative ones for the "others", in both cases the characteristics seem to cover the whole nation. But what is the "thing" that secures this time-resistant endurance? How is it possible that even environmental, social and historical developments do not influence and change the "national character"? Arthur de Gobineau said it was the race. But later, other factors that would give exactly the same results were proposed. Some perceived the language of the nation as the everlasting characteristic that secures the unchanged character of the nation, others the "culture" of the nation. It suffices to find one "thing" that does not change in time and the permanent character of the nation is supposedly demonstrated.

In the case of the Greeks, the "Greek language that exists from antiquity until today" is especially emphasized to show the continuity of the nation. There are other domains that are highlighted to "explain" the "thousand year old nation", too. The Greek "culture", usually associated to the "religion" is also seen as "permanent" and "unchanged", too. Race and blood are reminded sometimes, but these "justifications" are not preferred by officials and/or academics. Especially, Falmerayer is usually criticized because he tried to defy Greekness by references to their "impure" race. Quite often the "Greek education" (ελληνική παιδεία) is accentuated as the "thing" that secures the centuries long Greekness.

I will allocate some pages to the Greek language and the related myths. But before that I will present few popular myths (opinions?) that are based on the main myth of the "Ancient Greeks", either a) as believed realities expressed by their believers , or b) as myths, i.e., as popular "wrong" belief as expressed by the critics of these beliefs. I added some comments of mine in parentheses as well as short general information on the topic.

Nikos Dimou was one of the few and early critics of the passion or the frenzy with which (a big number of) the Greeks associate themselves with the Ancient ones. With much humor he wrote: "When a Greek looks at a mirror he sees either Alexander the Great or Kolokotronis (the hero of the revolution of 1821) or at least Onassis. But never Karagiozis (a funny figure of a traditional shadow play)... That is why the Greeks never excused the "mishellens" (the haters of Greeks) who painted their portraits. Poor About![127]... If a group of people believes that they are the grandchildren of the ancient Greeks they will be automatically unhappy. Unless they could forget them or surpass them" (Dimou).

The belief that that the modern Greeks are the grandchildren of the old legendary Greeks and that they share their positive (and negative) characteristics is expressed in various levels of persuasiveness. The one that is related to the academic historiography is somewhat more balanced, sophisticated and more "cautious". The well known Greek historian A. Vakalopoulos writes:

"The past of the Greeks continues to possess a tremendous strength and we are connected to it at a greater extent that we can imagine... Some inherited traits [καταβολές] influence at various degrees the formation of the human character, as it is accepted by psychology in our days, e.g., the inheritance of intelligence... There is not a common national Greek character as there is no anthropologically racial type of Greeks. Still, there exist some common characteristics that are found in all Greeks, irrespective of the geographical places and this shows the unity of the Greek nation" (Vakalopoulos, 1983, p. 38, 39, 48). He then mentions Thomas Gordon

---

[127] He means Edmond About (1828-1885) mentioned above and who wrote a book about Greece of 1850s. The picture of the Greeks was not flattering! (About).

whom he called "the best historian of the Greek Revolution". According to Gordon who took part in the Greek Revolution:

> "Those who are best acquainted with the Greeks, cannot fail to remark the numerous and striking features of resemblance that connect them with their ancestors: they have the same ingenious and active bent of mind, joined to a thirst of knowledge and improvement; the same emulation in their pursuits, love of novelty and adventure, vanity and loquacity, restless ambition and subtlety." (Gordon, p. 32).

Vakalopoulos also quotes long passages form Samuel Howe[128]:

> "Were there wanting any more convincing proof of the genuineness of the descent of the Modern Greeks from their illustrious ancestors, than that they speak the same language, which has undergone fewer corruptions that almost any other; that they employ precisely the same characters in writing; that they call places by the same name; that they inhabit the same spots; that they retain many of the prejudices, the manners and customs, that are recorded of the old Greeks; we say if more proof should be thought wanting, it will be found in the physical aspect, and in the character of the people. The same natural quickness of intellect, love of learning, attachment to country, vivacity, the same fickleness, the same deceit, are stamped in the character of the Greeks of today, as they were in the ruins of the Greeks of the older times." (Howe, p.17)

The popular and populist myths that are related to the Ancient Greeks, however, are more interesting. The contradictions, the aggressive criticism against the "mis-hellens", the anxious defensive argumentation and the anxiety to discover "similarities with the ancestors" disclose the mythic dimension of these theses. I will present some cases below.

ALEXANDER THE GREAT AND MACENONIA

This case is interesting, amusing with its eccentricities but also special because it has political consequences, too. In modern times the controversy on "Macedonia" lasted for decades and was discussed internationally: Were the Macedonians Greek? Was Alexander the Great a Greek or a Macedonian? Or a Macedonian Greek? I will not answer these questions, leaving this part to the reader. I will only present some "situations" related to this problematic and I will try to show that there should be a myth or a number of myths behind these skirmishes. At least this was my suspicion due to a number of personal experiences.

---

[128] Samuel Howe (1801-1876) was an American physician who took part in the Greek Revolution of 1821.

I have not been especially interested in Alexander until in a conference on human rights in Greece in 2001, an academic participant quoted some passages from a speech by Alexander. I marveled how "modern" this student of Aristotle – as I had heard from my childhood – sounded. That speech by Alexander was as follows:

"I wish you all to be happy with this peace since the war now is over. All human beings hereon will live as one people, in union and for common success. Consider the ecumenia [all world] as your home country, with common laws where the wise will govern, irrespective of race. I do not differentiate the humans as Greeks or Barbarians the way some brainless people do. I am not interested in the origin of the citizens, neither their race in which they were born. I only look for one criterion: Virtue. For me every good foreigner is a Greek and every bad Greek is worse than a Barbarian. When differences will occur, you will not resort to arms, but you will solve them peacefully. If needed I will be the arbitrator. You should not see God as an authoritarian governor but as father of all; so that your behavior will be like the one of brothers in a family. On my part I consider you all equal, white or dark skinned. And I do not want you to be the subjects of this commonwealth but participants, partners. I will try to make all these that I promise to be done."

I asked the participant the source of this speech. She looked perplexed and she said she will check it out and will call me. She didn't. So I called a few times and I insisted for the reference. She said that "it was a very well known text" but she is not sure from where she had copied it. "I think it is from Arrian" she said eventually. I read all the books of Arrian but I did not find that speech. I found it in the internet.

I had suspected there was something fishy with this humanitarian, anti-racist speech. It was too "modern". The equality of the citizens, the world peace, the peaceful resolution of differences with arbitration, the single God who is the father of all – three centuries before Christ - the citizens being partners in the commonwealth... If it had been phrased a little more carefully I might have believed it as authentic. It proved to be a myth that is encountered in various sites.[129]

My gain from this story was my reading the books of Arrian. There, I encountered another aspect of myths. People exert serious efforts to preserve them. The worries about the Greek identity of Alexander the Great is so big that sometimes even mentioning of the Ancient Macedonians and Ancient Greeks as two distinct groups causes an anxiety that leads people to the point

---

[129] For example: https://www.facebook.com/orlkarditsa/posts/1442506332553784/

of censoring the ancient texts. (Remember "confirmation bias" mentioned above.) This I found out as I read Arrian. In the Greek editions of *The Anabasis of Alexander* of Arrian(os) there are cases where the characterization "the Macedonians and the Greeks…" is translated as "the Macedonians and the other (the rest of the) Greeks…". Not all Greeks, of course, but some disregard the original texts as they translated them in a way that does not to harm a belief. The Arrian texts that I read were in two "languages", in Ancient Greek (on even numbered pages) and in Modern Greek (on odd number pages). It seems that the urge was so great that the forgery was done even though there was a great risk that it could be easily traced.[130]

In Greece in general Alexander the Great is seen as a Greek with positive characteristics. An able Greek warrior, to begin with, who conquered the then known world proving the superiority of the Greeks. In the textbooks, for example, he is praised for his other merits, too. In 1976 he was presented as trying to secure "order" in the neighboring countries, he was praised for extending civilization to the East and respecting the religion and traditions of the countries he conquered. And thus the world marveled the Greek civilization (Kamaterou, p. 159, 168). In 1988 the Greek identity of Alexander is more stressed but some "austere" measures that he took against his enemies are mentioned, too. He was also presented as a great politician who respected the conquered people (Aktipas, p. 182, 184, 198). In last year's textbook the "respect" part is omitted but his contribution in spreading the Greek language and his "generosity" are preserved (Katsoulakos, p.98-106).

However, there is also another completely different version of Alexander the Great. According to that interpretation Alexander is not all good but rather all negative: Cruel, despotic, and disastrous to Greeks. In a study in Greek about the myths on supposedly "great" historical figures the following Greek personalities are presented under the following titles: a) Alexander the Great (356-323), "the grave digger of Hellenism"; b) Constantine the Great (272-337), "vicious and corrupt"; c) Theodosius the Great (347-395) "the exterminator of ancient Greek civilization". (Simopoulos, 2010).

According to Simopoulos, history is distorted by presenting Alexander as a hero and a proponent of civilization and silencing his tyrannical side. To criticize Alexander is seen as an attack on national beliefs, whereas he actually enslaved free Greek cities and enforced their subjugation. He caused the decline of the ancient world. He left corpses behind him along his path to Europe and to Asia. He executed the enslaved male defenders of the cities

---

[130] See: Book 3, Chapter 22 (Arrian, 1992) and Book 7, Chapter 12 (Arrian, 1992b). Other Greek and English translations read "Macedonians and Greeks". See: (Arrian, 2004 & 2004b), and (Arrian, 1884). The original Greek text is clear: "… εν τοις άλλοις Μακεδόσι τε και Έλλησι…" and "… προς τε Μακεδόνων και των Ελλήνων…".

that he had captured, such as Thebes, Tyre, Gaza, selling women and children as slaves.

This 190 page study on Alexander the Great is a criticism of historiography, too. He accused many historians, ancient and modern, who exalted Alexander, either following ages-long stereotypes or satisfying the political ideologies of colonialism and imperialism. Simopoulos' point of view is close to a Marxist interpretation of history, judging the past with rather modern criteria. Interestingly, his objection is also the same: He criticizes the historical approach which evaluates the deeds of Alexander with criteria of the age of imperialism and romanticism, not considering the pain and ruin that Alexander caused.

The problematic of how and according to which criteria a historic figure should be "judged" will not be discussed here. What is of importance is how some historical events may be evaluated so differently: by some as facts and by others as myths and vice versa; and in both cases with great passion and confidence. The numerous theses and arguments of Simopoulos cannot be all presented here, either. It is a very lengthy endeavor. I will only present some of the subtitles of his text which they give a fairly good idea of the scope of Simopoulos' criticism on Alexander:

> Phillip (Alexander's father): The worst enemy of the Greeks; Unethical, a bully, drunk, lecherous; The conspiracy of Alexander to kill his father; He kills all the heirs of the throne; The abominable genocide of Thebes; He destroys the Greek cities of Asia Minor; Honing the swords by the massacres; The greatest drunk of history; Maniac of fame, arrogant, perverted, insane; Shameful "persianification" [becoming Persian] and demand for allegiance; Personally killing friends and partners; Forced demand to be worshipped as god; Twelve years of terror and disasters; Death due to excess drinking; The idol of Roman imperialism; The myth of Hellenistic period and the decay of Hellenism; Crude forgery of history; The delirium of hymnologists; The gloomiest pages of Greek history.

The praise of Alexander is understandable: His story is flattering to nationalist identity. But what are the drives and the needs that produce the attacks, especially by the Greeks, on the positive image of the "Great Greek"? These assaults are not easy to explain. There were furious reactions in 1993 when a journalist, Takis Mihas, called Alexander the Great "the slaughterer of peoples" (σφαγέας των λαών). The "explanation" of the action of Mihas then given was not very persuasive. A bundle of arguments with no coherent connection between them were voiced in order to explain the drives of Mihas.

It was argued that he worked for the Human Rights Watch of George Soros (SIC), that he wrote articles in Wall Street Journal claiming that there is "deep anti-Americanism in Greece", that he interviewed (Jew) Hobsbawm who claimed that the Greeks do not have Greek origin, that he has close connections with center-right Greek political party (New Democracy), that he was connected with the "Logical Front" movement (a group advocating peace) allegedly initiated by NATO; that he had been an editor in the journal published by the "rather secret agent" (πρακτοράκος) (M.Dimitriou).[131]

The head of the extreme rightist organization Golden Dawn G. Mihaloliakos explained Mihas' evaluation as follows: "Mihas is right to consider Alexander the Great a slaughterer of people since Mihas is a liberal and for the laws of the market the national heroes and the myths are useless ruins of a world that exists no more." He further added that he (Mihaloliakos) is against internationalism and neoliberalism which both are against nationalism.[132] One is left with the impression that Mihas is somehow involved with "foreign" forces that are not friendly to Greece. But why? Was Mihas a paid traitor?

This argumentation against Mihas (and against people who think like him) can only be understood when the myth that incorporated all these – Soros, Wall Street Journal, the origin of Greeks, NATO, the political parties in Greece and the traitorous agents that work against Greece, liberals and newliberalism – is explained. This will be done further down, when the more recent myths will be presented. For the moment, it is worth noticing that the issue of the "Ancient Greek" is very up-to-date and that the myths always exist as two poles: With supporters on one side and the opponents on the other.

SURREALIST SUPPORT OF THE ANCIENT ANCESTORS

I hesitated if I should include this category in this study because these myths are too extreme, rather marginal, quite naïve, even absurd. They are also very funny and entertaining though, at least to me, and I think that the readers deserve to smile now and then as they read about the core national myths, i.e., the heartbreaking shortcomings of the sapiens.

I did not find reliable numbers as for the extent of these beliefs. One is inclined to think they should not be very widespread since they do not sound very sound! On the other hand and contrary to expectations, various very peculiar myths and beliefs are quite popular. For example, we know that 46% of the Greeks believe that the earthquakes are related to the climatic

---

[131] See for example: https://athens.indymedia.org/post/97357/
[132] https://ethnikismos.net/2016/07/16/εθνικισμος-και-αστικος-πατριωτισμο/

changes[133]; 34% believe that the Darwinian evolutionary theory is not true[134]; and 33% believe in the chemtrail conspiracy theory and that they are being sprayed for nefarious purposes by some bad agents.[135] And there are many, worldwide, who after thousands of deaths still claim that there is no Covid-19 pandemic. Therefore, a high percentage in surrealist theories should not be excluded readily.

I think three (plus one extra) Greek surrealist myths are related closely with the subject matter of the Ancient Greeks. I will present them in an outline. The first is what Dimosthenis Liakopoulos says, writes and publishes. He is a Greek journalist, writer and publisher. For many years he advertised on his TV program various products and mainly his books, mostly written by him. I did not read any of his books but I watched tens of his TV programs in which he spoke about the content of his books and his views. I feel confident that I am aware of the main message of his theories. I watched his presentations with great interest, especially when I was in low spirits and in each case laughed wholeheartedly. I marveled his creativity. Each time I thought that he had reached the peak of his daring fantasies but in his next program he presented something new that exceeded one's wildest imagination.

These are some of the main characteristics of the Greeks and the Ancient Greeks according to Liakopoulos. The Greeks came to Earth from Sirius (the star) by flying saucers. He almost proved this because he showed a photograph of one of these saucers. It was a very clear photo and one could read its name in Greek capital letters: ΔHMOKPATIA (democracy). Actually, the Greeks were about three meters of height. There are skeletons of these tall ancient Greeks but "they" hide them from us. He was fortunate that one night, it was late midnight, as he was walking in a remote district of Athens he saw some people that were carrying a very long case, something like a coffin, which they accidently dropped it. Then he saw the bones that were inside. It was a human skeleton of three meters. An original Greek, in other words. "They" collected the bones and moved away in a hurry.

He also showed us photographs of Greek installations on the Moon. The Greeks have also built cities in China but very deep under the surface of the land. We understand that the Ancient Greeks were a very special nation. Culturally they invented all kinds of machines, even computers and developed all branches of science. Whatever we use in our days are actually originally started by the ancestors of the present-day Greeks. The Greeks have many enemies but also a really strong and royal friend: The Russians. By the way,

---

[133] Eurobarometer Special 479, Question QB2.5, in 2018. The average of EE is 53%. Highest is Portugal (74%) and lowest Sweden (28%).
[134] Polling and Analysis, December 2013.
[135] See: Metron Analysis, 2020.

the Russians have a huge military base eight kilometers below Istanbul. They are there waiting for a good cause, no doubt.

This kind of stories were heard for a couple of years and tens of books on these topics were advertised. I presume that there should have been a considerable number of buyers otherwise these programs would not have proved economically feasible to continue.

Another personality that advertises Greekness, but on a classic nationalist basis, actually on a racist basis, is Konstantinos Plevris (born 1939). He is a lawyer and writer with political activity in favor of the extreme right. He tried for his fascist and anti-Semitist writings. He appears systematically on TV programs and he speaks mostly about the ancient Greeks. According to K. Plevris the Greek nation is not like the rest of the nations. He demonstrates this superiority by many examples. The Greek language is the first language that started all other languages; there is nothing that the whole humanity added to what the Greeks have developed as philosophy; the ancient Greeks excelled the modern scientists, too, they have developed even the "atom": this word is Greek.

One of the most original theses of K. Plavris is that the Greeks excelled in all because they never had democracy. That democracy started in ancient Greece is a myth according to K. Plevris. Even in Athens of Pericles the leaders were not elected but chosen by lot. Alexander the Great and the emperor of Byzantium never resorted to democracy. When eventually democracy was appropriated by the modern Greeks, the result was the dichotomy of the nation and social disasters.

There is a difference between Liakopoulos and K. Plevris, even though both exalted the Greeks as superior to all other nations. Plevris is a typical and ideologically dedicated fascist, Liakopoulos is a rather good salesman. In the first case, the pride of being a Greek is self-sufficient; in the second case the success is related to the income from the sales, too.

There are some other personalities that propagate surrealist views about "the superior Greeks and the superiority of Greekness" that I think it is not necessary to mention all here. For example, Kyriakos Velopoulos, too, started as a salesman on TV programs and now he is a member in the Greek parliament as the leader of his political party being elected getting the 3,7% of the voters in July 2019 elections. Presumably, his sayings were well received. Among the many praises for the ancient Greeks – and the mentioning of the very many Greek enemies, worldwide –he also sold some letters by Jesus

Christ, written by his own (Christ's) hand writing (SIC).[136]

Surrealist ancient Greek appearances were popular among the Golden Dawn (Χρυσή Αυγή) extreme right political organization, too. There are, however, harmless followers of the ancient Greeks, too, that exhibit their admiration for the way of life of the "ancestors'. The "Twelve-Goddists" (δωδεκαθεϊστές), e.i., those who believe in the Olympus Gods of ancient Greece are of this kind of admirers. The adherents of the ancient attires and way of life form a "group" in Greece which mostly meet and perform in public at certain days. They declare that they are not Christians but they are tolerant to any religious and/or ideological belief. This seems to be an aesthetic adherence to the ancients. A photograph will be of use in this case.

The next chapter is about the myths that are related to the Greek language. This is an important topic and worth allocated a separate chapter to it. As I was trying to arrange my material, however, I came across a blog (Αρχαίος Τόπος) that dealt with the language issue in a special way. The theses advanced seemed to be more fitting to be classified under the title "surrealism" rather than "language". The writer is anonymous and the block deals exclusively with Ancient Greece. Here are some excerpts about Greek language (my translation from Greek and my comments in parentheses):[137]

---

[136] For the TV sale video see: https://www.youtube.com/watch?v=KmsW9ljLdO0. See also Kourdis (in bibliography) for an article on Velopoulos-Liakopoulos. Also: https://www.researchgate.net/publication/311843652_The_Velopoulos-Liakopoulos_Phenomenon_A_semiotic_approach_to_the_explosion_of_Greek_conspiracy_theories_and_urban_legends_in_the_economic_crisis

[137] ΕΛΛΗΝΙΚΗ ΓΛΩΣΣΑ (Η ΑΡΧΑΙΟΤΕΡΗ – ΤΕΛΕΙΟΤΕΡΗ ΚΑΙ ΜΗΤΕΡΑ ΟΛΩΝ ΤΩΝ ΓΛΩΣΣΩΝ) | ΑΡΧΑΙΩΝ ΤΟΠΟΣ (wordpress.com)

"The Greek language: The oldest, the perfect one and the mother of all languages (this is the title)… What is beyond any comprehension is the fact that in the Greek alphabet there is a hidden mystic invocation. If the letters are put in an order an ancient prayer which praises the Light and the Spirit appears magically. This is done by adding to the alphabet the verbs that are missing (SIC) and we get this: ΑΛ ΦΑ, ΒΗ ΤΑ ΓΑ! ΑΜΑ ΔΕ ΕΛ ΤΑ ΕΨΙΛΩΝ, ΣΤΗ ΙΓΜΑ ΚΑΤΑ ΠΑΛΛΑΝ ΔΑ (ΙΝΑ) ΜΗ ΝΥΞΗ, Ο ΜΙΚΡΟΝ (ΕΣΤΙ) ΠΥΡΟΣ (ΔΕ) ΙΓΜΑ ΤΑΦΗ ΕΨΙΛΩΝ, ΦΥ(ΟΙ) ΨΥΧΗ, Ο ΜΕΓΑ (ΕΣΤΙ)… (Then a meaning is assigned to each letter -Why? - and we get an ancient text which is also given in modern Greek.) We get:[138] 'Wise sun, you are the light, come to the Earth. And you, seen sun, send your rays to the clay that is heated. Let the I live, let them stay on the vibrant Earth. Do not let the night reign, which is the small, the small risked the disappearance in the cooked mud, and let the Spirit develop, which is biggest, the most important of all.' When we learn the Greek alphabet we voice this invocation unconsciously. Also some studies showed that the study of ancient Greek improves the (human) thinking. It is not a coincidence that an American study on artificial intelligence has shown that two computers needed ancient Greek to have a logical discussion between them… According to the last count, the Greek language has 6 million words…. Pythagoras listened to the music of the celestial Spheres, which means we have a language that is related to the flow of the universe… The Creator used arithmetic for the creation, so our language necessarily is related to the source… So we reach to the conclusion that the origin of Sanskrit is the Greek language… The reading of Homer has a positive effect in synchronizing the breathing and the heart pulse.. so it is good for

---

[138] This is the text in modern Greek. I did not understand why he "added the verbs" and how he reached to this invocation. «Νοητέ ήλιε, εσύ που είσαι το φως, έλα στη Γη. Κι εσύ, ήλιε ορατέ, ρίξε τις ακτίνες σου στον πηλό που ψήνεται. Ας γίνει ένα καταστάλαγμα για να μπορέσουν τα Εγώ να ζήσουν, να υπάρξουν και να σταθούν πάνω στην παλλόμενη Γη. Ας μην επικρατήσει η νύχτα, που είναι το μικρόν, και κινδυνεύσει να χαθεί το καταστάλαγμα της φωτιάς μέσα στην αναβράζουσα λάσπη, κι ας αναπτυχθεί η Ψυχή, που είναι το μέγιστο, το σημαντικότερο όλων.»

heart diseases... Learning ancient Greek is good for dyslexia, too..."

It is surprising how one misses what is in front of one's eyes because the phenomenon is perceived to belong to a different category and therefore different! I noticed a similarity much later than my writing the above paragraphs. The funny appearance of the Ancient Greeks occurred in the years 1926-1932, too. That case was not ridiculed then however, but it was perceived as an effort to revive the ancient spirit. The well-known poet Angelos Sikelianos (1884-1951) spent a lot of energy and money (of his American wife Eva Palmer) to revive the "Delphic Festival". The effort was acclaimed by the critics of that time. People were dressed in ancient dresses; peplos, chiton, chlamys, etc. They were not criticized for that and on the contrary Sikelianos was nominated for the Nobel Prize for Literature in the years 1946-1951. As a rare case historian Y. Kordatos was outspokenly critical though: "Sikelianos psychologically was not very normal... He believed that he could revive the time of Pericles... He thought that he had messianic capabilities... He would appear sitting on thrones with priestesses lying at his feet... His wife, too, would wear the whole year sandals without socks..." The effort to revive Ancient Greece was abandoned when Eva left for good to USA and the money support stopped. (Kordatos,1962, p. 451-459).

15- Summary and Assessment

In this chapter we saw how a mythical story of the Greek nation was constructed or invented. For others this process was one of "finding out and becoming conscious of a national identity". In this context the real and/or imagined Ancient Greece and the East-West relations and the related mutual images were discussed. The role of Greek "westerners" and "easterners" was analyzed by - presented the case of Fallmerayer, of Helleno-Christianity, of Alexander the Great and some surrealist cases of "Ancient- worship".

Looking from today's perspective at the above national narratives and at the different evaluations of the past and the present of the "Greeks" which were believed and propagated from the last two decades of the 18th century to the first quarter of 19th, and keeping in mind what was discussed in the previous Chapter 1, one may note the following beliefs and/or myths and how these changed within a relatively short time:

- Myths on the side of the "conservatives":

1) The Ottoman Rule was the will of God.

2) The Ottoman State was beneficiary.

3) The western revolutionaries were "atheists", antichristians and against the Church.

4) The Greek revolutionaries were like these westerners, atheists etc. The Revolution was not needed and it was a mistaken act.

5) (When the Greek Revolution was successful and the Greek nation-state was established) The Orthodox Church presented itself as having helped the Greek Revolution, i.e., the "national cause". See: The ethnic-martyr Patriarch and the Holy Banner of Lavra Monastery.

6) In the domain of education the Church was active through the Secret Schools since the Turks were negative, and the Ottomans were not seen as "beneficiary", but on the contrary a danger to our religion and identity.

7) The westerners, too, were not condemned as "atheists" and all-negative, even though the Church retained its dogmatic reservations.

8) The Ancient Greeks were not directly opposed by the Church

- Myths on the side of the "modernists":

9) The three millennium long uninterrupted existence of a Greek nation.

10) The identification of the Modern Greeks with the Ancient Greeks.

11) As a consequence, the superiority of the Greek nation.

12) The positive West (Enlightenment, Romantic world).

13) The negative invader, oppressive, etc Other, i.e., the Ottomans and the Turks.

14) (And after the founding of the new nation-state) The Byzantine Empire was accepted as Greek and as a positive state.

There are some important messages that one gets from the above: First, some of these beliefs that existed and/or appeared at the beginning of the 19th century are still encountered among the Greeks of the 21st century. Second, it is of interest to see that the Greek Enlighteners who opposed the myths (or the beliefs, if one prefers) of the "conservatives" created their own myths/beliefs. In other words, to oppose and reject some myths does not necessarily mean that one is distant from some other myths. Myths may be rejected but this does not mean that other myths are not appropriated instead.

Finally, one may easily see how the old controversy between the "conservatives" and the "modernists/nationalists" was superseded and how a new national myth secured the "unity of the new nation". Probably the greater step in this direction was the instilling of religion in nationalism – Helleno-Christianity. That was a "project" not unique to Greece and was put in practice in other countries, too (Grigoriadis). To understand this "instilling" the role of Fallmerayer should be considered.[139]

We noticed that there were decisive changes of views of the combating groups. The criticism of the "conservatives", i.e. the Church and the opponents of the "atheist West", vis-à-vis their enemies subsided, especially after the founding of the Greek nation-state. On the subject of the "pagan ancients", too, the voices were lowered. Especially in the issue of the Ancient Greece, they even came to the point of noticing some affinity of the Ancients with "our nation". In a site dedicated to the Christian Orthodox religion we read the following.

> "The fruitful Christian perception of the ancient Greek civilization started with Apostle Paul who, being a Jew with a Hellenistic education, in his speech to the Athenians showed his affinity to the ancient Greek civilization... Many modern thinkers point out that any opposition to Christianity and to the Orthodox Church is a paramount anti-Greek position. In the domain of the arts, too, the ancient Church used the Greek language and taking the pagan symbols attributed to them a new meaning and purpose... Therefore, the new religion borrowed all the known means of expression and did not deny any [Ancient] art... The Church only criticized the pagan practices which in essence they were not all of them Greek products, but foreign barbaric influences, for example like the Dionysian deities which came from the East and which basically were worshipped by the uneducated people and which were not accepted by our big philosophers."[140]

In this discourse we notice a) the term "our philosophers", b) the paganism that is not actually "ours" but a foreign eastern barbaric trend, and c) the Orthodox Christianity which is closely related to ancient Greece through its language and its symbols. No doubt this is a completely different view of ancient Greece and its relation with the Church. In our days, it is not surprising to find similar views in various sites that are close to the Church and/or to conservative, traditional and "national" understanding. E.g.: "In an age when the Greek dodekatheon (Twelve gods) was the dominant belief, the Greek philosopher Socrates believed in a single and only God. Even though Socrates lived four centuries before Christ he is justly considered the herald of Christianity."[141]

---

[139] The role of religion in forming a nation is much more complex than the summary presented here. There were, for example, old oracles and messianic myths that the nationalist made good use of them to serve their plans (Hatzopoulos, p. 83, 87). There were all kinds of frictions and intrigues among Orthodox, Protestants, Catholiscts, etc, during the critical years of the national revival (Gazi, 2009).

[140] https://www.pemptousia.gr/2017/06/ti-proselave-ke-ti-aperipse-apo-tin-archea-ellada-o-christianismos/

[141] http://www.pontos-news.gr/article/164933/sokratis-enas-proaggelos-toy-hristianismo

The old antagonism between the "atheist revolutionaries" versus the Patriarchate has subsided, too. We saw above how after the success of the Revolution the Patriarch who excommunicated the revolutionaries turned to a "nation-martyr who died for the revolution". A Greek researcher summarizes this change as follows: "It is clear that from hereon the 'studies of the Ancients' (αρχαιμομάθεια) and the Ancient world in general will not be 'left' to the enlighteners since it was possible to find ways to associate the Ancients with the tradition of the Church"(Gazi, 2004, p. 127). The West, too, in our days, even though it is somehow different and distant from "us", the Orthodox Christians, it is not the main enemy of "ours" any longer.

The radical, Jacobin and determined anti cleric romantics of the time of the Greek Revolution do not exist anymore, either. With the founding of the new state they have accepted the Church as a reality and they respect it, since the people respect it, and they agree that the Byzantine Empire was a Greek Empire which represented a significant civilization. The Greek historiography, the textbooks that express the official state view and every-day discourse voice this conciliatory approach as a "common sense" that does not need to be demonstrated or proved.

This peace-making mood and desire formed the synthesis of Helleno-Christianity as explained above. The synthesis operated as an agreement between rival groups who declared on what they share common beliefs: They are all Hellens, the glorious Ancients are their ancestors, their common language is Greek (Hellenic) which is a very old and rich language, the Greek revolution was fought by all the nation and so all Greeks – atheists and priests alike – have equal involvement in it and the Revolution was a just cause since the "Turk" was the oppressive and invader (who is not god-sent any more but the national Other).

In other words, all those fights, skirmishes and mutual condemnations of the last quarter of the 18th century and first decades of the 19th century between opposing groups were the birth-pains of a national ideology. They came to a culmination by the formation of the Greek nation. The truce was a need but also the expression of the formation of the nation. A nation needs a persuasive story upon which a consensus should be achieved. A unifying story (or a myth) that expresses an accord on the basic issues secures a harmony which is one of the basic aspects of any nation-state.

When the past antagonisms are seen from this perspective, the agitating conflict about the origin of the Greeks, i.e., if they are the grandchildren of the ancient Greeks or of a number of ethnicities or even of Adam and Eve or of Neanderthal man – acquires a special meaning. The whole effort was to claim the legacy of superior civilization. By being the continuation of the glorious Greece, modern Greeks, too, obtain the same credit. That is why, when Fallmerayer shed doubts on the ancestors of modern Greeks, "all Greeks", as a nation, objected. The main concern was not the origin of the Greeks per se but the need to legitimize the connection between a glorious past and the present. The question was if the modern Greeks were "civilized" or not. Any suspicion on the legacy of the glorious past was seen as a bad intention jeopardizing the greatness of the modern Greeks.[142]

The theoreticians of Nationalism produce models akin to these developments. For example, they explain the formation of a nation as a process of "construction" or of "imagining" a group of people with a common history and identity. But when this ideology of nationalism is seen in a more detailed way we notice its intricacies. I quote in length a passage that I believe is of importance:

"The myths that are related to and secure the operation of the societies are abstractions, simplified stories that soothe down historical experiences and are dictated by the need to lessen the contradiction and make possible the communal coexistence... The myths are the 'myths of coexistence'... These myths are basically the 'foundation myths' of modern European nations... The founding myths [of the nations] or the 'myths of coexistence' are not lies or completely imagined constructs. On the contrary, they include support of the common social experiences and this aspect is the force that keeps the myths alive securing their practical usefulness... In this sense these myths try new syntheses, create heroic narrations and decisively ignore whatever reminds social detachment and partition, stressing whatever helps the continuation and the common course of the people... These founding myths, as it is the case of all myths, cannot cope with serious rational criticism... The modern professional historians and political scientists perceive their mission as one that has to criticize these myths and even to reject them... But societies feel that they need these myths in order to exist" (Kitromilidis, 2007, p. 176-180).

P. Kitromilidis concludes his article with a question whose answer he stated does not know: "How will we use our right and need to criticize the myths without causing harm in the society that needs them?"

This evaluation and approach to "national historiography" – which is not solely related to the Greek case but covers "national discourses" in general,

---

[142] In a site that voices "national sensitivities" we read about the "anti-Greek myth" that there is not a continuous Greek nation from antiquity until today: "This is done to diminish the greatness of modern Greeks. They say that those ancient people had Hippocrates, Pythagoras, Perikles ... [But] for each one of them there corresponds today someone called G. Papanikolaou, K. Karatheodori, E. Venizelos... There is no doubt about the continuum of the Greek nation." This is a very popular and widespread understanding. (https://www.politischios.gr/parembaseis/oi-2-megalyteroi-ethnikoi-mythoi).

poses a problematic:

A) Are all national constructs, national societies and national historiographies "national myths"?

B) Is their criticism needed, required, useful and recommended, or should they be left as they are and maybe even be reinforced since they are operational, useful and necessary?

These and similar questions were probably posed for the first time by Edmund Burke in 1790 in his *Reflections on the Revolution in France* and lately by Yuval Noah Harari, as mentioned above.[143] They are important and challenging questions and I will try to express my opinion on them at the end of this study. Actually, the whole effort in this study is related to these questions. For the moment and in a few words my reaction to these is as follows:

Many and maybe all national constructs seem to be myths, but they are myths only to those who do not agree with these myths and do not see them as necessary and useful. The believers of the myths, however, see only understandable explanations and/or facts. In other words, in our times there is a movement against *these* myths. (In fact, all through history there was always some resistance and/or opposition to myths, projecting alternative myths.) The deconstruction of *these* myths will possibly give rise to new myths. And irrespective if the opposition to the existent myths hampers or not the existing national unity and eventually the social coherence, such a radical move signals a new need and usefulness for a new societal grouping. The new set of myths may be seen as a new and closer-to-the-needs- of-the-times "construct" and order. Naturally, any new group which proclaims a new identity proposes also its own "truth" (or "myth", for those who do not share the same belief). This new claim is as legitimate as the previous claims – myths – which have been criticized. In other words, all myths do not have similar normative "values"; their worth is historically ranked and determined.

After this "parenthesis" I turn to "the Greek myths about the ancient Greeks". It is the existence of a group of people (and me among them) that consider that a big part of Greek historiography is "mythical" that makes it so. In their absence, a claim of myths and as a consequence the myths themselves do not exist. Any myth appeared as such only when it was disputed and challenged by somebody. A rejected and discarded myth is normally replaced by a "true story" or a new "myth", its assessment depending again on its reception.

---

[143] Harari used the term "imagined orders" and Burke "pleasing illusions" but the meaning they gave to these terms is akin to the meaning I give to "myth" in this study. (Harari, Burke).

At this point a distinction should be made between a "myth" and a "mistaken belief". Both are "wrong beliefs" – always according to the unbeliever observer; but their differences are the following:

1) A mistaken belief (or knowledge) may change easily and even immediately once new data is introduced. For example, I may believe that Penguins live in the North and South Pole. If a trustworthy source corrects me in this matter I will change my mind without any difficulty, since the information is not related to ideological, religious or identity issues. To accept that the Penguins live in the South Pole has no effect on my life style and my existential worries.

2) A myth is something more than knowledge and information. It is a guide to think, to evaluate and to give meaning to one's life. It is related to one's identity, to one's beliefs on which one builds his/her ethical values; it is therefore difficult to be abandoned. If, for example, a gynecologist explains to a believer that it is highly improbable for a virgin to give birth, this does not secure an immediate abandonment of a religious conviction (myth). To be persuaded to abandon a myth presupposes the abandonment of a set of deeply believed other "truths".

3) A myth is a social phenomenon. It is a shared belief that unites the members of a group. To abandon a myth means leaving the group one belongs to. If the mistaken belief is only a personal matter then that may be named – apart from the simple and obvious "a mistake"- by using terms such as paranoiac belief, ignorance, prejudice, stereotype, hallucination, bipolar depression, psychosis etc.

The term "Ancient Greeks" refers to a basic national myth with a long history and many phases. In practice it propagates the message that "we the Greeks are worthy people because the famous and superior Ancient Greeks are our ancestors." This myth appears often in tens and hundreds different versions. Some typical examples will be presented below, in the next chapters.

***

CHAPTER 3

THE GREEK LANGUAGE

ERNST CASSIRER, KEITH THOMAS AND MYTHS

When a study on myths reaches the point to make room for "language", the book of Ernst Cassirer *Language and Myth* comes to mind. This work provides important insights into language and myth. Cassirer discussed the close relation of phenomena which at first glance seem to be apart. For example, he tried to show that without a sound knowledge of what "language" is it is not feasible to judge what the "things" and the "processes" are: "[T]he analysis of reality in terms of things and processes, permanent and transitory aspects, objects and actions, do not precede language as a substratum of given fact, but that language itself is what initiates such articulations, and develops them in its own sphere" (Cassirer, 1953, p. 10).

Cassirer also tried to show that language and myths have a common source: "[I]t is evident that myth and language play similar roles in the evolution of thought from momentary experience to enduring conceptions, from sense impression to formulation, and that their respective functions are mutually conditioned. Together and in combination they prepare the soil for the great syntheses from which our mental creation, our unified vision of the cosmos springs" (p. 43). And again: "That myth and language are subject to the same, or at least closely analogous, laws of evolution can really be seen and understood only in so far as we can uncover the common root from which both of them spring... And this common center really seems to be demonstrable; for, no matter how widely the contents of myth and language may differ, yet the same form of mental conception is operative in both. It is the form which one may denote as *metaphorical thinking*. .. The real source of metaphor is sought now in the construction of language, now in mythic imagination; sometimes it is supposed to be speech, which by its originally metaphorical nature begets myth" (p. 84). With reference to Max Müller[144] he states: "[T]here is mythology now as there was in the time of Homer, only we do not perceive it, because we ourselves live in the very shadow of it ... Mythology in the highest sense, is the power exercised by language on thought in every possible sphere of mental activity"(p. 5).

Cassirer, in *An Essay on Man* posits humans in a special world: "[M]an does

---

[144] Max Müller. "The philosophy of Mythology" appended to *Introduction to the Science of Religion*, London 1873, pp. 353-355).

not live in a world of hard facts, or according to his immediate needs and desires. He lives rather in the midst of imaginary emotions, in hopes and fears, in illusions and disillusions, in his fantasies and dreams" (Cassirer, 1944, p. 43). "Hence, instead of defining man as an *animal rationale*, we should define him as an *animal symbolicum*" (p. 44). "Language, myth, art, religion, science are the elements and the constitutive conditions of this higher form of [human] society ... Mythical thought is, by its origin and by its principle, traditional thought ... To call [a myth] into question would be a sacrilege. For primitive mind there is no more sacred thing than the sacredness of age... Any breach of continuity would destroy the very substance of mythical and religious life" (p. 280-281).

Cassirer in the first part of *Myth and the State* (1946) stresses the role of the myths and especially of the rituals. "At bottom the different schools saw in the magic mirror of myth only their own faces. The linguist found in it a world of words and names, the philosopher found a 'primitive philosophy', the psychiatrist a highly complicated and interesting neurotic phenomenon (Cassirer, 1946, p. 11)... Myth is one of the oldest and greatest powers in human civilization. It is closely connected with all other human activities - it is inseparable from language, poetry, art and from early historical thought. Even science had to pass through a mythical age before it could reach its logical age: alchemy preceded chemistry, astrology preceded astronomy" (p. 22). "[W]hat we wish to know is not the mere substance of myth; it is rather its function in man's social and cultural life. In this regard most of the previous theories remained inadequate because they failed to see the real problem" (p. 34).

The rituals and the emotions, however, seem to have a special importance. It is as if they precede myths. "When performing a religious ritual or ceremony man is not in a mere speculative or contemplative mood. He is not engrossed in a calm analysis of natural phenomena. He lives a life of emotions, not of thoughts. It has become clear that rite is a deeper and much more perdurable element in man's religious life than myth (p. 24) ... A feeling is a much more general fact and belongs to an earlier and more elementary stratum than all the cognitive states of mind (p. 27) ... Myth is the epic element in primitive religious life; rite is the dramatic element. We must begin with studying the latter in order to understand the former" (p. 28). "Art gives us a unity of intuition; science gives us a unity of thought; religion and myth give us a unity of feelings" (p. 36) .... "Nevertheless the legend is not a mere fairy tale... it refers to a certain 'reality'. But this reality is neither physical nor historical; it is ritual" (p. 42).

But myths are not simply emotions. There is one more step to go behind the emotions. "Myth does not arise solely from intellectual processes; it sprouts forth from deep human emotions. Yet on the other hand, all those theories that exclusively stress the emotional element fail to see an essential point. Myth cannot be described as bare emotion because it is the expression of emotion. The expression of a feeling is not the feeling itself - it is emotion turned into an image" (p. 42). "Linguistic symbolism leads to an objectification of sense-impressions; mythical symbolism leads to an objectification of feelings ... In his magical rites, in his religious ceremonies, man acts under the pressure of deep individual desires and violent social impulses. He performs these actions without knowing their motives; they are entirely unconscious. But if these rites are turned into myths a new element appears" (p. 45-46).

> "Genuine myth does not possess [a] philosophical freedom; for the images in which it lives are not *known* as images. They are not regarded as symbols but as realities. This reality cannot be rejected or criticized; it has to be accepted in a passive way. But the first preliminary step on the new road that finally will lead to a new goal has been made. For even here emotions are not simply felt. They are 'intuited'; they are 'turned into images.' These images are crude, grotesque, fantastic. But it is just for this reason that they are understandable to uncivilized man because they can give him an interpretation of the life of nature and of his own inner life" (p. 47). "Myth could not give a rational answer to the problem of death. Yet it was myth which, long before philosophy, became the first teacher of mankind, the pedagogue who, in the childhood of the human race, was alone able to raise and solve the problem of death in a language that was understandable to the primitive mind" (p. 49) [145]

Reading Cassirer in order to acquire insight to utilize in my study on myths I was left with a question. The key words and concepts - apart from myth and language - that predominate in the above paragraphs and that made an impression on me were the following: emotions, primitive mind, primitive man, rituals, sacred and sacrilege. The myths are closely related to these concepts. They are all found in the first part of *The Myth of the State* titled "What is myth?" The sections of this theoretical part read as follows: "The structure of mythical thought", "Myth and language", "Myth and the psychology of emotions" and "The function of myth in man's social life".

The second and third part of the book is on the history of political theory. Part 2 is about "The struggle against myth in the history of political theory"

---

[145] Cassirer elsewhere stressed again the importance of emotions and beliefs in matters of religion: According to him religions are not founded on logic or on ethics; they are born due to the fear of supernatural powers and the human desire to control these powers. Feelings and fantasies play a decisive role. The need to prevent superstitious dangers created the idea of God (Cassirer, 2004, p. 70).

and it is a critique in this field covering a domain from Plato to Enlightenment; and Part 3 is about the "The myth of the Twentieth Century" and precisely on "hero and race worship", with a rather indirect reference to Nazism. This critique follows a philosophical methodology and/or a method of political science. Surprisingly, the concepts developed in Part 1 were not utilized. So I was left with the impression that the analysis on language, myth, emotions, ritual etc., was about the "primitive man" and "primitive thinking".

The last chapter (Chapter 18), however, appeared as an effort to reevaluate "hero and race worship". It operates as a second and as a new reading of what happened in the 20th century, beyond the classical approach of philosophy and political science that was developed in Parts 2 and 3. It combined the "primitive mind" with the modern phenomena; i.e., the "primitive man" with Cassirer's contemporaries. This chapter is like an effort to show that "our different modern times" can be studied in relation to the past when some past human traits are still valid and in operation. I include here some passages from this chapter.

Cassirer explains that primitive societies do not recourse to magic but only when "man is confronted with a task that seems to be far beyond his natural powers" (p. 278)... "[A] highly developed magic and connected with it a mythology always occurs if a pursuit is dangerous and its issues uncertain. This description of the role of magic and mythology in primitive society applies equally well to highly advanced stages of man's political life" (p.279)... "The call for leadership only appears when ... all hopes ... in an ordinary and normal way, have failed... The former social bonds – law, justice, and constitutions – are declared to be without any value. What alone remains is the mystical power and authority of the leader and the leader's will is supreme law. It is, however, clear that the personification of a collective wish cannot be satisfied in the same way by a great civilized nation as by a savage tribe... Civilized man ... cannot entirely forget or deny the demand of rationality. In order to believe he must find some 'reasons' for his belief; he must form a 'theory' to justify his creeds. And this theory, at least, is not primitive, it is, on the contrary, highly sophisticated... Yet, if modern man no longer believes in a natural magic, he has by no means given up the belief in a sort of 'social magic'" (p. 280-281).

Then Cassirer shows what has survived until today from our ancestral primitive society is be adapted to modern times. He made a distinction between *homo magus* (magic using humans) and *home faber* (the maker human, who controls his environment by using tools): "The homo magus of former times and of primitive civilization became a *homo faber*, a craftsman and artisan... The modern politician has to combine in himself two entirely different and even incompatible functions. He has to act, at the same time, as both a homo magus and a homo faber ... It has been reserved for the twentieth century, our own great technical age, to develop a new technique of myth... The first step that had to be taken was a change in the function of language... [W]ords which formerly were used in a descriptive, logical, or semantic sense, are now used as magic words that are destined to produce certain effects and to stir up certain emotions... If we hear these words we feel in them the whole gamut of human emotions – of hatred, anger, fury, haughtiness, contempt, arrogance, and disdain. But the skilful use of the magic word is not all. If the word is to have its full effect it has to be supplemented by the introduction of new rites" (p. 282-284).

Cassirer continues his exposition of the modern political myths of 1930-1940 by analyzing concepts like freedom, propaganda, rites, political prophesy, destiny, the notion of race, culture, language, philosophy of history, all issues that cannot be repeated here. It is interesting that his understanding of the political tendencies of this period is in line with the views of Hannah Arendt on totalitarianism (Arendt, p. 489-490, 504). Both being born in Jewish families had "first hand" knowledge of the new political climate of their time. But they used different paths to reach to the same secrets of their special political environment: In the case of Cassirer this is a "mythical" one, in the case of Arendt a totalitarian one. Arendt exposed all the characteristics of this new political ideology; Cassirer tried to explain it, too.

Having discussed myths in conjunction with magic and with the past practices of the "primitive" societies and in relation to the modern political actors – who according to Cassirer "develop a new technique of myths" – it seems it is the right time to add Keith Thomas into the picture. K. Thomas in *Religion and the Decline of Magic* analyzes how the old primitive and traditional magic is presently challenged and mostly replaced by "modern" thinking. This analysis may shed light to the controversy that exists between the believers and unbelievers, actually the challenges of certain myths and of mythical explanations.

According the K. Thomas the primitive and/or traditional magical thinking was the result of a need to give an explanation to phenomena that could not be understood. "What the scientific revolution did was to supersede this type of reasoning... These primitive beliefs declined because they had come to be seen as intellectually unsatisfactory" (Thomas, p. 773, 774)... Thomas explains that in modern times with the increased popular literacy, the control of epidemics, of rationalizing the markets, the increase of transfer of information (e.g., newspapers), the provided security (e.g., due to insurance possibilities) etc., magical thinking – I add myth making, too - "declined". The notion of "probability" started replacing the understanding of uncontrolled "random" happenings (p. 785). According to Thomas the difference between the 18th and the 16th centuries lies not in the achievements but in the aspiration of many who felt that they can do something with what was once seen as an uncontrolled environment (p. 788).

"The methods of the scientists were different from those of the magicians. They stood for controlled experiment and innovation (p. 793)… It is therefore possible to connect the decline of the old magical beliefs with the growth of urban living, the rise of science and the spread of an ideology of self-help" (p. 797). But decline means only "decrease". Magical and mythical thinking is still present in everyday living, sometimes not being noticed and sometimes being criticized. Another question has to do with "science" the capability of which for a final solution to "reality" is disputed, too. Thomas expresses his skepticism with a rhetoric question, which reminds the reader that the magical and mythical thinking may exist under the cover of "science", too:

> "If magical acts are ineffective rituals employed as an alternative to sheer helplessness in the face of events, then how are we to classify the status of 'scientific' remedies, in which we place faith, but which subsequently, are exposed as useless? (p. 799).

16- The Greek language – its history and the fierce discussions

The Greek language was an object of heated discussions among the Greeks the last two centuries.[146] It caused existential worries and public tension. This issue was fought in two main axes:

A) The first axis was a practical one and it had to do with the kind of the Greek language the Greek state and the nation would use as an official and everyday language.

B) The second axis was (and still is) a theoretical one: Is the Greek language "one", i.e., a continuum from antiquity to the present time, naturally with changes in time, or is Modern Greek a different language from ancient Greek?

At the time I was writing these lines (December 2020) there arose a third issue being discussed: Should the Greek language "take" and use English words and expressions (loans) (e.g., lock down, take away) or should the Greeks be cautious in this matter and use Greek words instead. Actually, this discussion is part of both axes since both are about "our language, its merits,

---

[146] Roderick Beaton explaining the development of the 18th century wrote: "The Greek language was an evident and indisputable common denominator linking pagan ancient Greece, Christian Byzantium, the present-day Orthodox elites of southern Europe and a broadly dispersed series of rural communities, each with its own dialect. The notorious Greek 'language question' emerged in the mid-1760s, at a time when the elite of the 'Orthodox commonwealth' had identified themselves with this language to such an extent that they felt the need to codify it" (Beaton 2020, p. 24).

its value and the dangers that it faces".

These debates are indirectly connected on the basis of the Greek national self-identification. Various national myths accompany the whole problematic. Here, I will first summarise some well known relevant historical developments and then I will evaluate them and present the myths that are related to the Greek language.

The Greek language belongs to the Indo-European language family and it has the longest documented history of any living Indo-European language, of about 3,500 years. Its alphabet arose from the Phoenicians and became the basis of the Latin and Cyrillic ones, among other writings. In antiquity Greek was spoken as lingua franca and it became the language of the Bible.

This language passed through various periods and "transformations". In ancient Greece there were various Greek languages, like the Proto-Greek; the Mycenaean (15th century BCP); the Greek of the "classical period" with its various dialects (Aeolic, Doric, Ionic, Attic); the Koine (Κοινή), i.e., the dialect of ancient Athens which was used widely and for centuries as a lingua franca starting with the Hellenistic years and used as the language of East Christianity, naturally with continuous changes. During the Byzantine time a special Greek that resembled ancient Greek was used by the educated classes especially in writing.

The official language in the Byzantine Empire, i.e., the Medieval Greek, was an eclectic middle-ground variety, actually a fusion of Ionian with Attic, the dialect of Athens. The Greek Orthodox Church preserved its traditional language, too, which resembles the Koini language. In the modern era two varieties of Greek were used, the vernacular Dimotiki and the Katharevousa, (the "pure"), a compromise between Dimotiki and Ancient Greek which was mostly used for literary and official purposes. This state of "two languages" is the notorious "diglossia" that caused a lot of strife among the Greeks. It was only in 1976, that Dimotiki was declared the only and official language of Greece, having incorporated some features of Katharevousa. This language gave birth to the Standard Modern Greek which is used today for all official purposes, in education and everyday use.

In our days the diglossia discussion is usually seen an unfortunate event, as a futile civil strife that could have been avoided. According to the well-known Greek linguist G. Babiniotis: "The language fight of the last two centuries that turned to a linguistic civil war [started] on the 19th century. Until then … the written language and the oral one coexisted without a controversy. The language problem started at the end of the 18th century… With the events known as Evangelika (1901) and Orestiaka (1903) the language problem turned to a war where even blood was shed" (Babiniotis 2015, p. 24, 25).

Evangelika riots took place on the streets of Athens in November 1901. They were protests against the publication in the newspaper of a translation of the gospel of St Matthew into Dimotiki. The disorder reached a climax on November 8, on "Black Thursday", when eight demonstrators were killed. Then the Greek Orthodox Church banned any translation of the Bible into Dimotiki. These riots marked a turning-point in the history of the Greek language question and the beginning of a long period of bitter antagonism between the demotic movement and the proponents of Katharevousa. The Orestiaka also were riots on November 6-9, 1903 due to an ancient tragedy performance in Dimotiki.[147] The demonstrators were organized by the defenders of Katharevousa. In 1911, a private school was accused and persecuted of teaching atheism and of sexual molestation when it tried to use Demotiki in its education program.

The diglossia discussion first started on whether the language of the Greek people (Demotic Greek, *Demotiki*) or a cultivated imitation of Ancient Greek (*Katharevousa*) should be the official language of the Greek nation. The period is of importance: The contrasting ideas appeared before the Greek Revolution of Independence and the issue was about the prospected new Greek nation state, that is to say at the end of the 18th century. These were the years when nationalism and romanticism shook Europe both politically and culturally. Greek men of letters like E.Voulgaris (1716–1806), Lambros Photiadis (1752-1805) and Neophytos Doukas (1760-1845) were for an archaic language and I. Moisiodax (1725–1800) and D. Katartzis (1725-1807) were for the simpler demotic/colloquial/vernacular language. With the founding of the modern Greek state (1830) the "middle way", Katharevousa proposed by A. Korais (1748–1833) prevailed.

Arnold Toynbee evaluated these developments as follows:

"In the nineteenth century, when the Greek Orthodox Christians' feeling towards the West had changed from contempt and hostility to admiration and receptivity, it might have been expected that one of the first fruits of this cultural conversion would be the liberation of the Modern Greek language from the dead hand of a Hellenism that had been resuscitated in Greek Orthodox Christendom before the beginning of this Christian civilization's long encounter with its sister society in the West. Unfortunately for the Greeks, however, they imbibed the toxin of nationalism from the same Western spring; and this had the effect of heightening the nineteenth-century Greeks' consciousness that their language was lineally descended from the

---

[147] The word "Evangelika" refers to the Gospels (in Greek "Evangelio") and means "about the Gospels"; "Orestiaka" originates from the ancient tragedy Orestes by Euripides.

Ancient Greeks, and that their ancestral Orthodox Christian Civilization was affiliated to the Hellenic. These irrelevant historical facts led then to take refuge in the cultivation of linguistic archaism, and to denature their mother tongue by forcing into it as gross an infusion of Attic Greek vocabulary, inflexion, and syntax as they could compel this living language to swallow. Thus, on the linguistic and literary plane, the Greeks' 'reception' of modern Western culture, whose distinctive gift it was to use living vernaculars as its literary vehicles, had the paradoxical result of fettering the living Greek language instead of liberating it" (Toynbee, p. 469).

In the 1880s the movement in favor of Dimotiki and especially in the field of literature started gaining ground. In 1888 I. Psycharis initiated a sharp break in favor of Dimotiki by publishing his book *My Journey*. Soon the "other side", the proponents of Katharevousa, used the word *malliari* (hairy) pejoratively against Dimotiki. The controversy turned to a political fight. A bishop (G. Mavromatis) declared that Dimotiki was the same as anarchism, socialism, atheism. And in the 1901, 1903 and 1911 the fight reached its climax as mentioned above.

The subsequent years and up to 1976, this language strife was in the agenda as a political issue. In general the "left" was for Dimotiki and the "right", including the colonels of the 1967-1974 dictatorship were for Katharevousa. In those years it was enough to utter a single sentence – in Katharevouse or in Dimotiki - and one's political and ideological position would become apparent. At times the issue turned to a left-right fight, rather than a linguistic issue.[148]

17- The Greek language and its myths.

The Greek language has its own myths. The phenomenon can be phrased the other way around, too. The need for myths – in the sense meant by Cassirer and Thomas above - might have created, among other references, mythical stories about a language. In this second case it is the mythical worldview that has ended up with a mythical language. In any case, there are two levels of myths that are related to Greek language: A) What is being discussed within the Greek society as a "myth", in the sense that some perceive some linguistic phenomena as false, lies and not true; and others counting on them as true and of importance. And B) as myths on the language but which go far beyond the language itself, reaching the domain of identity and national ideology. I will start with the simpler ones, the "apparent" myths that are also widely discussed.

---

[148] For a short history of Modern Greek language see: Clairis, 1983 and 1984); Mackridge, 2014.

There is a book in Greek, titled *Ten Myths for the Greek Language* edited by Giannis Haris where ten experts on language exposed these myths. G. Haris wrote the introduction. I will simply mention the main arguments presented in the book (Haris, 2007).

In the introduction it is mentioned that similar phenomena of myths are seen in other languages, too. In the first article by D.N. Maronitis it is stated that four approaches are noticed: 1.The origin of the Greek language is presented as a mythological and even as a theological event; 2. The Greek language is shown as superior to other languages; 3. Mythological instead of scientific explanations are proposed for the study of the language; and 4. Myths are constructed to prove a close relation of "one language-one blood" (in the sense of one nation). The Greek language is presented as a "linguistic generator" that creates valuable literary texts. These Greek myths present a continuum, of a language and of a nation, from antiquity to our day. Actually, this introductory article summarizes some very basic myths of Greek language (Maronitis).

In the second article Evangelos Petrounias discussed the origins and the etymology of the Greek lexicon. He mentioned the basic changes that occurred in the Greek language the last centuries and how ancient Greek words passed into Latin and then came back again into Greek as loans in their new form. Some words were taken directly from foreign languages into Greek [κομπιούτερ/computer] and some are loan translations / calques [ουρανοξύστης/ skyscraper]. It is a myth that these words are Greek. Some ancient words have a completely different meaning in present-day Greek, too (Petrounias).

The third article (and the third myth) is written by A-F Hristidis and is about the misinterpretation of the role of the "katharevousa" as a transition language that connects the ancient to the modern one, demonstrating, in a way, the unity of the language. The ancient language is seen as the "basic one" and the creator of the Greek identity and of the new nation-state. In these schemata the teaching of ancient language in schools has been considered necessary. Hristidis, on the other hand, is for a "humanistic approach to the language which is against myths". This myth creates an imaginary controversy between the old and the new alive language assigning at the same time a priority to the old one (Hristidis, 2007).

A. Frangoudaki wrote about the fourth myth, the so called superior languages. She criticized the myth of "the deterioration of the language" and she explained that changes are normal and in harmony with the course of any language. There are no "superior" languages. "Historically, all languages that once were considered superior belonged to expansionist and imperialist societies". "Some Greeks dream that by speaking ancient Greek they would possess the old grandeur" (Frangoudaki, 2007).

The fifth article is about the "mistakes" that are claimed to occur in modern spoken Greek. For the author these new choices of words are the signs of the changes that occur, as a normal process, in the Greek language (Theophanopoulou). In the sixth article the unjustified complaints (and myths) about the loans of words from foreign languages and mainly from English is being discussed (Anastasiadou). Veloudis in the next article showed that the special "strange" Greek that the new generation uses is actually a richness of language and not a problem (Veloudis, 2007). The eighth article is a criticism against the view that traditional orthography should be treated as if it is a sacred issue (Karantzola). In the ninth article S. Moshonas tries to show that speech precedes writing (Moshonas); and the last article is about the misconception of rich and poor languages (Kakridi-Ferrari, 2007).

Two short comments before I present some more "myths": The above myths do not actually sum up to ten since there are some issues that are repeated. The criticized and claimed "superiority" of the Greek language was discussed in at least three different articles and the "changes" that occurred in Greek language in three or four articles. My second comment is that some arguments seemed to be about technical linguistic issues (e.g., loans, orthography, etymology) rather than myths.

The editor of the above book published another book - *Language, the mistakes and the pathos* - where he presented various controversial issues of the Greek language (Haris, 2003). I think his criticism of H. Giannaras (Χρήστος Γιανναράς) is of importance because it is directly related to "myth and language". Giannaras claimed that the Greek language does not exist anymore because of its complete deterioration! The ironical title of Giannaras' article in English and Latin - "Finish Graeciae" - was intended to show that the Greek identity is lost since the traditional language is hampered. It becomes apparent that most of the discussions on the Greek language is distant to linguistic issues and, on the contrary, at least for people who think like H.Giannaras, is directly or indirectly connected to some political and ideological worries. Harris accused Giannaras as being "populist" (Haris, 2003, p. 103).[149]

Maro Kakridi-Ferrari presented as "basic myths" of language the following

---

[149] According to the detailed analysis by A. Heraclides, G. Giannaras is a "religious nationalist" who perceives a Greek nation with permanent characteristics from antiquity to the present. This nation is the antithesis of the Catholic/Protestant "West", with its own culture, religion and way of thinking and perception of the world. It follows that the Greek language should be as close as possible to the primordial Greek. The changes that occur in the Greek language are, therefore, understood as "deterioration" of the paternal language that is directly connected to "our national being". (Heraclides, p. 81-89).

four: 1. The change of language is understood as wear and decline; 2) This happens because we move away from an older form of language that was superior; 3) This happens also because we make bad use of the language (mistakes, loans, etc.) and 4) The things get worse as young people use a special harmful language. "Even though these perceptions are myths they are, however, real as their consequences" (Kakridi-Ferrari, 2007b, p. 199-223).

Another book on Greek myths related to the Geek language is Nikos Sarandakos' *The Language with Hurdles*. Among other issues, he allocates 80 pages to present seven main "myths on the [Greek] language". All seven are presently existing beliefs in Greece. Sarandakos gives detailed explanation on how these myths were propagated as well as examples of their use. (Sarandakos, p. 21-99). I will only enumerate them here, without elaborating. They are the following:

1. When the USA was founded in 1776 there was a voting among the leaders of the new nation to decide what the new language of the nation was going to be. Greek lost by only one vote and English won.

2. The Greek language has six million words and therefore it is the richest language on earth.

3. The Spaniard members of the European Parliament proposed Ancient Greek to be the official language of the European Union.

4. The Apple Company has decided to teach ancient Greek worldwide because they have noticed that this language enables people to think creatively, to create new ideas and thus return to the roots of civilization. The English companies encourage their staff to learn ancient Greek.

5- Tens and hundreds of words in Latin, English, Spanish, Turkish etc. that exist in the Greek language are shown to be "actually" originally Greek words. This is demonstrated by showing how these words sound similar to Greek words: (e.g., rap from rhapsody; debate from dio-vima (two stands), Turkish meze- appetizer from ancient Greek μέζεα -genetic organs of animals, etc.).

6- English is claimed to be "actually" a version of the Greek language by declaring all Sanskrit origin words in English as Greek words.

7. The Greeks have reached Polynesian Islands from Peru before the Incas and this is proved by the hundreds of Greek words that exist in the Polynesian local language.

Having reached this lowest possible level of naiveté I will add a few more arguments (myths) about the grandeur of the Greek language and of the Greeks in general to complete the series of similar claims. Some are found in books and journals, some others on the internet:

- Greeks compose a nation that lived for 20 million years. It is also stated that the flying saucers carry on them the sign E (for ΕΛΛΗΝ – Hellen) which shows that there are Greeks even in the outer space (Haris, 2003, p. 421).

- That modern Greeks are not the continuation of Ancient Greeks is claimed by "the followers of the internationalist proletarian communism and of internationalist capitalism of globalization … These people serve foreign interests… [Whereas] language is the most valuable treasure of people…It is proved that Greek is the oldest language on earth and that foreign powers now try to present modern Greek as separate from the ancient language… Some mis-Hellens (haters of Greeks) try to deprive Greeks from their paternal legacy, the language … Language and history are the strongest binding powers of Hellenism".[150]

- Greek is spoken for 25 centuries… "Greek has been the only language that is spoken without interruption from antiquity to our days. (Its endurance) makes Greek language an exemplary case for all languages.[151]

- There is only one Greek language that presented some differentiations in time… This gives us the right to boast (καυχόμαστε) of speaking the language of Plato, but also the duty to learn our old [ancient] Greek… (This sentence is referenced to Babiniotis, as explained below)[152]

- Sanskrit originated from Greek. The American Journal of Physiology states that the Greek hexameter of Homeric epics influences positively in synchronizing breathing and heart beating. It also cures heart problems. Learning ancient Greek helps to cope with dyslexia (See: footnote 156).

It is clear that the basic myth – "argument" for some – about the Greek language is its supposed superiority. Papanastasiou analyses the myth of the "superiority" on the Greek language showing that this exists in various levels, from the more pseudo-scientific to the completely absurd one. For some the close relationship of the Greek with other languages (Sanskrit, Latin, etc.) is recognized but the role of Greek, as the "mother of all languages" is still supported. At another level, the similarities between Greek and other languages are not explained, as it should, by their common source but attributed to loans of the "Others" from the Greek language. At a lower level the Greek language appears with metaphysical origin: a language associated with the harmony of the universe, the first language on Earth and the like, as explained also above. "The modern Greek society appears to be rather

---

[150] This is a long article (of about 3,000 words) by Sokratis Siskos dated 23 March 2018, https://www.eproodos.gr/post/i-adialeipti-syneheia-tis-eniaias-ellinikis-glossas.
[151] https://www.alfavita.gr/epistimi/246899_i-poreia-tis-ellinikis-glossas-ana-toys-aiones
[152] Η Ιστορική Συνέχεια της Ελληνικής Γλώσσας – Μιχάλης (wordpress.com)

vulnerable vis-à-vis this excess of love for the ancient people and nationalism" (Papanastasiou, p. 99- 100). Giakovaki, too, with reference to the writings of A-F. Hristidis shows that the "special case" of the Greek language is supposedly proved by the fact that languages like Latin have created various languages but themselves have disappeared, whereas Greek is still intact. (Yakovaki 2007, 43-67).

VARIOUS APPROACHES TO LANGUAGE AND MYTHS

To approach myths in this lighthearted way is pleasant. (I hope you enjoyed the above myths!) One is surprised with the ignorance and the foolishness of the "others" and feels satisfied with himself. To present the above naïve beliefs about the Greek language as *the* myths about the Greek language curtails the possibility to notice the more important myths related to language. Almost all or at least the greater part of Greeks will agree that views like the above are exaggerations; and having said so, will feel that they have immunity to myths. In short, to present the above or only the above as "the language myths" results in hiding, actually camouflaging the most important myths.

Some beliefs are supported as true and as realities but criticized as false ideas and myths by others on a much more serious and "scientific" level. There still exists a controversy if the Greek language is "a single one" or two or even many more languages – i.e., Ancient, Middle Age and Modern Greek. For some a "single Greek language" corresponds to recognizing a national unity which incorporates Ancient Greeks and Modern Greeks. For example, the well known historian A. Vakalopoulos in his book about the character and the identity of modern Greeks mentions the common religion, customs, interests and the will to form a nation and then he points out the importance of the language: "The Greeks, differently from the other European people had ... historical memories and an identity that corresponds, in a sense, to the 'relics of ancient Greece', to the belief that we belong to the same ethnic group [γένος], that our roots are in the ancient glorious past ... which together with the only and special language in the world comprise the binding character of the society" (Vakalopoulos, 1983, p. 49.)

The belief in the "superiority" of the Greek nation is expressed in various myths, as we saw above, sometimes in a very simplistic way. But the same view is defended by academics and "scientists", too. The "Greek language" is of importance because it is used as a documentation of the "continuous existence of the Greek nation" and as a consequence, due to the connection to the Ancient Greeks, of "our" national grandeur. In other words, the controversy on the Greek language – one language or more than one - is a basic issue and many myths are related directly or indirectly to this theme. We read, for example:

> "It was first Howe [Samuel Gridley, 1801-1876] who noticed that there is no greater proof that the Modern Greeks have the ancient ones as their origin; since as their descendents they used the same language with their ancestors… they also live in the same geography, the toponyms are the same, and many of their perceptions and traditions are like the ones of the ancient Greeks" (Vakalopoulos, 1983, p.54).

The greatness and the uniqueness of the Greek language and its determining role in forming the Greek identity is a self-understood reality for most Greeks. I will quote linguist Babiniotis in length because he is known as the prominent supporter of the "one language" view.

> "The Greek language is not simply one language out of the existing 2,700 languages that are presently spoken on Earth, it is a special, an historical and culturally unique language – and this is recognized widely … The past and the present of the Greek language as well as its future are complementary aspects on the same course, of the single language, undivided within time, space and in the mouth of the Greeks who spoke this language for forty centuries… It is time for all of us to understand that there are no Greek languages but only one single Greek language with unavoidable differentiations in time and place… This gives us the right to boast (να καυχόμαστε) that we speak the language of Plato, but also put on us the obligation to know our 'old Greek' so that we use and understand our Greek better… [But today] we are left with an artificial and inflexible language. The language deteriorated very fast. We solved the language problem [by accepting Dimotiki] but we are left with the qualitative problem of a language that is being constantly deteriorating… The language of the people is their basic national characteristics. It secures its identity and its self-knowledge. The past, the present and the future of the people are experienced and expressed by their language… The teaching of ancient Greek, as well as the ancient and Byzantine tradition, that is to say, the historical aspect of the Greek language is a necessity" (Babiniotis, 2015, p. 11-29).

The careful reader probably has already noticed that:

A) The sentence "we have the right to boast of our language" was met previously in a blog with reference to Babiniotis, showing the close connection between academic and popular discourses.

B) Some mythical simplistic and naïve expressions are somehow linked –

as if they are communication vessels - to the academic and the scientific discourses; popular beliefs and the academic ones converge.

C) But most importantly, it is seen that the criticized myth above - in the books by I. Haris and N. Sarandakos – were actually critical views against the views expressed by academics like Vakalopoulos, Babiniotis, Giannaras and many others. This is in practice the way the "language war" is being carried out. And the realities of some are myths for the others.

There is a package of arguments that go together with the "one language" theme: The Greek language is in danger, it is deteriorating, foreign word loans are harmful, ancient Greek should be taught at schools, the Greek language is special and superior; and at a less frequency the conviction that there are "enemies" of the Greek language. One may find this kind of argumentations within various unexpected contexts. For example, in the introduction of a book about "the foreign words in the Greek language" where about 10,000 word loans are presented, we read the following: "We all need to understand that these 'new invaders' [meaning the Greek words of foreign origin] are probably more dangerous of the tens [loans] of the past. It is those that disrupt the national identity, that in the name of a so called internationalism violate the borders, distort the consciousness and convert one of the oldest nations into mimics of alien examples of doubtful values" (Konstantinou). One wonders if the book is intended to inform and teach the reader or to warn him not to use these words that are included in the book and in the Greek dictionaries.

One may encounter similar phobic views unexpectedly in any kind of topic. For example, according to the head of the Church of Florina Avgoustinos Kantiotis, Alexander the Great extended the use of the Greek language around the world and thus facilitated the translation of the Old Testament into Greek. And because of all these the Greek language became "the pioneer in the spreading of Christianity".[153] The reader understands that the Greek language – and indirectly the Greeks – are special due to their positive contribution to Christianity.

18- Summary and Assessment

The myths on language mentioned above supported the following view: "We are a great nation because we are linked through our language to a glorious past; we should preserve this traditional language; otherwise our language and our grandeur are harmed". The other components and the various myths are corollaries and/or variations of this basic myth.

The over mentioned views and/or myths are actually the consequence of

---

[153] https:www.sakketosaggelos.gr/Article/318/

other more basic beliefs: they are related to nationalism and to romanticism. Greece as a modern nation-state is a product of Romanticism. The projection of the Modern Greek nation to a three thousand years old epoch is essentially a romantic endeavor. (Beaton, 2009). The strongest binding power in the process of becoming a nation and forming a nation-state was language: "The key to this process of self-discovery was language. The Greek language was an evident and indisputable common denominator linking pagan ancient Greece, Christian Byzantium, the present-day Orthodox elites of southern Europe and a broadly dispersed series of rural communities" (Beaton, 2019, p. 24).

The romantic aspect of the Modern Greek existence and naturally of its language is often voiced: "Demoticism can be seen as part of a Greek Romantic movement that began in the Ionian Islands with the poet Dionysios Solomos in the 1820s and 1830s, was interrupted by half a century of Athenian Romantic pseudo-classicism, and re-emerged in the 1880s. In the ... [writings] by Delmouzos in 1911, we can almost hear the voice of Johannes Gottfried von Herder, the herald of Romantic nationalism, who had died one hundred years earlier" (Mackridge, 2009b).[154]

K. Dimaras, too, reminds the romantic aspect of the phenomenon of Modern Greece: "Greece is, par excellence, one of those nations that can be characterized, by the appropriate expression, romantic." (Dimaras, 1985b).

Romanticism and nationalism, however, belong to the same era and presumably cannot be studied separately. Furthermore, the Greek case of language and identity can be best understood when studied in light of what was happening in Europe in the same centuries. According to Joep Leerssen, "The romantic return to the roots of popular culture was not just a parallel to a Rousseauesque call for a return to nature and innocence, it was given an urgent agenda of national identity politics as a result of Herder's philosophy. Indeed, the rise of romantic nationalism in Europe may be seen, to a very large extent, as the outcome of a fusion between the influences of Rousseau and Herder" (Leerssen, 2006, p. 101). He also showed that over nineteenth-century Europe "political Romanticism" was widespread and that Dionisios Solomos in Greece was an example (p. 117). The "language reform programs", too, were typical to this climate all over Europe (p. 140). There was often a strife on which language was best to choose: the one of the older days which was pure and prestigious or the contemporary spoken language of the people. "The first and most fundamental of such debates took place in Greece, where a battle raged between those who advocated a purified, classical Greek (katharevousa) and those who endorsed the popular speech of the

---

[154] Romanticism and nationalism was discussed above, in Chapters 1 and 3, too.

common people (demotic)" (p. 201).

In other words, the Greek linguistic strife even though naturally had its peculiarities it was a "normal" European social phenomenon – closely related to Romanticism and Nationalism. This aspect of the Greek linguistic "problem" is not often highlighted. Especially, the fact that the linguists shared national and nationalist drives is often missed. Even though many researchers have stated that the Greek language is perceived by many Greeks as the "essence" of the Greek national identity – whatever "identity" in this case means - the nationalistic meaning of this identity is not made clear. Irrespective if one is for Kathrevousa or for Dimotiki, if one is a rightist or a leftist, conservative or modernist, language has been for them an important issue. I.Psyharis, who in 1888 gave an impetus to the movement in favor of Dimitiki explained his understanding of language and nation as follows:

> "A nation in order to become a nation [SIC] needs two things: To widen the borders [of the country] and to develop its own literature. When it shows that it is aware of the value of Dimotiki, when one is not ashamed of this language of his, then we see that there is really a nation. The nation needs to expand its physical but also its spiritual borders. My struggle is for these borders…. The nation is our basic purpose… The national, the holy, the only duty is to make a language that all would speak and write." (Mentioned in Kordatos, 1973, p. 131-132).

A. Frangoudaki, too, reminds the reader of the national sensitivities of Psyharis. His book, she writes, symbolizes in a clearest way the ideology of the Dimotiki movement vis-à-vis the nation and how it was influenced by the French Enlightenment. Psyharis was for civic nationalism, if one names his vision by a modern terminology. "The national problem is the ultimate priority" (Frangoudaki, 2001, p. 123, 124).

Frangoudaki, characterizes as myth the conviction that the Greek language is "impoverished" by the loans from other languages. "This is a social myth since the change of languages is a normal phenomenon in all languages… This view has turned to a self-understood reality and its central argument is that this happened because the language moved away from 'its roots'. The supporters of the myth of impoverished language pointed to where these roots were leaving no doubts in this matter: The roots of the Greek language are found in Homer" (Frangudaki, 2013, p. 132). Then she takes one more step and associates the linguistic controversy to its national dimension. She mentioned the xenophobic and supposed "foreign rule" and influence and the refuge to an imagined national past: "In short, it is not the language that is at stake but it is the nation again" (p. 133).

And again: "The basic point of the historical language issue is the relation of the language to the nation. Hundreds of pages have been written to defend Katharevusa and to condemn Demotiki, and as many pages on the other side to defend Demotiki and condemn Katherevusa. In all cases the writers referred to the nation and to its interests when defended "the" national language" (Frangudaki, 2001, p. 14-15). According to a linguist expert "Nationalism encourages people to say 'we' and 'you' to refer not only to synchronic imagined communities of their own time, but to diachronic imagined communities that include people who lived thousands of years ago" (Mackridge, 2009, 332).

The case of romanticism and its relations with language is complex. Romanticism has two references which in first glance seem contradictory. Artistically, romantics were admirers of Ancient Greece, i.e., of the "past". Byron and Shelley are typical examples, as already mentioned above (Chapter 2). It is easy to imagine that some Greeks tried to look nearer to the ancient "ancestors" to benefit image-wise. On the other hand, philosophically, say according to J.J, Rousseau, romanticism gives credit to and praises the "simple man", the one who is closer to nature, the unmolested, the noble savage and as a consequence it refers to the "present". This view directs to the "people" and language-wise to vernacular.

The Greek thinkers were influenced by Rousseau, by the national unification movements in Italy and later they were inspired by Johann Gottfried Herder and by the Brothers Grimm who highlighted the superiority of the "people". Supposedly different disciplines, e.g., linguistics, historical and folklore studies that have operated complementarily during the nation-building period, they were all influenced by both the nationalistic and romantic movements.

Therefore, one may conclude that "diglosia" strife – i.e., which language to choose - was and is a civil war within the movement of romanticism: Some followed the artistic path of the "past" and others the philosophical one of the "present".

However, the fight about whether there is "one Greek language" or "various Greek languages" is an impasse because it is carried out with words that are not defined. Situations of this kind are usually called "dialogue of the deaf" (dialogue de sourds). For example, in a single sentence of the kind "The language of the Greeks of today is the same with the one used by the Ancient Greeks, naturally with some unavoidable changes that occurred in time", various meanings are attributed to the key words "same", "language of the Greeks" and "Greek". The sentence has so many different readings that it may be considered meaningless.

For "same" the dictionaries give the following definitions: one without addition, change, or discontinuance; identical; indistinguishable; of equal in size, shape, value, or importance; exactly like each other; having the same quality; resembling in every relevant respect. Naturally, the proponents of "one language" do not mean "same" in this sense since they clearly accept that "some changes due to time did occur." So the word "same" does not suit this case. But what is then a language – say, Modern Greek - that is not the "same" as the other – Ancient Greek? Is it a different language? Is it a resembling one? Is it related to? Offspring? Descendant? Heir? Successor? And if it is one of these and not the "same", can that be seen as "one language"? Questions and dilemmas of this kind are blind alleys that create insuperable controversies. It is like asking if an old man at his 90s is the same with the baby that was born 90 years ago – it is a deadlock! Actually, if there is ever going to be an answer to a similar question that would be a matter of an ad hoc definition or an administrational decision that issues identity numbers for the newborns. Words like "same", "change" and "one and single" are philosophically and linguistically complex meanings.

The best that one can say in this particular case is to speak of "change" avoiding words like "one", "same" and/or "different". That is what A. Frangoudaki did with reference to Psiharis: "The proof of the continuity of the Greek language is that it is being spoken for centuries…The evidence of its continuity is the change and the distortion (αλλοίωση) of the language" (Frangoudaki, 2001, p. 133). The persistence in using the word "one" has to do with the ideological conviction (or myth) of the "*one* Greek nation all through history". It originates from a prerequisite of nationalist worldview.

The word "Greek" is also problematic. During the era of the rising of nationalism nations were assumed and named as Greeks, English, French, etc. These nations spoke the corresponding national languages: Greek, English and French, etc. There is no problem with this scheme provided it is not doubted and challenged. Who is a Greek? Is the one who calls himself so? If this is the case the ancient Macedonians and the Byzantines cannot be called Greeks. Is the one who speaks Greek? In that case the Karamanli "Greeks" who spoke only Turkish should not be Greeks; and the Cretan Turks (Tourkokritiki) who spoke only Greek – and who were deported from Greece as Turks - should be Greeks. And more interestingly: Can a speech impaired person be a Greek? Are we, today, liable to redefine who the Greeks were irrespective of how they defined themselves centuries ago? Or are the Greeks of today the ones defined so by the Greek constitution of Modern Greece? In that case language is irrelevant; both Grekophones and Turkophones, citizens of Greece, are Greeks alike.

Years ago and in a humorous mood – now I am serious! – and trying to challenge nationalistic perceptions I had made a list where sixteen different definitions of "Greekness" were presented, most of them contradictory to each other or self-exclusive; and some of them in practice were defining Turks! (Millas, 2002, p. 35-36). I mean that nationalist paradigm incorporates contradictions (and myths) and the issue of the Greek language is not exempt. Therefore the sentence "The Greeks speak Greek" is open to many doubts; and the sentence "the Grecophones spoke Greek" is a tautology.

Furthermore, all myths are not of the same importance. Some are predominant ones, even taboos. The cases that are discussed publically as myths are the beliefs that are already doubted, challenged and probably prone to be changed or abandoned. Almost all of the myths mentioned until this point in this text are of this "discussable" kind! The taboo ones are uncomfortable to read and unsafe to write about. Touching a taboo had been always risky; actually that is why they are called taboos.

The question "Who is a Greek?" is related to a taboo myth. It challenges an identity; an identity that is very fragile. The correct approach - correct in the sense of being in conformity with the constitution and laws of Greece – is to replace the word Greek with Grecophone when the language of the Grecophones is the issue at hand. In spite of the widely shared belief, all nationally Greeks do not speak Greek. The popular belief is not surprising since many myths are experienced as widely shared realities. I remind Cassirer's words mentioned at the start of this chapter: Myths are not regarded symbols but realities. And for what I call taboo he said "To call a myth into question would be a sacrilege"

In a small booklet on the "Linguistic Alterity in Greece" I found out that some of the Greeks of Greece speak (as their mother language and some as their only language) Albanian (αρβανίτικα, αλβανικά), Vlachs' Aromanian, (ρουμανική, μεγλενίτικη, ιστρορουμανική), Macedonian/Bulgarian, Turkish (of the Christians and of the Muslims), Bulgarian (of the Muslims), Romani and some more languages that are spoken by smaller groups (Baltsiotis, 2003). Teaching Greek to the children of language groups like these, naturally, presents some problems that have been under investigation lately (Apostolidou, Tsitselikis, 2003, Tsitselikis, 2012, p. 429-544).

According to S. Beis the efforts of the Greek state to secure the primacy of the Greek language reached the point of exerting "force and police repression, for example, prohibiting the use of the language [of Slavic of Macedonia] even within the houses or organizing massive oath taking ceremonies in certain villages in 1950s" (Beis, p. 330). The article concludes explaining why the Greek state does not recognize the languages of some minorities: "The logic of the modern Greek nation-state which relates to the political and the cultural dimension of identity, i.e., the issue of nationality, still exists as the official understanding until today" (p. 333). L. Baltsiotis proposes the term "complementary national myths" for the myths of ethnic groups – basically Vlachs and Arvanites – that support the thesis that they are Greeks and the continuation of the Ancient Greeks. In some cases the language of these ethnic groups are presented even as Mycenaean (Baltsiotis, 2007, p. 348). There are various "explanations", actually myths, of why these non-Greek speaking communities do not have Greek as their mother language: They were forced to change their languages by foreign powers, they served foreign powers for a long time, etc. The Greek academia quite often presents these groups as "bilingual" and they silence their mother language. The supporters of the official national ideology, concludes Baltsiotis, are not willing to accept the existence of "non-Greek" entities within the Greek geography (Baltsiotis, 2004, p. 354).

The widely believed, accepted and voiced "our one (and single) Greek language which all Greeks speak" is the cornerstone of Greek national grand narrative. According to Mackridge, "the Greek language has often been viewed by Greek intellectuals as a monument that requires constant maintenance and occasionally restoration. *Katharevousa*... was the outcome of such a restoration project" (Mackridge, 2011, p .20). A. Frangoudaki presents the crucial relations between romanticism, nationalism and language:

> "The national myth of origin is common in all ethnic groups and its old ideological mission was to collect the evidence that will provide the right to become a nation-state... All national mythologies talk of their sleeping princes that met in the wilderness after many centuries her prince who woke her up from her cultural sleep with a kiss and brought her again to life so that she 'continuous' her unending course in 'history'" (Frangoudaki, 2001, p. 121)

> "The closest the language that the Greeks 'speak' is to the language of the ancient ancestors, the more 'authentic' Greeks are considered; and as a consequence they deserve to be respected and recognized by the other nations... In short, from the moment the language controversy appeared it has been closely related to the basic corner stone of national ideology, the classical archaeology" (p. 104, 105).

Sometimes (nationalist) efforts are made to cope with the Greeks that do not speak Greek, but only other languages. "In the absence of linguistic evidence other criteria of national identity were invented. Briefly the nationalist discourse insisted that linguistic 'de-hellenisation' did not necessarily lead to the loss of national consciousness. For, although many Greeks adopted foreign languages, they never lost their ties with Hellenism, which conserved itself as an entity. Consciousness, therefore, emerged as the ordering principle of community, as an all-inclusive concept able to accommodate both Greek-speaking and non-Greek-speaking populations. Consciousness was perceived as a primordial quasi-metaphysical sentiment, shared by many, if not all, 'non-Greek-speaking Greeks' and sharing not only individual but collective behavior as well." (Exertzoglou). In other words, there are various, but self-excluding principles that can be chosen at will to prove "Greekness" and all related national meanings.

At the beginning of this section I had stated that there are two levels of "language myths": those that are being discussed as myths and the ones that actually go beyond language, to the domain of identity and national ideology. The grand national myth of Greekness and national identity which is resistant to criticism lies in the second level. Cassirer correctly reminds "sacrilege" when this myth is challenged; because this myth is experienced as something sacred by its believers. "To call [a myth] into question would be a sacrilege. For the primitive mind there is not something more sacred thing than the sacredness of age... Any breach of continuity would destroy the very substance of mythical and religious life" (see above).

It always strikes me when I hear the expression "the holy place" which many Greeks choose to use for the Parthenon, for that pagan monument! It is seen holy and sacred because there lies the basic national myth. Again Cassirer: "It has been reserved for the twentieth century, our own great technical age, to develop a new technique of myth... The first step that had to be taken was a change in the function of language... "[W]ords which formerly were used in a descriptive, logical, or semantic sense, are now used as magic words that are destined to produce certain effects and to stir up certain emotions." The "holiness" of Parthenon can be thus explained.

The myths related to the Greek language are of a different category from "the Greek language as a myth". In the second case the language itself is questioned as a myth. The same analogy applies to the cases of "nation" and of "Greekness". Myths *about* these concepts are acceptable. But handling them *as myth* is something like a sacrilege. And it actually is, once the "nation" is experienced as sacred. According to the historian Hugh Seaton-Watson, "nationalism has become an *ersatz* religion. The nation, as understood by the nationalists, is a substitute of god; nationalism of this sort might be called *ethnolatry*" (Seaton-Watson, p. 465). This is the way the taboo feelings arise.

Other historians and political scientists defined nation and nationalism with terms like "imagined" and "constructions". These terms do not mean that nations do not exist or that nationalism is not associated with a real set of feelings. But they clearly infer that they are not eternal and essential objective realities. In our times nations and nationalism are studies as historical entities; that is to say as realities that have a beginning and consequently an end. This new interpretation creates its followers and its dissidents and, naturally, the appearance of the related skepticism and doubts, voiced as "myths".

The Greek language is not a simple issue of linguistics. It is a crucial component of a national identity. I will discuss some more myths of both kinds – *myths about* X and X *as myth* – below and I will assess all the findings further down.

And a last moment addition to this chapter. On the days these were written (December 2020-Janary 2021) the discussion about loans and infiltration of foreign words stirred up again in Greece. The apparent occasion was the qualities of the dictionaries that appeared in the market of Greece the last few years and the "correct use" of the Greek language. The "national identity" and the nationalist ideology were almost completely silenced in this strife. There was, however, an interesting article which approached the dictionary of G. Babiniotis in a unique perspective. Hagen Fleischer made use of the examples given in this dictionary to show how nationalist images, stereotypes, prejudices disclose an ideological tendency (Fleischer). I present a few examples of how some words were used in sentences in this dictionary (the words are underlined). Fleischer wanted to show that national identity was expressed by the inverted image of the Other vis-à-vis "us", with reference to my book *The Imagined Other as National Identity*, too.

> "The USA is a country of *business (μπίζνες)* and of richness", they *launch (λανσάρουν)* strange fashions; they interfere in our internal affairs without *excuse (απροκάλυπτα)*; they are positively *biased (μεροληπτικοί)* in favor of Turkey; many believe that the richness of the *West (Δύση)* is attained against the Third World; the statements of the German ministers mean *interference (επέμβαση)* in our internal affairs; the Greeks are the descendants of Ancient Greeks as it is seen from the *continuation (συνέχεια)* of the Greek language and their *traditions (παραδόσεις)*; the Greeks have the right to feel *proud (υπερήφανος)* of the history of their country; hospitality is the *characteristic (χαρακτηριστικό)* of the Greek people; some foreign powers want to impose relations of *vassalage (υποτέλεια);* there is an *eternal (αιώνια)* hatred between Greece and Turkey; during the revolution of 1821 the Turks *impaled (παλούκωσαν)* and/or *flayed (έγδαραν)* alive the Greek captives; ask a person who was in the destruction of Smyrna to tell you what Turks *mean (εστί).*

The above case renders an opportunity to see how nationalist understanding is expressed in various cases. The central theme of this ideology is twofold: "We are superior" and "the Other constitutes a danger".[155] This simple view may appear in almost infinite cases, contexts and opportunities and under various circumstances. Once it is expressed by someone in one case it is almost certain that it will appear in other cases, too.

Above (3- Summary of a study on images) I showed that many parameters are associated:

> Some parameters are directly related. 1- the critical attitude towards one's state (recognizing or not negative acts of "our state" against the Other), 2- the degree of preference of the West and "western values" and 3- the distancing from religious affinity are, all three, directly related (and proportional) to having a positive or negative perception of the Other. It becomes also clear that one does not need to ask many questions to find out what group one belongs to, suffice to know any of the perceptions (parameters) mentioned above (i.e., the West, "our" religion, the Greeks, "our" state) and one has a fairly good chance to know what the other parameters are. In other words, there is a very high predictability and a high correlation factor in these parameters which operate in packages.

This means that nationalist imagery is not limited to one or a few subject matters. If this understanding exists, it is reflected in all issues. If "we are unique" it follows that some Others will compose "a danger for us"! Our uniqueness, superiority etc., go with the Other who has various negative characteristics. In other words, national haughtiness pairs with xenophobia; in all cases these are related to language, to history, international relations, to sports, to arts, etc. An isolated "nationalistic" utterance should not be interpreted as a coincidental case; most probably it is an indication of a special understanding.

***

---

155 That the Other is inferior is not needed to be repeated; our superiority is a precondition of that.

PART TWO

MYTHIC THINKING

CHAPTER 4

SENSITIVE / TABOO MYTHS

In the first part of this study, following a preface on "myths", some well known Greek national myths related to the Church, to the Ancient Greeks and to the Greek language have been presented in three separate chapters. In this Second Part the national myths will be discussed from a different perspective. The basic question that will lead this part is: Are the national myths *related* to the nation, to the Ancient Greeks and to the Greek language, or are the Nation and the Church *myths themselves*, creating a series of secondary national myths? This question is justified since almost all the myths mentioned above were directly and/or indirectly related to a national discourse and belief. If the question proves meaningful then national myths will obtain a new meaning.

The historic appearance of the nations, the national identity and my definition of a nation as consensual and contingent have been discussed above (Preface, 3- The meaning of words: National). At this point I want to introduce the belief in the nation and nationalism and show its relation to myths.

19- The Nation as Myth

Contrary to what some nationalists believe "nationhood" is not based on objective criteria, such as race, language, religion, culture and the like. At the dawn of the nation states and nationalism, entities of this kind were suggested to explain the phenomenon of nationhood. In our days, this is not accepted by the experts on nationalism and by the greater part of the academic world. The last decades two new aspects are seen as "true": A) Nations and nationalism are relatively new phenomena and B) they are mainly "believed" and/or "imagined" situations.

Ernest Renan as early as 1882 in "What is a Nation?" had stated it quite clearly: it is not the race, the language, the religion or the geography that make a nation, but "A nation is therefore a large-scale solidarity, constituted by the feeling of the sacrifices that one has made in the past and of those that one is prepared to make in the future. It presupposes a past; it is summarized, however, in the present by a tangible fact, namely, *consent, the clearly expressed desire* to continue a common life. A nation's existence is, if you will pardon the metaphor, *a daily plebiscite*, just as an individual's existence is a perpetual affirmation of life." [My underlining, and in the rest that follow, HM] (Renan).

Carlton Hayes in 1931 opened a new way in studying nationalism: "In the eighteenth century, rather suddenly, emerged a philosophy of nationalism... It promised a way of escape from the crazy evils of the time to a logical millennium of the near future, and *faith* in just such a millennium was a marked trait of eighteenth-century thought" (Hayes, p.13). Elie Kedurie in 1960 used the verb "invent" to explain nationalism: "Nationalism is a doctrine invented in Europe at the beginning of the nineteenth century"(Kedourie). The way for a modern interpretation of nation and nationalism was widely open.

Hugh Seton-Watson in 1977 wrote: "I am driven to the conclusion that no 'scientific definition' of a nation can be devised; yet the phenomenon has existed and exists when a significant number of people in a community *consider themselves* to form a nation, or *behave as if they formed one*" (Seton-Watson. p. 5). He also makes a distinction between old and new nations. "The old are those who acquired national identity or national consciousness before the formulation of the doctrine of nationalism. The new are those for whom two processes developed simultaneously: the formation of national consciousness and the creation of national movements. Both *processes were the work of small educated political elites*" (p. 5, 7).

Anthony Smith in the 1970's expressed similar ideas: "Of all the *visions and faiths* that compete or men's loyalties in the modern world, the most widespread and persistent is the national ideal.... [N]ationalism can adapt the vision, the culture, the solidarity and the programme to diverse situations and interests. It is this flexibility that allowed nationalism continually to re-emerge and spread, at the cost of its ideological rivals, *from 1789* until today." (Smith, 1979, P.1, 4). Later, as a kind of answer to B. Anderson, Anthony Smith introduces the concept of *ethnie* (or proto-nation by others) meaning that nations are not created out of the blue but there is a prehistory behind them. But still, A. Smith recognizes that nations belong to modern era as a novel phenomenon. "To say that *modern world* is a 'world of nations' is to describe both a reality and *an aspiration*. The legitimating principle of politics and state making today is nationalism, no other principle commands mankind's allegiance" (Smith, 1989, p. 129) Most interestingly, A. Smith stresses the importance that myths played in the creation of the ethnic groups and as a consequence eventually the nations: "What I shall be arguing is that the 'core' of ethnicity, as it has been transmitted in the historical record and as it shapes individual experience, resides in the quartet of 'myths, memories, values and symbols' and in the characteristic forms of styles and genres of certain historical configuration of populations.... Special emphasis is laid on what is termed the 'myth-symbol' complex, and particularly that 'mythomoteur' or constitutive myth of the ethnic polity; both indicate the vital role of *myths and symbols as embodying the corpus of beliefs and sentiments which the guardians of ethnicity preserve, diffuse and transmit to future generations."* (Smith, 1989, p. 15)

In 1982 John Breuilly talked of nationalism as a means of *modern times* to get power by controlling the state (Breuilly, p. 2). Next year Ernest Gellner wrote "In fact, nations, like states, are a contingency, and not a universal necessity .... Two men are of the same nation if and only if they share the same culture [or] if they *recognize* each other as belonging to the same nation. In other words, *nations maketh man; nations are the artifacts of men's convictions* and loyalties and solidarities" (Gellner, p. 6, 7). And Benedict Anderson used the word "imagined" to explain and define the nations: "In an anthropological spirit, then, I propose the following definition of the nation: it is an imagined political community – and imagined as both inherently limited and sovereign" (Anderson, p. 6).

Eric Hobsbawm in 1990 stated how difficult it is to define "nation". "How indeed could it be otherwise, given that we are trying to fit historically novel, emerging, changing and even today, far from universal entities into a frame work or permanence and universality?" (Hobsbawm, 1990, p. 6). In this case I underline the words "historically novel and emerging". (p. 6). And Liah Greenfeld in 1992 adds: "The only foundation of nationalism as such, the only condition, that is without which no nationalism is possible, is *an idea*; nationalism is a particular perspective or a *style of thought*. The idea which lies at the core of nationalism is the idea of the 'nation'... [I]n early sixteenth century England [the word 'nation'] signaled the emergence of the first nation in the world" (Greenfeld, p. 3-4, 6).

The list of historians, political scientists, sociologists, etc. that see nations and nationalism as a "new" phenomenon and as a "perception" can be extended. There are, however, many and sometimes great differences among the academics on this issue. Some see the "beginning" of the nations in the 18th century, other, as early as the 16th. Some as "cause" of the appearance of nations see the economic developments, others the need for sovereignty and others the old-time cultural heritage. What I want to keep from the above is the two aspects of nations: they are new and operate as perceptions, as what the members of the nations believe. As I have already mentioned the words used to indicate this aspect of the nations are: expressed desire, faith, invented idea, considering themselves, behaving as if, process worked by elites, aspiration, myths and symbols, belief, sentiment, artifacts of men's convictions, an idea, style of thought, imagined. All these adjectives that characterize the "nation" express a related subjective belief.

Some specialists of "nation and nationalism" see a new rhetoric of "us" versus the "other", a new perception of "a world of nations", a new interpretation of the past, the present and the future as the common aspect of this new ideology (Ozkirimli).

All these eventually bridge nations and nationalism to perceptions, to images, to beliefs, to ideologies and eventually to myths. It was a surprise to me to read William McNeill's article "Mythistory, or Truth, Myth, and Historians" (1986) as I was writing this chapter. He used the motto that I used above – One's absolute truth is the myth of the Other – and I felt a little disappointed that I had not been really original! On the other hand, I felt reassured of my approach and hereon I can refer to an authority as I make my point.[1] Here is what McNeill wrote about truth and myths.

> "What seems true to one historian will seem false to another, so one historian's truth becomes another's myth... The principle source of historical complexity lies in the fact that human beings react both to the natural world and to one another, chiefly through the mediation of symbols. This means, among other things, that a theory about human life, if widely believed, will alter actual behaviour, usually by inducing people to act as if the theory were true... What a particular group of persons understands, believes, and acts upon, even if quite absurd to outsiders, may nonetheless cement social relations and allow the members of the group to act together and accomplish feats otherwise impossible... Shared truths that provide a sanction for common effort have obvious survival value... Yet to outsiders, truths of this kind are likely to seem myths... Everything suggests that this sort of social and ideological fragmentation will continue indefinitely...

> "Partially autonomous professional idea-systems have proliferated in the past century or so. Those most important to historians are the so called social scientists – anthropology, sociology, political science, psychology and economics – together with the newer disciplines of ecology and semeiology. But law, theology and philosophy also pervade the field of knowledge with which historians may be expected to deal. On top of all this, innumerable individual authors, each with his own assortment of ideas and assumptions, compete for attention. Choice is everywhere; dissent turns into cacophonous confusion; my truth dissolves into your myth even before I can put words on paper."

Chris Lorenz, twenty three years after McNeill, enriched the theme of mythistory by giving also credit to what has been dared in this direction. In

---

[1] I was surprised with W. McNeill for a second and a personal reason, too. His book *History Handbook of Western Civilization* (University Chicago, 1953) stays in my bookshelf from the 1960's. It was assigned as a textbook in my university years in a course called "Humanities". I used the book for decades but as a "textbook", not paying attention to who the writer was. It was only recently that I understood why I had liked this book so much.

his article he pointed the following: 1) The "scientific" history could not generate a consensus comparable to that found in the natural sciences; 2) Myths, as shared truths are necessary for groups and cultures to survive; 3) Historiographies and myths build a world of heroes and emotional rituals, liturgies, symbols similar to what religions had done. 4) The nations (the emotional communities) are creations of the historians who act as "mythmakers"; 5) Nationalism, like religions has cults, sacred dogmas, nation as God, heroes as martyrs, etc.; 6) The line between history writing and myth making is blurred; 7) It is possible to show that the mythical character of modern "scientific" historiography was set from the start, "from its inception", as seen in the works of Leopold von Ranke and Wilhelm von Humboldt; 8) This history of historiography was repressed because historians did not dare to face these aspects of their work. (Lorenz, 2011, p.35-55). [2]

I will interpret all these in the end of this study. Here I will only highlight a few points and ask questions that are related to some sections above and that will lead to the next ones.

1- W. McNeill enumerated the very many fields of academic disciplines as if he stresses the need of "multi-disciplinary" studies (mentioned in Preface, above, too).

2- The myths operate as catalysts that merge supposedly unrelated fields of knowledge and of human activities: For example, history, religion and faith, language, as well as studies on primitive and modern man, science and art, all interrelated on the basis of "myths". It is indicative how philosopher Cassirer and historian McNeill speak the same "language" even though they have different starting points.[3]

3- Many "stories" of the past, myths for others, are the founding beliefs of the nations. Therefore, the role of the myths is important and usually prioritized.

4- Group psychology of many mammals – especially of bonobos – show resemblance with the human (national) solidarity, and findings of this kind carry the issue of myth to new fields of studies, e.g., to sociobiology and neuroscience.

5- And a question that should be answered in the following chapters: If most Greeks (and most humans worldwide) believe in myths on matters of religions, and again on matters of nationhood, is it possible to think of any

---

[2] The Greek historian Antonis Liakos, discusses the close relation of historiography and myths with reference to the related article of Chris Lorenz refraining, however, from reaching to a kind of conclusion (Liakos, 2007, p. 48-51).
[3] One may safely assume that William McNeill (1917-2016) was influenced by E. Cassirer (1874-1945) especially considering that Cassirer wrote *Mythical Thought* and *Language and Myth* in 1925.

human society that is not basically founded on myths? Is it ever possible to live without myths?

20- Religion as a national myth

The scientific and/or academic study of a myth differs from experiencing a myth. In the second case the myth is a belief perceived as a true story, and its defiance causes resentment. In such a situation the believers feel as if they are not respected, that they are insulted and provoked or betrayed. Furthermore, almost all of the myths presented above in the first part are cases which have been "discussed" at various times among the Greeks as of their validities, i.e., if they are actually myths or legends or absolute realities or real situations that include some minor mythical parts. In all cases, however, it is as if there is an implicit social consensus that it is legitimate to discuss these issues.

There are some other myths, however, which have not been or could not be discussed as freely as the above. Some of these are "new myths", not yet fully opened to discussion or myths that are seen as indispensible for the religious and national identities. These may be called "sensitive" or "taboo" myths. My first experience with "sensitive" myths goes back to my youth.

I was in the primary school, about ten years old, when we the students discussed among ourselves how babies are born. I explained what I had learned at home: The priests bless the couple that gets married in church and that's it! Two girls had another explanation, the classical one which they described in some detail, too. I was so embarrassed that I still remember vividly that moment. I wished I had learned the truth at least from boys and not from girls! My parents had deceived me and I had believed in a myth! That time I was not aware of the word "myth" and I said to myself that the whole story was a "lie".

My second experience with "lies" in my youth had to do with God. As a child I had two important questions that could not be answered convincingly by my elders: First, why did God who had created fish for us to eat created them with bones which stuck in my throat? Second, why did my elder brother die so young before given a chance to be tried as of his loyalty to the commandments of God so that he would be judged accordingly? Presumably my parents' explanations were not very convincing, so the day I heard for the first time the "non-existence of god" – I was about fourteen – I decided that that view had fewer contradictions.

This second revelation in my life, i.e., God's nonexistence, was a more serious situation than the birth of the babies. This was not a "myth of childhood", because it did not belong to the category of myths that are being abandoned in adultery. The heroes of the fairy tales that once excited us or put us to sleep at night, Cinderella, Little Red Riding Hood and of course the ever existent Snow White and the seven Dwarfs were all forgotten after a while, but not Christ and his Twelve Disciples, nor Satan. Mainly because, they were recounted repeatedly.

That there is a God or alternatively some spiritual powers that need to be somehow worshiped is almost a universal reality for a very big part of human race, children and grownups alike. The first four major (populous) religions, Christianity, Islam, Hinduism and Buddhism make up the 78% of the world population, 31%, 25%, 15% and 7% respectively; together with some other beliefs the religious world population amounts to 84%. The nonreligious population amounts only to 16%.[4] According to Richard Dawkins "God" is a "delusion", i.e., a myth (Dawkins). Christopher Hitchens and many others tried to prove the nonexistence of God and that religious beliefs do not correspond to realities (Hitchens). But God exists for most people and this belief is a "democratic reality": the atheists are only a minority in our time.

This imbalance between majority versus minority established the almost unquestionable dominance of the myth of religion as a fact. In our days the reputable status of religions and their non-inclusion in the category of myths is the consequence of the existence of social imbalance of powers. The religions of our time enjoy a protection not only against criticism under the understanding of "respect of beliefs" but also against their possible study within a general category of myths. Present-day religions enjoy their disciplinary/academic autonomy.

If Dawkins and his devotees are right then religion is one of the most prominent myths of humanity at present. I presume that a few centuries ago the non-believers were even fewer. This does not mean, however, that the "delusion" is declining. Its retreat may be contingent and may rise again. I will come back to this issue further down. At this point I should add that in Greece Greek-Orthodox Christian religion is part of the Constitution of the Greek state. Right at the beginning there is a reference to the "Holy Trinity". This prestige secures religion its autonomy from other disciplines of social sciences.

Present-day statistics show that the Greeks (of Greece) are among the most religious six people in Europe. Their religion, attending masses and praying are considered important. Also they believe in God (92%) and they are "sure" about this by a 59% (Millas, 2021).[5] The non-believers are about

---

[4] List of religious populations - Wikipedia. This figure may be lower. In the footnote about this figure we read the following: "Nonreligious group includes agnostic, atheist, secular humanist, and people answering 'none' or no religious preference. Half of this group is theistic but nonreligious.

[5] Eastern and Western Europeans Differ on Importance of Religion, Views of Minorities, and Key Social Issues | Pew Research Center (pewforum.org)

6%. This makes it difficult to speak about religion in the context of myths.

The instilling of religion to the Greek national discourse was discussed in Chapter 2 above with respect to "Helleno-Christianity". This combination of national myth with a religion (or with religious story/myth) was an "annexation" of religion by nationalism rather than a mixture of the two parts. Starting with the establishing of the new Greek nation-state the Greek Orthodox Church made use of nationalism and national ideals to secure its legitimacy. It is enough to look at the myths that the Church appropriates and how it defends its relation to them. All three myths discussed above – the Secret School, the Holy Banner and the Nation-martyr Patriarch – play this role. The Church tries to show how it served the "national cause", how it educated the nation, how it helped the national revolution and how the clerics sacrificed their lives for the nation.

This "modern" role of the Church is distant from the teaching of Christ, of peace and of its ecumenical mission. It is national and this is clearly stated. Church's importance is claimed on the ground of its input in nation-building. In other words the modern story of the Church composes a section of the more general Grand National Narrative: "The Church, too, contributed in the national fight". All religions and particularly Christianity of any version experienced various different missions and alliances. The one mentioned here is related to the era of nations and nationalism. This new role of this particular Church makes it a new church, somehow different from its predecessors.

As for the question, if the Church was *forced* to take this decision or if it decided to comply with the new national ideology *voluntarily* may be irrelevant. Normally, decisions are taken freely because individuals and institutions are forced in that direction.

21- A check list for "nationalism"

Once nationhood and religions are associated to myths, the sphere of this study widens substantially. It may be seen as becoming a new kind of a study. The association of the three – nationhood, religion and myths - is justified since ideologies and religions are related to feelings and beliefs, as it is with myths. Looking at all the above mentioned Greek myths – the Secret School during the period the nation was enslaved , the national-martyr Patriarch, the patriotic and holy Lavra Monastery, the "glorious" Ancient Greece, the Greek language that renders pride to the Greeks worldwide – they all seem to be complementary parts of a greater basic myth: the Greek national story/myth. And naturally the definition of myth obtains new dimensions.

Taking into consideration what has been said about nationhood until now in this study, national(ist) rhetoric seems to have some characteristics that run horizontally through all nations, irrespective of the possible historical, cultural and/or economic differences that may exist among these nations and nation-states (Ozkirimli; Millas, 2016). Six characteristics of the nation – which I call "the check list of six points" is a good guide to see if a text, a discourse or a picture is nationalistic, and if it is, to what extent:

1- The nation is considered the main reference point and the source of legitimacy of many actions. It is the central "value" that gives meaning to "national" decisions. The preservation of the nation – with its history, its borders, its language, its sacred heritage and culture, etc. - is the basic idea and an ideal whose rationale does not need to be demonstrated.

2 - The world population is perceived to be composed of nations. There is a dichotomy on the basis as "us" and the "other(s)". Other possible classifications, e.g., based on religions, classes, gender, education, geography, ideology, etc., which would transcend national divides are not considered by the followers of the national paradigm. The nations are imagined to be in a Darwinian kind of competition, and the "others" usually are seen as rivals, enemies and threats.

3 - The nation is perceived to be composed of "homogeneous" citizens. The nations have "characters". Therefore, stereotyping is a normal phenomenon: "we" are positive, the Jews are not. In the case of Greeks the Turks are, in the last resort, negative: invaders, cruel, etc. To think of the "other" as being composed of personalities ranging from positive to negative renders holistic national thinking obsolete. "We", normally, have many merits. "We" are old (ancient), brave, creative, noble, honest, righteous, clever, generous etc. – and humble. The "other", in general, is never better than "us". "We" are "proud" of our past, identity and the like, and very sensitive to criticism on these matters, e.g., when national myths are disputed. The (negative) "other" is indispensible in order to define the "self" and specifically national identity.

4 – Not only are the national characteristics perceived as homogeneous at a certain historical moment, but they are also considered to persist throughout history. Therefore the (real or imaginary) ancestors are of great importance. If "they" prove defective, "we" should be seen equally defective. Therefore, stories and myths about heroic and great ancestors become necessary and "sensitive" issues.[6]

5 - A difficulty with national perception (national paradigm) is how to determine what is the "constant" that secures the unchanged identity, the

---

[6] A study on Greek textbooks showed that three ideas were systematically exhibited: the continuity of the Greek nation from antiquity until today, the role of the Church and the heroism of the Greeks (Aggelopoulos, p. 319-334).

Hercules Millas | **181**

permanent character and the unity of the nation throughout history. Race, language, religion, culture and character of the nation are some "constants" which have been proposed. But eventually – as explained above – a persuasive answer to this important (and essentialist) question has not been found. However, all these old ideas, from race to culture, are still used by the proponents of nationalism, even though quite often in an indirect way.

6 - As Renan in 1882 had said, nations also "forget" and "miss" whatever contradict the above perceptions. Forgotten are the negative actions of "our nations".

For many, however, and among them myself, the above assumptions are not true. What is true are the following: Nations are relatively new formations; they are not composed of citizens that have a single character; the world population is composed of all kinds of groups and individuals, not only of nations; "we" are not only under the threat of "others" but we have all kinds of relationships, positive, negative and neutral, with our wider environment; the Manichean "positive us versus the negative other" is an exaggerated nationalist phobic perception; and "we" normally are not ready to accept "our" wrong-doings, this being a tendency leading to oblivion and lack of self-consciousness.

It is clear that that there is a divide between nationhood and all the related assumptions and beliefs, on one hand, and the critics of these on the other. When some believe in something and others disbelieve it, then the case where "one's truth is the myth of the other" is reached. In other words, nationalist discourse (and paradigm) is perceived as a myth and an object of study. The crucial step is to see all the manifestations of nationhood as myths and myths as expressing nationhood. If this step is taken, and I do not see why it shouldn't, then a huge number of social beliefs become objects of study as myths. Anything national and/or religious is included in the study of myths.

On the other hand, the national and the religious beliefs cover almost all aspects of life in our era of nation-states: the political sphere with the related ideologies, programs, prejudices and stereotypes; the religious sphere with the related various group affiliations and daily practices; the ethical sphere with the corresponding values and understandings; the various aesthetic worlds of these groups; the arts and literary texts that correspond to these spheres; the interpretation of the past and present of these, e.g., historiography. Even the most seemingly "innocent" manifestations are part of national and/or religious beliefs and quite often presenting difficulties in distinguishing the difference between the two.

It is widely argued, as we saw above, that nationhood is an existing real belief, in the sense of being influential and determinant in shaping our way of thinking and behavior, but still historically new and "imagined", in the sense of being a human construct. But for some, "tradition", too, is invented; and I have in mind *The Invention of Tradition* (of Eric Hobsbawm, 2012 &Terence Ranger). Others (Ronald Fritze, for example) claimed that knowledge, too, may be part of a set of myths; see for example his *Invented Knowledge*. Michael Billig in his *Banal Nationalism* showed how nationalism may be present and active in domains where we normally do not suspect. I edited, too, *The so called Innocent Nationalism* (Millas, 2010) where it was shown how nationalism was present and active within domains we think are distant of ideologies and mythical beliefs such as, cartoons, stories for children, TV series, pictures on banknotes, toponyms, Olympic Games, football, newspapers, songs, church and folklore. (see bibliography for all studies mentioned).

It is understood that the topic of myths and its relation with nationalism, religions, ideologies, tradition and other domains of social life necessitates a multi-disciplinary approach. The problem that normally arises, however, is not the very wide scope but the meanings that are given to words such as myth, ideology, belief, religion, tradition, history, etc. Once these "words" are perceived as corresponding to "different" categories, and as belonging to separate academic spheres, any "multi" approach turns to self-deceiving process: the effort to relate the supposedly "different" issues is also a process that re-confirms the differences. (See: Preface; 4- A tentative assessment, To Be "Similar"/ "Different")

Whereas, all human behaviors and beliefs may be handled, as such, under one heading. The name to be given to this "one heading" is secondary. What is of importance is to see that human behavior is a single phenomenon, that should be studied making use of all hitherto human knowledge and not as dispersed academic approaches. The scattering of human reality to many different domains was discussed above. At this point the question is how to continue with the Greek (modern) myths.

I will try to avoid the "academically scattered approach" to human behavior, naturally making use of all knowledge in my possession. I will make first a list of "myths" that exist among the Greeks, not elaborating, since that would require a number of volumes! I will make a distinction between issues that are being discussed as "myths" among the Greeks and issues that are not discussed, either because they are not perceived as myths or because they are "taboo" issues. And at the end I will venture a final assessment.

22- Some Taboo myths

All myths are sensitive but some are much more, they are almost treated as taboos. When the believers of a myth are much more numerous relative to the ones who challenge it the reaction is greater. However, this is not the major reason of having "very sensitive" myths. The myths can be seen as the basic ones and their derivatives. The basic ones are the above mentioned "nationhood" and the Church that is instilled to the national discourse. The Secret School, just to mention an example, is a byproduct of the main national myth.

Any myth that challenges the derivatives of the main myth can be tolerated to a certain extent. Such a challenge, i.e., calling a belief "myth" may be experienced as an insult by the believers but this is different from an "attack" to the basic myth itself. In our days in Greece the *reputation* of the nation and/or the Church can be discussed as myths but not their *existence* with equal freedom. This explains the centuries-long violent reaction of the Church against atheism, too: Church perceives an attack against its being.

To call a nation a myth triggers different sentiments than calling Holy Banner a myth. Many can endure without the story of the Banner; but to "lose" the sense of national belonging is different. I will give a few examples of some sensitive issues to end this chapter. It is illuminating to see what an agony prevails in producing an explanation to what is experienced as a challenge to the national story (myth).

THE OTHER AS NATIONAL IDENTITY

As was mentioned above with respect to the "check list" of nationalism, the (negative) "other" is indispensible in order to define the (positive) "self" and specifically the national identity. The Turks are mostly seen as the "historical other" (Millas, 2007). This myth of stereotyping a nation was seriously challenged mostly by academics starting in the 1980s. The criticism was first directed to the xenophobic education and to the textbooks that propagated this prejudice (Heraclides, 1980; Ahlis; Frangoudaki, 1978, 1997; Millas, 2001). Then the Turks were "re-evaluated" and presented in a balanced manner, either in a social context or in view of the bilateral political relations (Theodoropoulos, Pesmazoglou, Heraclides, 2001, 2010, Millas, 2004.).

The Turks are not the only "foreign Others"; the "West" as Catholics and Protestants or as capitalists, imperialists and exploiters, or simply as "foreigners" are seen as a threat by a section of the Greek society. Some of these cases were presented above.[7] Besides the "foreign others", however, the "internal others", too, constitute another cluster of myths which interestingly operates not so much as an accusative discourse but rather by silencing the issue. The presence of Greeks – citizens of Greece – who do not speak Greek as their first (native) language constitute a problem to those who equate

---

[7] See, for example: Chapter 2- HOW THE GREEKS PERCEIVE THE "WEST" IN 1800 AND TODAY. See also: Veremis, p. 99-108.

Greekness to Greek language. What do we do with those who challenge the assumption that "our nation" is composed of Greeks who speak Greek? The nation was supposedly based on the assertion of a unity and homogeneity, mainly attained by language and religion. But the existence of language and religious "minorities" within the nation is a challenge to *that* meaning of "nation".[8]

There are different approaches and corresponding "solutions" to the problem. Sometimes both the state and the "minority" members – usually a section of the minority - construct a story (a myth) that is compatible with the "uniformity of the nation". Populations that speak Wallachian (Βλάχικα / Αρωμανικά) and known in Greece as Βλάχοι (Wallach or Vlach) may be defined as "bilingual" to handle the problem. For example, Babiniotis dictionary defines Βλάχος (Valch) as a bilingual Greek who speaks βλάχικα Wallachian" (Mackridge, 2011). Then follows a long explanation to clarify the ethnic origin of the Vlachs:

> "Contrary to what foreign interests and political expediencies have formerly attempted to impose (they even established a Romanian school in Yiannina to teach to Vlachs ... as a "minority" their supposedly mother language, the Romanian!), whereas today scientific research has established the truth, which is widely accepted. The Vlachs who are Greeks [Ellines] by descent and consciousness, are bilingual Greek herdsmen and livestock breeders ... who along with Greek they speak a dialect descended from Latin. [Wallachian, Koutsowallahian, Aromounic [Βλάχικα, Κουτσοβλάχικα, Αρωμουνικά]. Their linguistic (not ethnic!) kinship to the Romanian is due to the fact that both the Aromanian and Romanian go back to the common source, the Eastern or Balkan Latin. The Greeks who adapted the Latin language, the Vlachs, spoke this language which was strongly influenced by Ancient Greek" (Babiniotis, 1998).

In the rest of this paragraph the distinguished linguist gives examples of Ancient Greek words that are encountered in the language of the Vlachs, thus demonstrating their ethnic origin. Another well known dictionary simply defines the Vlachs as "Greeks who speaks Greek and Wallachian" without trying to get involved in the ethnic origin of the Vlachs (Academy).

There are various "explanations "of the origin and the ethnic identity of

---

[8] The "recognition" of minorities based on "differences" of language, religion, ethnicity, etc., is an intrinsic problematic of some nation-states, in the first place: they declare equality of all citizens but they "recognize" differences and act according to these differences. But "difference" from what? It is as if the minorities are not in tune with a certain "norm". Whereas, any free and voluntary grouping of the citizens - political, ideological, occupational, gender wise and likewise, according to language or religion – ought not to constitute "minorities" that are not in tune to a norm but simply equal citizens that exercise their right of assembling and forming social groups. This problematic is beyond the scope of this study.

Vlachs which for the non-partisans in these are simply myths (Katsanis, p. 221-231). It is wrong, however, to think that the Vlachs are shown as Greeks only by the Greek authorities. Some Vlachs self-identify themselves as Greeks, too. According to a Vlach historian "starting from the time of the Latins (6th century) Greek consciousness was firmly established among the Vlachs" (Sotiriou, p. 29). Then by references to well known Greek Vlachs he states that "The Vlachs as middle class created the Modern Greek Renaissance ... and created all the cultural centers of the Greek state and the University of Athens by their donations" (p. 33).

Toward the end of this book some incidents of the year 1905 are mentioned but not very well explained. "The Vlachs of Greece faced many restrictions and discriminations in using their language... Some [paramilitary] Cretans caused the alienation of a small group of Vlachs which had joined the side of the Romanians, Italians and Scopians. The Athenian side reacted violently during this period of foreign propaganda thinking that by imposing prohibitions on the use of the language of the Vlachs would limit the foreign propaganda, These methods caused the opposite results of what were expected and these bilingual Vlachs... are now the most ardent haters of the Greeks " (p. 75-76). It seems that the relations between the "Athenian side" and the Vlachs who were "haters of Greeks" were quite tense.

In an article in a Greek paper, six possibilities are mentioned for the etymology of the name Vlach. In the first three the word is associated to Ancient Greek words (βληχή/bleat, βλίχαν/frog, βλάχρον/fern), the next is the Greek βράχος/rock and the last two are the latin flaccus (big ears) and the Egyptian fellah/shepherd, but this last etymology, according to the writer should not be true.[9] Fellah is also a Turkish word which means peasant or Egyptian peasant but this would infer that the Greeks carry Turkish names which made the etymology contestable. The non-Greek sources have a very different description of Vlachs:

> "Vlachs are any of a group of Romance-language speakers who live south of the Danube in what are now southern Albania, northern Greece, the Republic of [North] Macedonia, and southwestern Bulgaria. Vlach is the English-language term used to describe such an individual... The name Vlach comes from a Celtic tribal name recorded by Caesar as Volcae and by Strabo and Ptolemy as Ouólkai, and it was transferred from Latin to Gothic as *walhs*. In Gothic, from which it entered Slavic, the ethnonym took on the meaning "foreigner" or "Latin speaker." The form Vlach reflects South Slavic metathesis, while the name of the former Romanian kingdom of

---

[9] See: Οι Βλάχοι: Η καταγωγή, η γλώσσα, και η μακραίωνη ιστορία τους (protothema.gr)

Walachia reflects East Slavic treatment… In Greece the Vlachs, like other Christian minorities, have no language rights. Books of Vlach folklore and linguistic studies have, however, been published there, and occasional folklore performances are permitted".[10]

The Arvanites are Greeks that speak a language called "arvanitika". According to the dictionary of Babiniotis the etymology of the word comes from the Albanian Arbena, changed to Greek Ἀρβανα. Then follows a long explanation. "They are Greeks of an old Albanian origin … closely related to the history of Hellenism and having fought in the national liberation war against the Turks and the other invaders, the Arvanites are in Greece from the 14th and 15th century. They have been ethnically, culturally and socially integrated into the Greek community with the only exception of the language Arvanitika which is a dialect of Albanian. Gradually this language receded … and in our days very few Arvanites speak this language" (Babiniotis, 1998).

For the language of the Arvanites one may find another definition, a tautology: "Arvanitika is a dialect of the Arvanites" (Academy). According to a study by an Arvanitis, K. Biris, the national origin of the Arvanites is Greek: "We see that starting from the early years of Byzantium …[the Arvanites] they are seen as Greeks [Hellens]… [These Arvanites] were bilinguals, they spoke the Doric Greek language and the language of the non-integrated Illyrians, and out of these two, Arvanitika eventually originated." Biris then mentions historians who characterized the Arvanites as having "Ancient Greek origin" (Biris, p. 16,17).

The non-Greek speaking communities, namely the Albanians and the Slavs, have been considered as cases that "make impure / bastardize" (νοθευτές) the Greek pure blood (Skopetea, 1988, p. 186.) Some other times the Albanians and the Arvanites are seen to mean the same groups (Baltsiotis, 2012, p. 355). In the 19th and early 20th century there were four theories related to the Albanians in the Greek public discourse: a) They are a different race but not a nation; b) Albanians are Greeks; c) Albanians should not establish a separate state; d) It is to the interest of the Albanians to be part of Greece (Skoulidas, p. 390-391).

A more recent anthropological case study on a village of Arvanites where the relationship of Arvanites-Albanians was studied revealed that the identity issues are much more complex than the myths on communities. The natives Arvanites of the village Gerbei (latter named Midea, by an ancient Greek name), in north Peloponnesus, who have been traditionally "leftists" and as a consequence faced problems with the Greek state, felt quite close with the immigrant Albanians that reached Greece the last decades. The villagers'

---

[10] Vlach | European ethnic group | Britannica.

explanation was that they both used a language through which they could communicate, that they shared some values and behaviors (they were honest, industrious "like themselves"), that the Albanians were discriminated like themselves and that Albanias honored their language and identity being expressed through an official status of the state. The researcher noticed two identities, first a political one, and later the appearance of an ethnic one among the Arvanites of that village. (Athanasopoulou, p.246- 250, 261).

Lambros Baltsiotis, an expert on minorities in Greece, calls the whole handling of these issues "national myths". "The formations of the *national myths*, which have been formed during many years and contain many contradictions…, are *constructed traditions* … that are expressed mostly as folkloric life… These national myths about the groups that do not speak the official language of the state may be called *complementary national myths*, since they are considered necessary, not only for the groups but for the national ideology in general" (Baltsiotis, 2004 , p. 344, 345).

Similar situations exist with the other non-Greek speaking groups and/or non-Orthodox Christians. The non-Greek speaking "Macedonians" of Greece is a very sensitive, even taboo issue. According to Hugh Poulton this "minority group" was not recognized, was suppressed not allowing the use of their language and was forced to reject their identity, names, etc. (Poulton, p. 162-171).[11] There always existed academics, journalists, etc., who criticized the policies of the state (for example, Kostopoulos, 2004; Heraclides, 2018), but these were confronted with hostility. We read, for example, the evaluation by a reader, against the skeptic of the official approach: "Mr. Heraclides in general is a special case. His book is addressed to personalities who present their prejudices as realities and there is no possibility to see this book as a valid evaluation of the Macedonian issue". The writer, instead suggests the books of Ioannis Koliopoulos, Sarantis Kargakos and Spiros Sfetas who, according to this reader present the "reality"[12]

The national/religious conflicts with the "minorities" are various and complex relations. Mazower, for example, has studied the case of the island of Tinos where Catholics were numerous. In the 1820s violent clashes erupted between the Orthodox and Catholic communities, and the Ottomans, French and Russians were also involved in some

---

[11] Also see: Η ιστορία για τη «μακεδονική μειονότητα», τα δικαστήρια και το «Ουράνιο Τόξο» | in.gr
[12] ΤΟ ΜΑΚΕΔΟΝΙΚΟ ΖΗΤΗΜΑ, 1878-2018

occasions. Eventually, a buried holy "Orthodox" icon of Virgin Mary was found – after a miraculous dream of a nun suggesting the place - and the greater Orthodox church of that time was built on that spot in 1831. King Othon visited the island and this church in 1833. This church is a pilgrimage place until today, and according to Mazower the local touristic guide books "forget" to mention the Catholic population of the island.[13]

The Turkish and "Pomak" speaking Muslim Greeks are another "problematic" issue. In general the Greek State and the Greek speaking Orthodox Christian society confront these communities with embarrassment and uneasiness. "The ideological and legal perception of the 'national self' or 'Greekness' was defined as 'Greek-speaking Orthodox' and excluded Muslims (or Jews)" (Tsitselikis, 2012, p. 535). The policy of the state concerning matters of these minorities was decided according to the development in international relations (Tsitselikis, 2004, p. 458). As for the educational system "the whole legal status of the schools [of this minority] is based on a mythical sphere" (Tsitselikis, 2003, p. 11).

"Defining" the non-Christian populations quite often acquires a tragic-comic dimension, especially when the issue is dealt with comparatively. The national myths compose mirror images; mostly they are opposite to each other but similar at the same time. The muslim Pomaks, for example, are appropriated by Greece, Bulgaria and Turkey:

> "The Bulgarians consider them part of the Bulgarian nation that was once converted to Islam by force during the Ottomans, the Turkish side see them as Turks who were converted to Bulgarians and the Greek thesis is that they are indigenous population that are related to ancient [Greek] Thracians ... The Turks claim that the word "Pomak" is related to "Patsinak" which comes from Petsenek [an old Turkish group], the Bulgarians see the word "pomagam" and "pomagaci" which mean to help and helpers" (Asimakopoulou, p. 278-279).

According to Baltsiotis, apart from the five "foreign" languages mentioned above there exist the Romani which can be encountered at any geography of Greece and five more, Armenian, Kurdish, Arabic, Italian and Judeo-espaniol speaking groups, languages that appeared mostly by the migrants that came to Greece from Asia Minor. (Baltsiotis, 2003). But the "internal others" are not only these: The Tsamides and the Jews existed, too. According to Y. Margaritis about 2,000 Muslim Albanians (Tsamides) of Greece were massacred in 1947 in a nationalist strife. In 1994 the parliament of Albania inaugurated the 27th of June as the day of "genocide" of the Tsamides. It is also mentioned that the Albanian side did not retaliate, "and this should be

---

[13] 26th Walton Lecture, The Gennadius Library, January 9, 2007.

reminded in these times of ours when many in Greece claim that the Greeks have taught what civilization means in the Balkans" (Margaritis, p. 171).

The issue of minorities in Greece has been a field where all kinds of national myths flourished. There have been efforts to explain the reason of this tendency, mostly "nationalism" and xenophobia shown as the cause. Almost always these supposedly local problems of the minorities were perceived as national and international cases related to some neighboring country, e.g., Serbia, Albania, North Macedonia, Bulgaria and/or Turkey. (Heraclides, 2004, p.43-57; Millas, 2004, p. 21-27

THE JEWS

According to some Greek researchers, few in number indeed, many of the cases mentioned above are dealt, not within a context of language, but rather as ethnic cleansing. They are taboo issues, too, since their existence jeopardizes the "character of the nation": On one hand, they introduce the problematic of some "non-Greek speaking Greeks", and on the other, the politically inappropriate attitude of the state towards its citizens.

The case of the Jews in Greece and the related myths are somewhat special and different from the myths of the "other groups" mentioned in this study: First, the images and the prejudices against the Jews are not special to Greece, but show similarities with what has been encountered in other societies of Europe. A traditional accusation had been that "they" crucified "our" Christ! Christ was a Jew, but the drama is not perceived as an internal matter of a community, but on a religious divide, reinterpreted anachronistically: The Jewish people killed our Christian Christ.

For centuries the image of the Jews was negative in Greece. By the 19th century the image of "the Jew" changed from the killer of Christ to the economic exploiter, too (Karabot, p. 226). This is clearly seen in the Greek literary texts. This image preserves myths about the Jews which reflect the thinking of Christian Greek vis-à-vis the "Jew" (Abatzopoulou, p. 117). "The usual scenario that is related to the image of the Jews, is the ghetto, the usurer, the miser father and the beautiful daughter… this is the beginning of a myth, and the stereotype and the myth are thus closely correlated" (p. 256). The Jews were often accused of killing and getting the blood of Christian children. It is recorded that between 1840 and 1930 there were more than thirty accusations of this kind in various cities of Greece, some cases causing the interning the Jews in ghettos (p. 201). Social unrest occurred and the interference of the state necessitated. The "burning of Juda" and the charge that the Jews played a role in the hanging of the Patriarch in Istanbul in 1821 were widespread, too. Especially in the 1940s, there were many articles in the newspapers demanding the "departure" of the Jews from Greece (Patrikiou, p. 245-258).

The last few decades there are researchers who voiced that the Jews suffered a lot in Greece, a fact that has been silenced almost completely until recently. This is a second characteristic of the Jewish issue. Jewish myth is one of replacing the facts with a more nation-friendly myth: Our Jew compatriots suffered only due to the Nazi Germans; there is no racism within the Greek society. According to L. Ventura

> "It is a paradox that even among those who adamantly condemn racism there are many who believe that there exist inherited unique Greek cultural characteristics – which, on top, they are perceived to be threatened because of Greece's integration to the European Union or because of globalization. We see that a section of the Left which fights racism, perceives the nation as a timeless outcome of a transcended Greek civilization" (Ventura, p. 197).

According to G. Margaritis "the Jews were massacred systematically in all areas where the Revolution [of 1821] was triumphant. In this way when the modern Greek state was formed in 1830 there were very few Jew communities left within its borders… The most well known massacres of the Jews are the ones of Tripolitsa, of Agrinio and Niokastro" (Margaritis, p. 99). As for the period of the Nazi occupation in Greece and during the deportation of the Jews for their extermination, "Neither the Resistance movement, nor the state official, nor the illegal press did react against what was happening. Relatively to the reactions in the same period in other European countries, the Greek society was passive, with no any positive results in favor of the Jews as the statistical numbers show … The Greeks saw the whole issue as one between the Germans and the Jews, not as one of Greece and of the Greeks" (p. 118, 122).

Mark Mazower recounts how the Jews of Thessaloniki were deported for the crematoriums in 1943 and how when a few of them returned they found their homes and properties having passed to the "Greeks" with no hope to get them back (Mazower, p. 443-461). These stories are little known within the Greek society; and instead the cases where the "Greeks helped the Jews" are highlighted – and these are numerous, too, especially in Athens. Some publications by Jews the last twenty years brought to light the details of the tragic story of the Jews of Greece (For example: Kounio-Amarilio; Nahmouli; Lampsa/Simpi).

Some Jews lately voiced more courageously this ugly side of their history. Esthir Koen remembered that when the Germans asked the Jews to gather in the square of the town of Ioannina within twenty minutes and as they were going there, children, oldies, pregnant women, "Not a single curtain moved, not a single tear was shed from the Greeks, no one showed some sympathy, I am sorry to say that. I suffer more because of this behavior, than of what I met in Germany. Because we implored many [Greeks] to let us stay outside the Jewish vicinity until the crisis was over, they did not accept that. We would have been saved."

There was another incident upon her return "home". "In 1945 I came back and I went straight to my house. A stranger appeared and stopped me. "Where are you going?' he asked. 'Home' I said. 'Do you know if your mother had an oven in the kitchen?' he asked and answered joyfully that surely she had. 'Then listen' said the man, 'if you dare enter, I will burn you in that oven, since the Germans did not do that to you'. I left and I never saw my house again".[14]

Apparently, this story is much different from what the Greeks know about the Jews-Greeks relations in their country. What is common in these stories about the "internal Others" is their silencing and/or their association with some real or imaginary "foreign Others". Except the Jews, all the other "minority Greeks" are perceived – but not openly declared - as nationally Others and connected to a neighboring (and rival or enemy) country, not as ethnic groups.[15] The silencing, on the other hand, operates mostly as a mechanism to avoid the "unpleasant forgotten events" that are directly associated with these "Greek citizens".

Tasos Kostopoulos, who published a book recounting the ethnic cleansings that occurred in the Balkans and in Anatolia in the years 1912-1922 and presenting the atrocities that the Greeks as armies or mobs did explained what triggered this study: When the public hysterical protest was voiced in 2007 about the history textbook known as the book of Maria Repussi,[16] a journalist, Themos Anastiasidis, in line with the protesters, had written that Greeks should stop producing myths about their history and present what is true. According to this "truth" the Greeks never resorted to atrocities against their enemies (in this case the Turks); there is not a single case of Greek violence in history. And Kostopoulos clarified: "This was the atmosphere in the media which showed what our National Ethical Education had created and forced me to write this book... In this study emphasis is given to the murders and ethnic cleansings by the Greek armies without silencing what all the other sides, the Bulgarian and the Turks did, too, but without self-

---

[14] The story presented by Stavros Tzimas, in Kathimerini, 5.12.2020. Esher Koen died five days prior this publication.
[15] It is of interest that in Greek there are not even words for "ethnic" and "ethnicity", except in some relatively recent academic texts that are written following universal practices (ethnotita, ethnotikos). The word "ethnos" in Greek is used to denote both "nation" as well as "ethnicity". In Greek dictionaries "ethnotita" is defined as "nationalité" or as "ethnos" (nation) (Academy; Babiniotis, 1998).
[16] The case of Repoussi textbook is discussed above in Chapter 2, 10- The Secret School: an exemplary myth.

censoring myself" Kostopoulos, 2007, p. 16).

Haris Athanasiadis, reacted to the systematic censoring of textbooks that crossed the line and deviated from the official Greek historiography. He mentioned some cases where textbooks were banned – in the years 2006-2007; 2002; 1965; 1919; and 1894-1917. He started with the case of Repussi and reminding what Antonis Samaras – a European Parliament member and Greek Prime Minister two years later - had said in 2007: "All those who try to demolish the traditional myths which strengthen the national consciousness are violating the Constitution. And the violations of the Constitution is not a matter of 'history' or 'education'. It is clearly a political issue and concerns all of us" (Athanasiadis, p. 45).

In other words, all the above show that the myths are protected and preserved, too. They are not only created out of some communal needs; they are perpetuated by the official state, too. This is done by direct interventions which produce a historiography of a special purpose; and/or some times by silencing some events that are not in harmony with a well-learned national history.

THE POLYTECHNIC EVENT OF 1973

After my over mentioned traumatic experiences – the birth of the babies and God who created fish with bones - my trust to my parents and to my environment was seriously shaken. I am a skeptic now and I look out for possible myths. To tie my personal story with the topic of this text, i.e., the myths, I will recount my experience of a "sensitive" Greek national myth. The story is about the Polytechnic student uprising against the dictatorial regime in Athens in 1973. I copy-paste from Wikipedia:

"The Athens Polytechnic uprising occurred in November 1973 as a massive student demonstration of popular rejection of the Greek military junta of 1967–1974. The uprising began on 14 November 1973, escalated to an open anti-junta revolt, and ended in bloodshed in the early morning of 17 November after a series of events starting with a tank crashing through the gates of the Polytechnic.... 17 November is currently observed as a holiday in Greece for all educational establishments; commemorative services are held and students attend school only for these, while some schools and all universities stay closed during the day. The central location for the commemoration is the campus of the Polytechneio. The campus is closed on the 15th (the day the students first occupied the campus in 1973). Students and politicians lay wreaths on a monument within the Polytechneio on which the names of Polytechneio students killed during the Greek Resistance in the 1940s are inscribed, while a catalogue of victims by the 7 year junta is uttered."

I will start my version of this story going thirteen years prior to the Polytechnic incident. Having been born, brought up and lived in Turkey the first thirty years of my life (1940-1970), I witnessed the political turmoil of May 1960. There were fierce student demonstrations against Prime Minister Adnan Menderes who was accused of being authoritarian and antidemocratic. There was a general censorship and the news reached us as rumors. The most convincing ones – convincing because everybody knew them – were about the hundreds of young people that had been killed by the police and the army during the protests. Their bodies were kept in the morgues of the hospitals or were secretly buried in mass graves and they were not shown even to their families. Their exact number was not clear but they were hundreds. There were other rumors, too, e.g., that some politicians were arrested as they were trying to fly abroad carrying kilos of gold with them, but I was personally excited about the killing of the students.

Eventually, a military coup on 27 May 1960 deposed the government and Menderes was arrested along with other members of his party. They were put to trial and A. Menderes was executed (hanged) on 17 September 1961. In the meanwhile the bodies of the dead students that were named "martyrs of liberty" (Hürriyet Şehitleri) were not found. On 2 June 1960 the Istanbul University decided to build a monument for these martyrs. The army announced that they are determined to find the dead. But they could not be spotted. The rector of the University of Istanbul declared that "We may not find the dead but we know that we have martyrs". Eventually, four young men could be detected who died during the demonstrations, some said by accident. They were buried in a "Martyrs cemetery".[17]

Living in Athens in 1973 I heard about the "big number" of students that were killed in the Polytechnic; tens of them, at least. The junta controlled the press and the news reached us as rumors. I was determined this time not be fooled. I was doubtful about the numbers from the beginning. The Junta fell eight months after the Polytechnic events. The result of the 17th November protests was a change in the hierarchy of the military Junta: During the "uprising" Y. Papadopoulos was toppled and Ioanidis took over. The Junta regime ended when it tried a coup in Cyprus against Archbishop Makarios (15 July, 1974) and when the Turkish forces invaded the island and Greece was not able to react. The Junta simply "disappeared".

One of the first initiatives of the new democratic regime was to try to publicize the identities of the murdered students. This was needed for different reasons. It was a public demand: the month-long secrecy of a tragic

---

[17] See: 27 Mayıs Darbesi - Vikipedi (wikipedia.org)

story had to be terminated and at least the parents of these young people had to be satisfied and compensated. The negative aspect of the Junta had to be demonstrated, too; this would have legitimized the new regime. The martyrs would be also the indisputable proof that the Greeks really exercised a resistance against the dictatorial regime and they did not tolerate it for seven years being passive spectators of the developments.

For weeks there were official pleads of the kind "please come and declare your losses in the Polytechnic, do not be afraid, the Junta is gone for good". But weeks and months passed and the names did not appear. Naturally, I became even more doubtful about the martyrs; and I followed daily the news about the related findings with special interest. After months some strange lists appeared. I remember one was about the people who were recorded as dead in the various hospitals in Athens on the 17th of November 1973. All were assumed to have died in the uprising and within the Polytechnic. Another list was about some people who were killed during the demonstrations on those days, but they died hundreds of meters away from the Polytechnic. Some eye witnesses described how a tank broke in smashing the gate of the school when there were students around; and the killings were thus assumed.

The story of the killings in the Polytechnic lasted for years and it is still discussed in the Greek blogs. The problem is that it is the supporters of the Junta or the extreme rightists who mostly challenge the story of the "martyr students". I remember Patakos, the number two of the Junta, who clearly stated that "there is not a single person killed in the Polytechnic." On the other hand, all the political party leaders, all university representatives and all public figures, every year on the 17th of November go to the monument of the martyrs and pay their respect to the students that died on the campus of the Polytechnic.

Eventually, thirty years after the events the historian Leonidas Kallivretakis (a member of the National Hellenic Research Foundation) published the most reliable report about the killed people in the events. The report includes the names, the photographs, the home address, the profession, the age of the 24 killed people, the total that could be confirmed, as well as the day, the hour and the location of their death. According to this report there is not any person killed on the campus of the Polytechnic. Five people died in various districts of Athens, twelve at a distance of 200 to 1000 meters from the campus and seven people in the neighborhood of the school. Four people were older than 57 years of age. Among the dead there are only three university students (one was injured in Patras, i.e., in another city) and three were high school students, one of them while she was on her home terrace (Kallivretakis).

The time of these deaths is interesting. The police entered the campus after the tank broke the gate, at about 3 in the morning of 17 November. Eight of the deaths occurred the previous day, late at night, before the attack. The rest after 10 o'clock on the 17th (six on the 18th); many hours after the attack. It is understood that the killing was not related to the attack against the students inside the Polytechnic.

There is no doubt that a determined protest by the students and killings of civilians is a fact. However, there is a mythic presentation of the events: "The police attacked the students and killed them"; this is not exactly so. The present-day public commemoration is about an invented event. This myth survived the reports' findings by a dexterous new interpretation of the past. Some distorted what the skeptics had said and re-interpreted the dispute: "They said there are no killed people, the reports have proved them wrong". Whereas the objection was to "the students that were killed on the campus by the police".

A more recent study of the event enumerates six myths that are associated with the Polytechnic event of 1973. The myths are about: the army that was supposedly violent; the "great number" of students that participated in the event; the USA that was allegedly behind the suppressing of the resistance; on how the students that participated in the events later made advantageous careers based on this event; that the Greek politicians were behind the events; and the mostly exaggerated issue of the "deaths in the Polytechic" (Gatos, p. 13-18).

There is an additional myth related to this Polytechnic event, too. This second defiance which is rarely heard in Greece is only lately voiced by Apostolos Doxiadis.[18] The Polytechnic uprising is seen by some as the social protest that ended the military dictatorial regime or – according to the second more convincing version – as the uprising that paved the way to the termination of this regime, i.e., the beginning of the end. It should also be reminded that this event is presented as a heroic act of the socialists of Greece. It is a leftist myth.

Doxiadis, in his autobiographical "personal novel" reports a different story (Doxiadis, pp. 911- 1040.) In a detailed narrative he described the course of the events of which he was an eyewitness and also in close contact with the actors of the uprising. At that time the dictatorial military Junta was trying to make concessions and to come to terms with the politicians leading to a transition to a more democratic regime, a development that eventually would

---

[18] Apostolos K. Doxiadis is a Greek mathematician and writer. He is best known for his international bestsellers *Uncle Petros and Goldbach's Conjecture* (2000) and *Logicomix* (2009), both earning various international awards.

have made the total return to democracy possible.[19] The 1973 uprising gave an end to *this* development and brought to power a more hard-core military regime under the leadership of D. Ioanidis.

Doxiadis criticizes the Polytechnic uprising as a harmful event. He recounts how, even during the events, a section of the students wanted to end the protest since their "message" had been conveyed and there was no need for further protests. During a voting, the students that wanted to continue the protests won by a small margin and the subsequent events gave the opportunity to Ioanidis to topple the more "reconciliatory" G. Papadopoulos.

23- A tentative assessment

In the second part of this study the framework and the scope are broadened. In the first part different myths that are seen as such in Greece were discussed. In the second part some "sensitive issues" as well as religion and nationhood were introduced as new cases for study.

In all cases, however, two factors were present: a) There were some beliefs which b) were disputed by others. Therefore, sentences of the kind "the Greeks saw X as a myth" simultaneously means that some other Greeks did see that X as a reality. This comment purposes to prevent stereotypes. Not "all" Greeks are meant when the term "the Greeks" is used.

By broadening the scope, new questions appeared. Many myths that were handled in the first part as special/distinct phenomena now appear as parts of a more general "myth". Religion and everything that has to do with the Church and nationhood, i.e., nation-state, national identity etc., appear as broader frameworks that incorporate the supposedly isolated singular myths.

The "broadening" had an additional dimension, too. New questions came to fore. Do the societies of the epoch of nation-states experience a unique mythical worldview - the way, for example, Europe experienced the world in a specific way in the Middle Ages? Is it possible that believing in myths is part of human nature – the way children get enchanted by fairy tales? Are the thinking and feeling of a child of a different sort from a grownup's or are they different only in their contents? What is the difference between a belief (myth) and knowledge? Are myths useful? Is it possible that producing myths is part of human nature – nature, in the sense of evolutionary development – especially considering that many other human behavioral inclinations are encountered in other mammals and especially in primates, too?

These questions will be discussed below. Starting first, however, with some "myths" which actually are perceived rather as "mistakes". But what is the

---

[19] This is also voiced by others, too. See: Veremis, p. 425.

difference between a mistaken judgment and a myth?

***

CHAPTER 5

NATIONAL MYTHS ARE OMNIPRESENT

This study on Greek national myths has reached to a certain maturity, however, at the same time bringing to fore new questions that necessitate new studies. In this chapter I will add some final comments, in a sense of a summary of the above and a general assessment.

24- Mistakes or myths

Many people by "myth" understand a mistaken belief that is not in harmony with reality. For example, if one thinks that our globe is on the shoulders of Atlas or that alien creatures from the outer space visit us daily, somebody else will judge that these are simply myths and definitely mistaken views.

But what if somebody thinks due to ignorance or due to misinformation that the lands cover a greater part of the surface of our globe than the seas? We know that the seas cover about 71% of the surface of the globe. Should we say that this person is *mistaken* or that he believes in a *myth*? In other words, what is the difference between a myth and a "wrong" knowledge?

Some common sense answers to these questions are the following:

1- If within a group there is a consensus about an opinion, that opinion is experienced as a true statement, as a reality and as knowledge. As long as that opinion is not challenged there is no discussion on its being a mistake or a myth, either. The size of the group may vary: It may be a small family group of some relatives, a local communion, a religious, a political or an ideological group or the whole world. At present the opinion/knowledge that the seas cover about 71% of the globe is not challenged; so we "know" that this information is neither a mistake nor a myth, it is a reality.

2- If, however, somebody has different numbers in mind, say, she thinks (or "knows") that lands and seas cover equal parts of the surface of the world, one may show to her a map of the world or some data of experts and thus demonstrate that a ration of 71-29 is more sensible. Normally, this person will change her opinion and will accept the true number.

2- The two cases above are about cases where opinions (knowledge which may be either true or false) are distant of myths: First, because there is no dispute on the issue and second because there is no "resistance" to the data. The person who had a mistaken idea about the size of the seas had no problem in accepting the presented data. In cases, however, where myths are involved "proving" the opposite is not so simple. In other words, things start getting complicated if knowledge is somehow related to "beliefs". For example, in a case where the past is being discussed and one claims that the world was covered completely by seas at the time of Noah, the argumentation to the contrary, or even the expression of doubts about this past will be met with a different psychological mood. The story of Noah as well as the source of this knowledge corresponds to a belief. In a case like this there will appear two different groups; those who believe in the story of Noah and those who do not and see the believers as following a myth.

3- In our days we may look back at and speak about a group of people, say of some villagers of the Middle Ages in Europe, and say that they believed in the myth of Noah because "we" (or at least some of "us") do not share that opinion. If all the above make sense, then a myth is different from a mistake because the first is a belief. Which means it is a part of a worldview and of an identity. That is why it is not easy to be abandoned. When one adopts a new rate about the sea/land relationship, his daily life, his relation with his group, his belief about the past and his expectations about his future do not have to change. But to show doubts about the story of Noah is a different situation for a believer. Many things need to be changed as soon as one accepts a new percentage of sea to land: his basic beliefs, his friends, his group in which he belongs, his perception of his past life, the every-day rituals and most importantly, the trustworthiness and legitimacy of the scriptures he believed.

Quite often a simple story that is expected to be discussed "logically", for example, about a historical incident, turns to a great historical, academic and/or social controversy. The reason is that the issue is directly or indirectly related to some myths. Some other times, some issues related to myths are silenced or shuffled in a way that they cannot be discussed anymore. All these are mechanisms which are put into action, mostly unconsciously, in order to defend and/or preserve some myths (beliefs, ideologies, etc.) that exist behind the apparent issue.

Here below follow some "stories" which in Greece appear as being related to some social and historical issues, but which are somehow connected to myths. They are cases that are related to the greater myth of "nationhood", to national identity and to nationalism, sometimes called "grand national narrative". This relationship – story/myth/nationalism – may be seen more distinctively if each story is controlled based on the "check list" of nationalism explained above (Chapter 4).

The myths that follow below will show also one of the main premises of this study: that the (modern) Greek myths –beliefs, ideologies, opinions and/or knowledge - exist because there are some other Greeks who do not believe in them. Starting from the time of Enlightenment and especially the last hundred years there have been many new interpretations of well established social "truths". All the myths presented above are the result of questioning, doubt, skepticism, challenge and defying of some kind.

The stories that follow are only some examples of theses "new interpretations". They are rather randomly selected, because an exhaustive list would require a voluminous work. What is of interest is that they are all directly and mostly indirectly in contrast or at least in disparity with the "grand national narrative" of Nationhood. They are stories that are usually challenged as "mistakes" but a closer look reveals that their contesters have another motive: to challenge or at least question a paradigm. This explains also the usual extreme counter reaction of those who are being contested.

25- A list of myths, mostly not recognized as such

National (and religious) myths are encountered in almost all social manifestations. I propose the following categories, mostly interconnected, just to facilitate their presentation.

A- Historiography, legends, literature, folklore ...

B- Politics, ideology, religion, conspiracy theories ("illusory pattern perception")

C- Cultural life: arts, museums, music, sports, science ...

D- The role of the state: laws, education, official festivities ...

HISTORIOGRAPHY, FOLKLORE, LEGENDS, LITERATURE...

By historiography the mythic heroic grand national narrative is meant. It may be about "our ancestors", for example the ancient Greeks, about the Greek Byzantium or the modern Revolution of the 1821 or the Resistance of 1940 or of 1973, etc. All these stories give the same message, but in various levels of persuasiveness: They honor and praise the nation and some of its institutions such as the Church and "us" as a nation. Several of these historical appraisals were presented above: E.g., the Ethnic-martyr Patriarch and the martyrs of the Polytechnic are two examples. The "unchanged character of the Greek nation and its continuity all through history" is the basis of this narration.[20]

The myths that are rather directly related to "history" are so many that even a list of them would not be exhaustive. Historian V. Kremmidas, widens

---

[20] See: H. Millas 2008 and 2008b.

the meaning of "myth" and includes to this term the purposive efforts to hide facts. He also gives few examples of lies/myths which are widely believed in Greece: The leading figure of 1821 Alexandros Mavrokordatos was disastrous for the nation; the Greeks always tend to start civil wars; all ills of the Greeks are caused by the foreigners; the rich Greeks generously helped economically the revolution of 1821, etc. (Kremmidas, 2021, p. 245-247). National myths are really omnipresent.

Folkloric studies are of a special significance. Actually, the interest in the "pure and genuine Greek people" among the Greeks started with Spiridon Zambelios (Σπυρίδων Ζαμπέλιος, 1815-1881) who showed a (national) interest in the folk poetry. Nikolaos Politis (Νικόλαος Πολίτης, 1852-1921), however, is considered the founder of this academic branch in Greece who published *The Traditional Tales of the Greek People* (Οι παραδόσεις του Ελληνικού λαού) in 1904 and which numbered 1,013 tales. Looking at this collection of stories, which are usually called "myths" and "legends", only a very small part of them is related to the Greek ethnicity/identity, either by direct reference to it or indirectly. Most of the stories are about some kings of unspecified time and creed, ancient pagan gods, Christ, saints, sky, plants, animals, dragons, magical creatures, magicians, demons, ghosts, sicknesses, fate, vampires, death, etc. Only about fifty of these stories can be considered to be somehow related to "Greeks", even though these were rather associated to Christianity. These tales, which one would question why they were called "Greek" – and not myths of Grecophones, for example - were placed at the very beginning of the series of the 1,013 stories, probably to give the tone that they all belong to stories "of the Greek people" (Politis, N.).

But another question is more important. Why were the miraculous stories of these people, such as the stories about demons, ghosts, fate, death and other metaphysical worries considered traditional stories and myths and no effort was made to collect the religious stories related directly to the Church, such as the creation of the world, the Annunciation, that is the pregnancy of Virgin Mary, the miracles of Christ, the resurrection, etc., and to include them to the "traditional stories"? A plausible explanation seems to be that mythical stories related to Christianity were separated from the world of myths to safeguard religion. These religious myths are classified under titles of scriptures and/or religion.

I will not elaborate on the folkloric aspect of myths even though it is a very rich subject. I will mention only two more examples to show that studies of this kind are organized, executed and presented in a way that will serve the process known as nation-building. They complete the national grand narrative of "one nation" whose members share a history, a language, a religion etc., as well as the six characteristics of the "check list" mentioned above.

I quote from the official site of a "scientific institute". "The Centre for Asia Minor Studies (CAMS) is a scientific institute involved since 1930 in the collection, research and documentation of information of oral and written historical tradition, as well as the publication of scientific studies and monographs related to Asia Minor Greeks. The CAMS was created when, following the 1922 disaster, Greece became conscious of the need to preserve the cultural heritage and history of the Asia Minor homelands through the memory of the refugees... Since 1962 the Centre functions as a legal entity of private law under the auspices of the Greek Ministry of Culture."[21]

The "preservation of the cultural heritage" was carried out in a special manner. Some of the Greeks that came from the central and south parts of Anatolia by the forced exchange of population of 1923 spoke only Turkish. According to the introduction of a volume dedicated to their oral histories, people of 47 localities (and villages) spoke Greek, some others from 15 localities spoke both Greek and Turkish and people from 99 localities spoke only Turkish. But the language used to record the memories of these Turkophones was only Greek. No remnant of the language of those Greeks was preserved and saved. The language and probably many other "Turkish" cultural traits are lost and will never be retrieved (CAMS).

This is the reason that makes folkloric studies susceptive to expediencies. The related memories are manipulated to suit the "check list" of nationalism – to numbers 1, 2, 3 and 4. Naturally, the end result in similar situations is closer to "imagined" situations, to invention of a tradition and to myths, rather than to the so called "scientific" research.

The case of Y. Kordatos, too, is interesting. The Greek national/nationalistic historiography was challenged from the first quarter of the twentieth century. Following the Russian revolution of 1917, the Marxist movement in Greece developed rapidly voicing an alternative worldview. Yanis Kordatos (1891-1961), a young lawyer who dedicated his life to history writing, in 1924 challenged the taboo of the Greek Revolution, claiming that it was not a national uprising against the Turks, but a class struggle of the oppressed masses against the oppressors who happened to be both Turkish and Greek dignitaries and landlords.[22] He published his studies in a hostile social environment, facing fierce opposition and threats, but insisted on claiming that modern Greeks were a new nation and not the "continuation" of ancient people. He was probably the first to use the term "ethnicity"

---

[21] History (kms.org.gr).
[22] Y. Kordatos was mentioned above a few times and this is not a coincidence. He was among the first who challenged the main Greek national myths. In this study he was mentioned in relation to the Secret School, the national-martyr Patriarch, the revival of the Ancient Greeks and the Greek language (Chapters 2, 4 and 5).

(ethnismos) to describe the Grecophone communities of the Middle Ages, distinguishing them qualitatively from the modern Greek nation (Kordatos, 1957, p. 24).[23]

As early as 1925 Kordatos criticized the Greek folkloric studies, too. He tried to show that the well-known Greek poem that ends with the line "a time will come that Constantinople will become ours again" and which is supposed to prove the Greek national consciousness that existed from the time the City was captured by the Ottomans (1453), was a recent construct (invented tradition) (Kordatos,1957, p. 34-37).

Alexis Politis, too, states that folkloric studies and the collected folk poems have been often changed to make them compatible with the grand national narrative. For example, traditional folk poems that were not against the "other" – the Turks, for example - were "adjusted" by adding some verses (Politis, A. p. 58=59). In other words the folkloric studies appropriated the mission of inventing an appropriate national past.

As of how literature operated parallel to historiography was explained above, in Preface.(Millas, 2004, 2008).

POLITICS, IDEOLOGY, RELIGION, CONSPIRACY THEORIES ("illusory pattern perception")

According to E.J. Hobsbawm there were "movements of popular revolt against alien rule (i.e., normally understood as meaning rule by a different religion rather than a different nationality) which sometimes appear to anticipate later national movements. Such were the rebellions against the Turkish Empire... Greece became the myth and inspiration of nationalists and liberals everywhere. For Greece alone did an entire people rise against the oppressor in a manner which could be plausibly identified with the cause of the European left; and in turn the support of the European left, headed by the poet Byron who died there..." (Hobsbawm, 1977, p. 172, 173).

Greek national revolution was, indeed, closely related to "Christianity"

---

[23] It is interesting to note that, even though Y. Kordatos negated the ages-long existence of a Greek nation, all his work covers the cultures and the people that the traditional Greek national historiography considered Greek – Byzantine and Ancient Greece. His interest was "the Greeks". A more careful analysis of this work may show that his approach is a combination of class analysis not completely disconnected with the national paradigm.

This blending of the two paradigms becomes apparent when the portrait of the Other *vis-à-vis* 'us' is examined. The Turks, the Other, still appeared stereotypically, as backward and generally negative, for "historical" reasons. This controversial approach is also found in subsequent Marxist historians who followed Kordatos. Nikos Svoronos (1911-1990), for example, who stated in the 1970s that the modern Greek national consciousness appeared for the first time in the thirteenth century (and not in ancient Greece), did not express a very different opinion about the Other either. In fact, Greek Marxist historiography did not revise the traditional image and "role" of the Other, even though these historians did not reproduce extreme nationalist stereotypes (Svoronos, 1985, p. 40-43).

(Millas, 2007). Not only because the popular revolt was understood as a religious issue by the revolutionary masses, as Hobsbawm wrote, but because even the leaders of the revolution, too, who were inspired by the French (class) Revolution, after a while preferred, for political reasons to present their fight as one against the oppressor Muslims who enslaved the Christians. This was a political decision, since, as Marc-Philippe Zallony clearly explained that in the 1820s, the European kings of the time were against the national liberation wars. (Zallony, p. 178).[24]

Starting from those years there is not a clear demarcation between national and religious identity. The constitution of Modern Greece starts with a reference to Holy Trinity. The myths that are related to the Church are in harmony with the "six items of the check list" of nationalism. The "other", i.e., the enemy or enemies of the "Greek nation" are not different among the secular Greek nationalists and the religious Greeks. The Turks, the Westerners (imperialists, capitalists, Catholics, Protestants, Jews, etc.) or the Muslims are common among the secularist and the religious Greeks. Many myths related to politics, national ideology, religious stories and the "other" compose closely related units. Many of the myths presented in this study and a great number of conspiracy theories can be classified as myths of this "common" kind.

There are many religious myths that combine the sacred and the national enemy. For example, in 1959 on the Island of Lesvos the graves of Saints Raphael, Nicolas and Irini were miraculously found. Dreams and ghostly figures guided the people to the point where they were buried. They are supposed to be killed by the Turks in 1463. They are therefore both religiously saints and martyrs and nationally heroes. Irini was only twelve years old when she died and therefore she is depicted as such in an Orthodox icon. Fotis Kondoglou wrote a 240 page book dedicated to the sacred event (Kondoglou). Local stories of mixed religious/national content are widespread in Greece.

A conspiracy theory is an explanation for an event based on a belief that

---

[24] Zallony's case was explained above, in Chapter 3, (17- Helleno-Christianity).

some powerful groups act in their own interests and against the well-being of others, usually against "us", even though there may be other more probable explanations. It is clear that such a theory is believed as true by some and as false by others. This definition of conspiracy theory is almost identical with the accepted understanding of myths in this study.[25]

As a term, "conspiracy theory" is relatively new. It entered everyday language in the United States after 1964 in connection with the report of the Warren Commission that investigated the assassination of Jack Kennedy. However, conspiracy theories in practice are both many and frequent all through human history. There are various ways in classifying them. A list mentions about nine main groups, each containing a number of cases as follows: 1- Core topics (12 cases); 2- Psychology (8); 3- Deaths/ disappearances (45); 4- New World Order (24), UFOs (36); 5- USA government (24); 6- Health (14); 7- Energy (2); 8- Sports (65); 9- Others (25); a total of about 190 cases.

Among these one sees well known cases like the conspiracies concerning Soros and Bill Gates in collaboration with the Jews; the chemtrail case where "they" spray chemicals by planes on "us"; the bad guys that impose a new world order; the intrigues of the pharmaceutical industry/there is no Covid-19, etc. In fact, stories that cultivate racism, national phobias, anti-Semitism, Islamophobism, anti-Western prejudices and similar phobic movements should be considered expressions of conspiracy theories. Naturally, often real conspiracies do occur and this fact reinforces the imaginary conspiracy theories. Conspiracy theories akin to these are numerous among the Greeks, mostly voiced on the internet.[26]

---

[25] I made use of the following sites in writing about conspiracy theories; naturally, the interpretation and the conclusions are mine:
https://en.wikipedia.org/wiki/Conspiracy_theory
https://onlinelibrary.wiley.com/doi/10.1002/ejsp.2331
https://en.wikipedia.org/wiki/List_of_conspiracy_theories

[26] Historically, many myths and stories were perceived as conspiracies with disastrous results and much pain. In the Middle Ages, antisemitism was a typical conspiracy theory. In medieval Europe it was widely believed that Jews poisoned wells, they had been responsible for the death of Jesus, and ritually consumed the blood of Christians, especially of children.

During the Protestant Reformation of the 16th century, anti-Catholic conspiracy theories had taken many forms. Even as late as 1853 it was claimed that the Catholic Church was secretly continued practicing the pagan religion of the ancient Babylon, as claimed by A. Hislop in his pamphlet *The Two Babylons*. Many well known persons had been called "Antichrist" in the past, including the Holy Roman Emperor Frederick II, the Russian emperor Peter the Great, Saladin, Pope John XXII, but also Benito Mussolini, Barack Obama, Napoleon Bonaparte, and Adolf Hitler in the recent past.

Biblical conspiracy theories appeared claiming that parts of the New Testament are false, or have been omitted. Various groups such as the Priory of Sion are said to suppress relevant information. It was claimed that Jesus and Mary Magdalene were lovers and that their descendants were secretly hidden in Europe. Among the Islamists there exists a conspiracy theory about a "War against Islam" expressed often as Islamophobism and on the other hand, among many westerners there exists the conviction that the Muslims exercise a systematic terrorist action against the Christian World.

It is of interest that according to the Judeo-Christian-Islam religion group the Demon/Satan is an "enemy" who conspires against God and "us". Satan drove Eva, the woman, to sin disobeying God (Genesis, 3:1-15). Christ was tempted by Satan for many days to deny God (Mathew 4: 1-11). We read that "there was a war in heaven; Michael and his angels going forth to war with the dragon; ... And the great dragon was cast down, the old serpent, he that is called the Devil and Satan, the deceiver of the whole world..." (Revelation, 12.7-9) In the Koran, too, Satan is in opposition to God: "Whoever takes Satan for a friend will suffer" (Nisaa, 18/19).[27]

These kinds of myths are numerous among the Greeks even though they are not recognized as such. Apparently, for reasons that have to do with a significant power imbalances that exists between the big number of "believers" in contrast to "unbelievers", the tendency in our days is not to treat existing religions as myths. Only religions that they do not have followers anymore are called myths. For example, the miraculous births that are mentioned in the Assyrian, Babylonian, Egyptian, Hellenic cultures are myths.

Conspiracy theories may be discovered in political theories, too. The intellectual group known as the Frankfurt School (in the1930s) was the subject of conspiracy theories which have alleged the promotion of communism in capitalist societies. The members of the Greek Communist Party are confident enough that the imperialist powers systematically conspire against the Greek proletariat. With a little imagination Marxism may be seen as a theory where the righteous fight the Satan (the proletariat against capitalism). It is as if Manichaeism and its bipolar understanding of the world exists horizontally in many (in all?) societies, either as "religions", as "ideologies" or as "scientific" explanations.

In other words, conspiracy theories may appear among fringe and small groups but they may become popular and mainstream beliefs, too. They may be widespread around the world and some may be held by the majority of the population. They may operate as a faith, a belief, as paranoia, etc., depending on who is judging. They are attractive for various reasons. First, conspiracy theories claim to explain what institutional analysis cannot. They appear to make sense out of a world that is otherwise complicated and confusing. Second, they conveniently trace all evil back to a single source, to the conspirators. Third, these theories are presented as special and secret knowledge unknown by others. So believers feel proud for seeing what others cannot. And fourth, they have a scapegoat function: the responsibility of all ills is not "ours" but "theirs".

A concept that helps in understanding this human behavior is the "illusory

---

[27] See: Bible and Koran.

pattern perception". People perceive patterns in world events, which in turn become irrational beliefs. Illusory pattern perception is a central cognitive mechanism accounting for conspiracy theories and supernatural beliefs; they help to make sense of the world by identifying meaningful relationships between unrelated events. For many it is difficult to appreciate the role of coincidence in generating pattern-like sequences. Studies have also shown that people with high education levels, or with strong analytic thinking skills, are less susceptible to irrational beliefs. However, in general, humans need to detect patterns in order to function well in their social environment and this leads them to imagine patterns in a chaotic world.

CULTURAL LIFE: LITERATURE, ARTS, MUSEUMS, MUSIC, SPORTS, SCIENCE

The Invention of Tradition by E.Hobsbawm & T.Ranger (Hobsbawm, 2012), *Banal Nationalism* by M. Billig (Billig) and other studies on how societies experience nationalism are already presented. A study on how literary texts express and establish national stereotypes were presented in the Preface above. The study titled *The so-called innocent nationalism* (Millas, 2010) mentioned above showed how sports, cartoons, literary texts, music, TV series etc., may express nationalism creating stories akin to national myths. To extend this present study to these domains not only will it be a repetition but it will also require a couple of volumes of writing. National myths are everywhere, as the nationalist ideology is widespread.

With due respect to scientific approach – of which, by the way, this study of mine humbly claims a share, too – my reservation vis-à-vis "science" is its occasional use as a free pass. People with a certain academic title behave as authorities on a subject, simply because they are officially recognized as scientists. Those scientists may be seen as unscientific, prejudiced, narrow-minded and irrational persons by other scientists. The titles "science" and "scientific" by themselves do not secure their claim of impartiality. If one needs additional – apart from the academic title - information to judge if what is called scientific is actually so, what is that information? This is a difficult question the answer. Thus, science becomes a word that obtains sense and acceptance, like the word "myth", only by those who perceive a quality of reality. Personally, I try not to use the word "scientific", since it has different meanings to different people.

THE ROLE OF THE STATE: LAWS, EDUCATION, OFFICIAL FESTIVITIES...

A nation state and its national ideology are of the same category; they may be conceived as a body and its breathing or as an entity and its functions. The constitution of Greece starts with a reference to the Holy Trinity and its Article 16 which is on education clarifies what its mission is:

"Education is the basic mission of the State and its purpose is to educate the Greeks on ethical, spiritual, professional and physical domains, as well as to develop the national and religious consciousness, as well as to form free and responsible citizens".

When our son started primary school in Athens and simultaneously started uttering negative adjectives against "the Turks", I checked the textbooks of the time out of curiosity and I discovered how the "negative other" is recreated and how "national consciousness" was "educated"! This stimulated my interest in textbooks (Millas, 1991). The state with all its manifestations acts in the direction that is dictated by its purpose of its existence: it feeds the national ideology. M. Billig in his *Banal Nationalism* has shown this mechanism so vividly that I do not think the "method" should be mentioned here again.

Nation-building necessitates and initiates a set of institutions and practices in addition to schools: Museums, archives that constitute the "canons" of "our past", monuments, national days and related commemorations, special holidays and memory days, state-sponsored historical and social studies of a specific type are some of the instruments that recreate what some call "national grand narrative". The purpose of this study is not to show these practices, but to show their mythical side.

CRITISISM OF FOUR NATIONAL MYTHS

It is not possible to present and evaluate all national myths that may exist in various domains of the Greek society. I will only present shortly four more cases which show how a) sometimes myths are criticized as "historical mistakes" or "wrong readings" without these being labeled necessarily as myths and b) how in these cases the main target is the core of the national paradigm, i.e., the basic concepts of nationalism.

Well known national personalities may sometimes be exalted with the intent to demonstrate Greek heroism or the Greeks' "strong points" and some other times national themes such as creating national Others may be advanced, but acting mostly unconsciously of the primary drives. These efforts are criticized by others, too. In most cases this opposition is based on arguments of true/false or real/imaginary. In all cases, however, the target of the criticism is the "national paradigm" and the Grand national narrative. The following four examples are of this sort.

A – The case of Makriyannis.

Ioannis (known also as General) Makriyannis (1997-1864) was a fighter of the Greek Revolution of 1821. He became famous in Greece with his *Memoirs* that were found by Yiannis Vlahogiannis and published in 1907 (Vlahoyannis). Another manuscript of his titled *Visions and Miracles* was also published both in printed form and in its original hand writing in 1983 and 1985 (General, 1983 & 1985).

Vlahoyannis exalted the *Memoirs* as a true narration of the events that cover the Revolution but the political events that followed the next decade, too. Makriyannis is presented as a dedicated fighter for the nation and a successful witness of the events because he was an un-educated person and therefore close to the people. The language he used is considered a good example of the genuine Greek of the people. The "General" is considered as the personification of the "soul of the Greek nation".

The highly respected Nobel winner poet Yiorgos Seferis in a lecture on Makriyannis in 1943 expressed similar views. "Makriyannis wrote – the story of his life – a very important book probably because he was illiterate" (Seferis, p. 228). He represented "the treasure of the soul of the race, as it is bestowed to us from past centuries and millenniums, from generation to generation, from sensitivity to sensitivity, persecuted and always alive... this is the common edifice of the great popular legacy of the Nation [Genos]" (p. 237). "If we want to really understand the Ancient Greeks we have to study the soul of our people. These words were said by Makriyannis in 1821" (p. 257).

There was criticism to all these starting in the1970s. Historian Asdrahas, for example, in 1975 expressed his reservation about the impartiality of the *Memoirs*: The "General" criticized all those who did not join his political choices and present himself as the sole righteous critic. "All the others distort reality and this is done consciously" (Asdrahas, p. 323). But the systematic criticism was not directed to Makriyannis, but to those who constructed a myth about him by Giorgos Yianoulopoulos in 2003. He analyzed what was written by Vlahoyiannis, Yiorgos Theotokas (a well known Greek author, 1906-1966), Seferis and Zisimos Lorentzatos (1915-2004). In all cases he pointed the nationalist reading of the *Memoirs* and of *Visions and Miracles*.

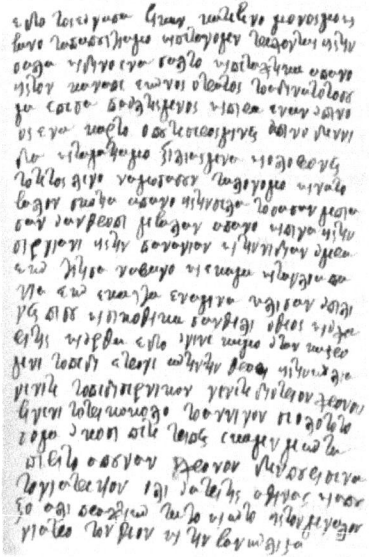

According to Yianoulopoulos, Makriyannis was not "discovered" as it is claimed by his supporters but constructed: Theotokas read the *Memoirs* from the perspective of romanticism (Yiannoulopoulos, p. 92) and Seferis in these texts "discovered" the centuries long Greek nature, in other words "our national nature" (p. 151). Lorentzatos was criticized due to his extreme religious reading of Makriyannis. Especially Markiyannis, probably not in a very mentally healthy state as some critics suggested, in *Visions and Miracles* tried to persuade the reader that he has visions of God protecting him and guiding him! This text expresses "the metaphysical bases of modern Greek ideology" (Yiannoulopoulos, p. 193). Loretzatos reads a text that is clearly against Enlightenment and Western World. (p. 196). Makriyannis infers that God is on his side and Lorentzatos follows in this mystic reading.

At present the image of Makriyannis is close to what Seferis said: a Greek that symbolizes the virtues of the nation. He is an idol. He is a national hero and by his deeply religious belief a model for the religious Greeks. Almost a metaphysical national figure, in good terms with God. His writings are seen almost as Holy Scriptures. There is no other way of explaining why the original of his hand-written manuscript of *Visions and Miracles* was published in spite of the fact that no Greek can read that handwritten text but only a few specialists. Is this text a sacred relic?[28]

B - The case of Rigas

This is another creation of a national hero. Rigas Velestinlis (1757-1798), is mentioned above in another context (in Chapter 1; 6- A Patriarch as a national-martyr). He is known in Greece as the first hero and the fore-runner of the Greek National Revolution. Everybody knows that! However, in his "Constitution" written in 1997, his best known political endeavor in which he clarifies in detail the state he has in mind, the sovereign citizens of this state are shown to be "All the people that live in this state with no distinction of religion and language, Greeks, Bulgarians, Albanians, Wlahs, Armenians, Turks and all others" (Article 7). It is clear that he had in mind a French-like revolution in favor of the "people" and against the "kings", but not a modern nation-wise "independent" nation-state.

In a detailed a study on Rigas and his "Constitution" it is clearly stated that within the New State that Rigas had in mind the Greeks would constitute a minority (Daskalakis, p. 63). In a study of mine I demonstrated that Rigas had followed closely the French constitution of 1793 where the concept of independence is absent (Millas, 2019). (In the American Constitution of 1776 the word "independence" is mentioned three times right at the beginning). In

---

[28] I wonder why I bought this book! I could not read a single word – I do not exaggerate. Probably I was carried away by the mood of the 1980s. The myths address their messages to our unconscious part of ours.

the Introduction of the constitution of Rigas the Ottoman State is characterized as "the most beautiful kingdom in the world" (See also: Psarras, p.165).

But in spite of this evidence Rigas remains the main visionary of the Modern Greek State. The most probable reason seems to be that the myths are not superseded by logical arguments. A second explanation is that the people who oppose this myth are fewer than those who insist in recreating the myth- especially with the backing up of the nation-state.

In support of the second explanation I add the following. Rigas is also known for his militant poem "March" (Θούριος) where, among other passionate expressions, he calls all people to join his revolution. In three points he mentions "the Turks and the Greeks who suffer under tyranny", "the wolves who torture the Christians and the Turks" and he urges "the Turkish local chief Pestvanoglou to join the revolution". A very popular comics magazine was distributed the days I was writing these lines with the newspaper I read. It was about Rigas. At the end the poem "March" was included. But what a coincidence, among the passages that were skipped were the ones where the Turks were mentioned!

The name that appears with the portrait of Rigas Velestinlis – Velestinlis means from the town of Velestino, "lis" in Turkish stands for "from" – has been changed without the consent of Rigas to Feraios, which refers to an ancient Greek town Feres. So the Greek hero now has a proper Greek name. This is part of the process of nation-building or ethnic myth-building.

According to Roderick Beaton, important changes occurred within the few years that passed from the time of the death of Rigas to the appearance of Adamantios Korais as a leading spokesman of the new Greek national ideology: "Where Rigas had allowed for all the religious and linguistic identities of the Balkans to buy into a new 'Hellenic' identity, the logic of Korais's position obliged him to exclude all those who were not Greek from his understanding of the 'nation'" (Beaton, 2020, p. 60).

C - The case of the Three Fathers of the Church

In Greek by the term The Three Fathers (Τρεις Ιεράρχες) the The Cappadocian Fathers, Basil the Great (330–379) who was bishop of Caesarea; Gregory of Nazianzus (329–389), who became Patriarch of Constantinople and John Hrysostom (347-407) are understood. The study of Effi Gazi is on how these religious personalities where integrated into the Greek Grand National Narrative. The complex relations between various social institutions, the national prioritizations and the conflicts of social agents show how the religious and the national discourses jointly create what the researcher calls "Helleno-Christian" ideology (Gazi).

The creation of Helleno-Christianity was explained shortly above (Chapter 2/13). The study of E. Gazi is about the step by step process that the past and especially Ancient Greece was integrated into the Christian Orthodox religion. This new narrative which was advanced by the Church and the academic milieu of the 19th and 20th century operated as a myth: The Three Fathers for centuries were a basic inspiration of the nation (Gazi, p. 57, 189, 239).

D - Xenophobia: The negative West

The mistrust against the Other, in this case specifically vis-à-vis the "West" is one of the basic characteristics of nationalism. In Greece this is expressed as "negative Pope or Protestants" by the Christian Orthodox believers; as "as capitalists and/or imperialists" by the socialist and leftists and or simply "enemies" or "friends of our enemies" by the patriots. These Others, naturally are presented as "always" harming "our national interests".

Alexis Heraclides (and Ada Dialla) in their book *Humanitarian Intervention in the long Nineteenth Century* show that the "West" not only did interfere in favor of the Greeks during the most critical time of Greece' modern history, in 1828-1832, but that was the first time in world history that such an act happened: "The Greek case, apart from being regarded as the first case of humanitarian intervention, providing the springboard for the emergence of the new concept, has a bearing on the evolution of international norms and rules of conduct instances of humanitarian plights in a number of ways" (Heraclides, p. 123).

It is known that it is difficult to prove what is right but easy to show that a premise is wrong: a single black swan may destroy the image of the swans! Thus the negative "West" proves to be a stereotype and a national prejudice.

25- Assessment

With this chapter, it is as if this study on myths changed perspective. The whole endeavor started with a number of myths that existed within the Greek society and reached to the outlook that myths are so widespread that one suspects they constitute the norm of human existence. National myths are encountered in all aspects of the societal life. One wonders if there is a myth-proof domain in human life.

Since a myth may exist only when there is a counter group that defies that mythical approach - *One's absolute truth is the myth of the Other* - the optimistic conclusion may be that at least there are those who reside on non-myth "sound and realistic" grounds. The pessimistic view is the suspicion that those who reject a myth may still as well believe in another myth. For example, renouncing animism may lead to a new mystic belief, the rejection of a conspiracy theory does not exclude the adoption of another.

Various findings mentioned above support the view that myths are central and necessary in human societies. Myths form the binding forces that secure the societal existence. (See: Chapter 3; E. Cassirer).[29] Other related studies show that myths enjoy a wide range of defensive arsenal. "Confirmation bias" lead people to find refuge in myths by creating unbeatable argumentations; "Boomerang effect" secures the inviolability of a myth (See: Chapter 1, The testimony of myths). Human thinking has a tendency to "perceive illusory patterns" in world events, which in turn become irrational beliefs and myths (see: this chapter, 25- A list of myths).

These findings lead this study to new questions. The starting point, which was to present the Greek national myths, turns to one of questioning "our" capacity to live in a world distant from myths. Even though what is said above about the Greek national myths are reasonably sound, the basic premise which was not stated but somehow inferred, that myths can be refuted, even if considered feasible, is not conclusive. Abandoning a myth does not mean leaving our probable cosmos of myths.

***

---

[29] As shown above some researchers expressed the view that myths are functional in uniting groups and helping them to face crises. This is partly true. "Myths" do that but not as "myths", but as beliefs or/and as "Truths" (with capital T). Once a belief and/or a Truth start being discussed as a "myth" it loses its function of being a reference of unity. The appearance of myths signals the end (or the beginning of the end) of a traditional belief and the probable appearance of a new one. This process reminds the "paradigm" model of Khun.

CHAPTER 6

OUR WORLD OF MYTHS

To write about the Greek myths has been one of my wishes for many years. The opportunity was given when the Covid-19 pandemic appeared. Now, mid-2021, as some signs appear that the prolonged and intermittent quarantine days are approaching to their end, my study seems to have taken the same course. This academic journey was pleasant and especially useful: time passed fast saving me from boredom.

It was during this Covid-19 period that I experienced how myths may appear all of a sudden. On the TV I watched how people explained why they did not want to be vaccinated: Some bad people want to place chips in our bodies; capitalist companies want to sell their vaccines and make money; "they" want to get rid of the old people not to pay pensions, etc. I heard that masks are very dangerous because we breathe through them the viruses that are accumulated on them!

According to my understanding all these show limited knowledge and unlimited self-confidence. At moments, I suspected low IQ. But doctors, too – who supposedly passed a demanding education and difficult exams to receive their diplomas – joined the dissidents and the skeptics. As the Greek proverb goes, "the soul of man is an abyss!" It is understood that "others" will say that it is me who believes in the myth of Coronovirus because I represent the interests of some companies or I am misled by my ideological bias or I have low IQ, etc! Anyhow, this case study on myths is about *my* views.

In this chapter I will put down some general conclusions related to all the above, but mostly some queries that came to my mind at the end of this study. Various other conclusions are already presented at the end of each chapter and often within the text itself.

27- Myths as general phenomena

This study is about national myths; and Greece is chosen as an example. Therefore, the whole endeavor can be read both as a limited one, that is, as the national myths of Greeks, but also alternatively, as a general one, as myths in human societies. The case of Greece and the Greeks was presented above in a relatively detailed way, making possible a special reading of the Greek society. One may see how Greeks perceive themselves, the others, their past, how they explain historical and social phenomena, who they see as a threat, what they see as a problem, etc. These perceptions can be read as issues of national identity. One may see how this identity is experienced, expressed and defended. Most importantly one may thus predict what the reactions of the Greeks will be – in favor or against – when they face certain situations and challenges.

For example, based on the above mentioned "Greek national myths" one may foresee with a considerable precision how some Greeks will react when facing foreigners who come in contact with Greeks. Some Greek readers may agree with my views and feel the way I do about the above mentioned issues. Most importantly, they may be more at ease when they meet the Greeks who express "strange ideas" (myths), since they will accept these myths as an expected "normal/usual" phenomenon. They may even realize that their own convictions appear as myths to others. "Knowing" all these will not secure transcending the myths, nor an agreement on contested issues, but may provide an explanation and probably understanding.

In other words, the believed and the refused "myths" within a nation show the way people think and to what different sections of the society believe in. That national myths are widespread in almost all domains of the society –from historiography to politics and from cultural life to laws and education - is explained in the previous chapter. Approaching a society through their national myths secures a holistic approach, too, since each myth exists in pairs (for and against), and this guarantees that the conclusions will not be stereotypically one sided, resorting to generalizations about that society. Each myth necessarily refers and brings to fore its adversaries, as well.

Looking at the national myths from this wider perspective one questions "myths" in general. There are many myths that are not national. One may remind the myriads of fairy tales and/or superstitions. All through history societies lived with myths of some kind. So, myths are many more than "national myths"; or, to phrase this differently, national myths compose only a part of all myths. It may be said that national myths are "modern myths" too – since nationalism is a modern phenomenon. But the crucial question becomes the following: to what extent do myths compose the conceptual world of human societies and what is left as non-myths?

SCIENTIFIC TRUTHS THAT CANNOT CONVINCE

Meanings such as "truth" and "reality" exhausted many philosophers who came up with various definitions and explanations; but all their claims were seen as unsatisfactory (myths?) by others. Popper tried to establish a "scientific approach" and according to many he succeeded. But the problem is not the demonstration and the "proof" of truth and reality; this proof should be convincing and persuasive. A scientific approach and/or a "proof" is good and useful only when it is accepted, i.e., when it is functional. If it is not accepted by others then we are in square one again. What is the use of a scientific proof that is not convincing at the same time? What is the validity of such a "proof"?

In my early youth reading Plato led me to communicate with my peers and the grownups around me trying to prove how I was right about my convictions by the use of "logical arguments". But the students of Plato who used to say "you are right, master!" were not around! It took me few decades to find out that persuasion works best only with those who are already in one's "group". Truth is what it is not contested; and this occurs only among people that share similar ideas, feelings, beliefs and principles, in short, a common identity.

A group of people is a "group" because they share beliefs. But also conversely, when some people constitute a unity – a group – then they show the tendency to share ideas, that is, "truths". Another, group will share different truths. And each group will see a "myth" – a mistake, an irregularity, something strange and wrong – in the belief of the other group. The above study disclosed the recurrence of this phenomenon.

Does this mean that "truth/reality" is always relative? This question can be answered only when the verb "is" is defined and explained. If "is" refers to an existence within a finite number of people, i.e., a group (family, village, religion, nation, humanity at a given time, etc.), then truth exists within the group and it is experienced – "it is" - as a non-contested reality. On the other hand, if by "is" one means an existence that transcends the finite group and is valid for all groups and especially for an infinite time span, then this existence refers to an imaginary world, probably to a mythical one. To discuss these alternatives with words such as "relative" and "absolute" means that the whole problematic is perceived as if it belongs to a world that is independent of the phenomenon of mythic thinking and feeling.

CAN MYTHS BE TRANSCENTED?

Another problematic related to myths is if their abandonment (renunciation, rejection) is possible or if what actually happens is their replacement by new beliefs. As explained above[30] myths are "necessary", or to use a more appropriate wording, myths are an indispensible and a "normal" phenomenon of human societies. According to various researchers myths reinforce the communal unity. Their abandonment may occur as a kind of paradigm shift, say, the way the Olympic gods were rejected and replaced by

---

[30] See: Chapter 3, 15. Summary and Assessment and Chapter 4, ERNST CASIRER.

a Christian god and saints. Or rejection may occur within a section of a society where "one's truth becomes a myth for the other". The question in both cases is: Is the phenomenon signaling abandonment or a replacement?

The argument of "necessary and socially useful myths" is based on a practical reasoning: Since myths exist and people constitute communities based on them, they are functional and useful. Exactly the opposite conclusion may be reached, however, based again on the same reasoning, namely, on the premise that opposition to myths sustains some other social groups and this turns the anti-myth stand "necessary and useful" for the existence of these groups. This conclusion is the outcome of the definition of myth: A myth can exist only if there is "another" group that perceives a "myth" – that is, a non-true belief. The refutation and negation of a myth is practically necessary and useful for the existence of the opposing group. In short, myths are useful and necessary for some, and harmful and not necessary for others. This argument legitimizes the right to criticize and oppose myths, once somebody perceives one. In modern civil terms, the criticism of myths is a democratic right, equally legitimate with believing to an irrational – for some -myth.

The above problematic directs us again the basic question: Do societies live always with myths, of one kind or the other? We see beliefs, religions, myths etc. beings substituted by other convictions of the "same kind". An interesting example of "substitution" that was presented in this study is the case of the Marxist criticism vis-à-vis the Greek nationalist historiography. Kordatos criticized the myth of the "secret school" and the character of the Greek Revolution of 1821 based on "scientific materialism"; but in our days other historians, and even Marxist historians, see bias and ideological misconceptions (myths?) in the analysis and the criticism of Kordatos (Melios). Maybe, more importantly is the criticism against Marxism itself. Just to give one example, for Robert C. Tucker Marxism is related to myths (Tucker). In this case – according to some – myths are succeeded by new myths.

28- Observations, questions and assumptions

CHILDREN AND GROWNUPS

Almost everything said in this study is related to human understanding, to feelings and to drives. Humans are perceived as rational and/or as emotional beings, who sometimes "think" and other times act unconsciously. Interestingly, children are dealt differently. Their behavior, their thinking and their judgment are presented as being associated to their age. All studies without exception show that children have a special way of thinking and "judging" and this depends on their age.

These studies show that children follow some steps in their thinking and judging as they grow up. For example, by age 2, children clearly show awareness of the difference between thoughts in the mind and things in the world. A crucial development occurs around 4 years of age when children realize that thoughts in the mind may not be true. By the age of 5 years, children realize that people talk and act on the basis of the way they think the world is, etc. Roughly, this is the perception of children of the academic and pedagogical world.

We all know that children also believe in fairy tales. They imagine situations; they may treat a piece of wood as if it were a ship, for example. They may think of flying to the moon or to a wonderland to meet Little Prince or Peter Pan. Children cannot distinguish reality from storytelling. Indeed, they are pretty irrational! If this is a human trait it means humans are "programmed" to "think" in this way in these early years of childhood. The question is: What assures us that humans do not think as they are programmed to think as they grow up? And if they are programmed what is this "program"?

Is the assumed demarcation of children "versus" grownups a decisive one, beyond question? Is this difference one of substantial change or of a change of degree or only of a different agenda? These questions, in a way undermine the self-image of the grownups who think that they judge situations based on (objective) observations and (logical) evaluation. The grownups normally do not enjoy being perceived as acting "childishly". The dictionary of my PC shows the following words to be related to the word "childish": childlike, babyish, immature, irresponsible, silly, foolish. Apart from not behaving politically correct grownups may have an overestimated image of themselves.

Children normally play. But grownups play, too, only they play different games: Football, athletics, actually all kinds of sports; but also cards, bets on lottery, etc. There are some special games for rich grownups, in the stock market, the artistically inclined play the piano, they act in plays, some others play even war games, virtual or real. Do the children imitate the grownups when they play "war" and when they quarrel, or do they all – children and grownups - express a drive for fight? Are these games among children and among grownups different due to their "kind" or are they "analogous" and only the rules are different? Why one does not suspect that the existence of myths – this tendency that persists in human societies – may be a human programmed way of thinking after the age of, say, fifteen!

Grownups are forced to abandon the fairy tales and the imagined games of their childhood when they face "reality". They cannot insist that they can go to the moon riding a magic horse, for example. They cannot enjoy such a myth either, because their knowledge and practice do not allow the games of their youth. But they can stick to different stories that cannot be easily "falsified": They may create stories (myths) that recount how people go and visit Hades and Heaven, for example. Grownups cannot insist on the existence of a Prince on a planet, since we have a perception of the universe that precludes such a story; but they can develop a story where families of Gods live on top of the mountain Olympus or in the "Skies". And myths on Christian saints outnumber the myths on Olympic gods. In other words, grownups create stories that differ from the stories of children, but still stories that by others may be seen and evaluated as myths. What is the difference believing in going to the moon riding a broom to meet a Prince and being accompanied by an angel to go to Heaven to meet a god??

UNDIFFERENTIATED VIRTUAL AND IMAGINED REALITY

I leave aside, for the moment, the temptation to reach to some conclusions based on the comparison of child/grownup and I pass to a second observation of mine. During the time I was working on this issue of myths I noticed something really strange with me. As I was watching movies on my video player, at certain scenes I was moved as if things were really happening in front of me. I empathized with the tortured people and/or tears of happiness came to my eyes when eventually the romantic couple was saved and got married!

In the very first chapter of this study (in Preface) empathy was explained and some of its characteristics presented: "Sociobiology shows that other animals, too, exhibit actions that resemble some social behaviors of humans, such as altruism. Frans de Waal showed that monkeys and especially chimpanzees exhibit empathy. Neuroscience understands empathy as an innate capability of the human brain that works unconsciously, yet it can be trained for special cases. Neuroscientists have discovered that people scoring high on empathy tests have especially busy mirror neuron systems in their brains… It is as if neuroscientists and philosophers reach the same 'understanding' with respect to the 'reality' even though they have different starting points. Some neuroscientists reminded the close relationship between their discoveries of the neurons and especially of the mirror neurons and the philosophical school of phenomenology" (See above, Preface, 2- A case of multi approach.)

In all cases, empathy is studied as a phenomenon experienced between an observer and an object, mostly a living object. This is the case with humans but with other animals, as well. However, my case in front of TV screen was different: I empathized with imagined situations, with "representations". The scenes of torture in the movie were really disturbing, so I tried to persuade myself that "actually nothing was really happening, that everything is on a DVD disk, that I could push a button and the images will disappear". But this logical thinking of mine did not stop my body from reacting as if the events were really happening in front of me. I noticed the same behavior each time I watched a horror film or a sad romantic scene. Each time my body acted independently of my "reasoning". There were some scenes so disturbing that I chose to shift to a different DVD since my self-persuasion that "nothing actually was happening" did not work. It was as if there was no connection between my body and my thinking. My body shivered, my hands sweated, my heart beats changed, tear drops appeared in my eyes, according to what I was watching – watching scenes that I was sure they were virtual.

The same phenomenon is observed with literature, too. A novel is experienced as a real situation, we sympathize with the heroes. A theatrical performance is watched as if it was not "played" by actors but lived by our compatriots. Representations are experienced as real situations. As people watch, hear or read, experience the virtual reality as "reality", a real existence. But what is of importance is the phenomenon that this perception of reality is not and cannot be controlled by our "reasoning" or "logical thinking".

29- A General assessment

It seems that the human brain has been shaped within the past million of years based on what it received through the senses: eyes, ears, nose (smell), touch. The brain itself, securely positioned in the dark scull, had to operate and to evolve based on what the senses provided. Within those million years living organisms barely had "representations" and definitely they did not have symbols like language, literature, art and their equivalents. "Representations" are new phenomena of only a couple of thousands of years. Therefore, I presume, without being an expert on this matter and being cautious with my assumptions, that our brain cannot differentiate signals sent by the eyes and the ears if these signals are "real" or "virtual representations". Our "reasoning" and analysis realize the difference, but the part of the brain that receives the signals and then sends the directions to the body, does not.[31]

For time immemorial our brain could only "sense" and "see" what senses allowed. Here "our brain" means all the stages that the brain has passed from its initial appearances in various living organisms – not only the human brain. The environment and the conditions in which the brain(s) developed was not

---

[31] This has been demonstrated by some tests, too. Subjects with normal brain function were positioned with their left hand hidden from their sight. They saw instead a lifelike rubber left hand in front of them. The experimenters stroked both the subject's hidden left hand and the visible rubber hand with a paintbrush. The experiment showed that if the two hands were stroked simultaneously and in the same direction, the subjects began to experience the rubber hand – what their eyes see - as their own; apparently misled by the couple "sight/touch". When asked to use their right hand to point to their left hand, most of the time they pointed toward the rubber hand. (See: Body transfer illusion - Wikipedia).

one that allowed analytic thinking – and it was one where "representations" did not exist. It was rather one where an immediate response to the senses was required. Probably because of such a legacy we do not possess a brain that differentiates a real scene from a representation. This is the explanation I gave trying to understand why my body experiences empathy, sympathy, fear, agony, joy etc. when my thinking is sure that "actually nothing is happening" on the screen of my TV.[32]

According to Daniel Kahneman, humans and other mammals are all emotionally driven due to our evolutionary history (Kahneman, pp. 408-418). In his *Thinking fast and slow* he demonstrated that many of our decisions are instantaneous and consequently not "rational" because of our evolutionary heritage. It is the belief that science precedes; and logic follows to confirm the feeling.

> "Why is it so difficult for us to think statistically? We easily think associatively, we think metaphorically, we think causally, but statistics requires thinking about many things at once, which is something that System 1 [our intuitive thinking, HM] is not designed to do." (Kahneman, p. 13) "Contrary to the rules of philosophers of science, who advise testing hypotheses by trying to refute them, people (and scientists quite often) seek data that are likely to be compatible with the beliefs they currently hold." (Kahneman, p. 81)[33]

A field that was not very well known to me, neuroscience, helped me notice and explain some phenomena that lead me to my, tentative if one prefers, assessment. According to S. Pinker "The study of human from an evolutionary perspective has shown that many psychological faculties (such as our hunger for social status and for risky sexual liaisons) are better adapted to the evolutionary demands of our ancestral environment than to the actual demands of the current environment. Anthropological surveys have shown that hundreds of universals, pertaining to every aspect of experience, cut across the world's cultures." (Pinker, p 101).

Pinker quotes R. Bialey: "There are different kinds of truths for different kinds of people. There are truths appropriate for children; truths that are appropriate for students; truths that are appropriate for educated adults; and

---

[32] This limitation of human brain, that is, its inability to distinguish the real world form its representation should be the source of the success of the literary type social phenomena. A film, a novel, a theatrical performance, etc, are influential because of their effect on humans, since what we "see" and imagine is akin to experiencing life itself. In other animals the closest to this phenomenon may be the "conditioning" where, for example, the dogs of Pavlov "perceived" an action nearing when their ears or their eyes sent a message of a specific noise or of a light flashing to their brains. That noise and flashing were a representative of reality for these dogs; we know that this is a "myth" of the dogs!

[33] This issue is discussed in a more detailed way above; see Chapter 1, 4- A tentative assessment, TO BE "SIMILAR"/ "DIFFERENT" AND STATISTICAL THINKING; MYTH AS A WORKING HYPOTHESIS.

truths that are appropriate for highly educated adults, and the notion that there should be one set of truths available for everyone is a modern democratic fallacy. It doesn't work" (Pinker, p. 131.)[34]

Why not add more?: There are truths that are appropriate for Greeks, truths appropriate for conservative and religious Greeks, truths appropriate for skeptic Greeks, truths appropriate for me, etc? And each of these "truths" naturally is being perceived as myths by others.

A theme that ran all through this study is that a myth is created and sustained in a group. A group (from a village to a nation and from an ideological to a religious community) exists because its members share a distinct way of thinking, imagining and myth-creating.[35] They share a special "reality" and "truth'. This conclusion seems to be in tune with the findings of Ludwig Wittgenstein and Thomas Kuhn[36]: That is, "truth" exists and is perceived according (relative) to a group.

According to Wittgenstein reality operates as (or in) a language-game. One may read the following sentences from his *Philosophical Investigations* (1953) and conclude that the various language-games correspond to various "groups".

> "But how many kinds of sentence are there? ... There are *countless* kinds: countless different kinds of use of what we call "symbols", "words", "sentences". And this multiplicity is not something fixed, given once for all; but new types of language, new language-games, as we may say, come into existence, and others become obsolete and get forgotten" (Wittgenstein, 2001, No 23).

Kuhn, a decade after Wittgenstein, advanced the thesis that "scientific findings" are in accordance to the paradigm that is "chosen": "When the individual scientist can take a paradigm for granted, he needs no longer, in his major works, attempt to build his field anew, starting from first principles and justifying the use of each concept introduced." (Kuhn, p. 19). And each paradigm corresponds to a new "reality".

Nations, too, are groups. According to Antony Giddens "the content of nationalism as a symbol system" is related to a "myth of origin, conferring cultural autonomy upon the community... Nationalism helps naturalize the regency and contingency of the nation-state through providing it myths of

---

[34] On the other hand, it is "democracy" which as a political system indirectly recognizes that "reality" is not registered objectively by the enlightened despots or by scientists, but by the votes of the citizens, that is to say, relative to the preference of the majority. And a proof of that reality is not required. That is why democracy proved an efficient, but especially a socially approved and pragmatic system. Actually "one set of truths for everybody" is a democratic *wish*; a relative truth decided by vote is the democratic *practice*.

[35] See above: Chapter 2, 8- The testimony of the myths; THE DEFENCE OF A MYTH: CONFIRMATION BIAS.

[36] See above: Chapter 1, 4- A tentative assessment; MYTH AS A WORKING HYPOTHESIS.

origin. But, at the same time, the discourse of national solidarity helps block off other possible discursive articulations of interest" (Giddens, 1985, p. 276, 221).

The present study showed that myths (and/or "truths", "reality", etc) are related and relative to groups. National groups, naturally propagate their special national myths. National myths vary from one nation to the other, that is to say they are "relative", but only in relation to the *various* national groups; within each group the myths are seen as natural realities. Within the groups the convictions are not relative, and they are even internalized as scientific truths. And, once there is a group whose members confirm each other there is no limit to what (absurd) ideas they may believe. As human beings we are against "relative truth" because the acceptance of such a state weakens and even annuls our private truths. The findings, however, seem to invalidate this assurance.

More importantly, humans are inclined to "explain" all phenomena by presenting or imagining a "cause". Accidental and/or unexplainable phenomena are all explained, if needed by stories that for others are only myths. It is not unusual that rejected myths are replaced by other myths. "Our mind is strongly biased toward causal explanation and does not deal well with 'mere statistics'. When our attention is called to an event, associative memory will look for its cause – more precisely, activation will automatically spread to any cause that is already stored in memory." (Kahneman, p. 182.)

Combining the peculiar capabilities of human brain with the suspicion that the thinking of the grownups is not diametrically different from the thinking of the children, one wonders if the mythical thinking is rather a tendency of humans, if not the rule. Humans believe in "stories", in symbols and in similar representations, often in rituals and in performances since the brain perceives all incoming messages as "realities"; or to be exact, without distinguishing between real and virtual signal.

According to the social scientist Howard Margolis there seems to be "a deep continuity between the mythmaking of primitive societies and the scientific theory-building of modern societies. Mathematics itself ... becomes the endpoint of a spectrum with primitive myths about monsters and ghosts near the other end." (Margolis, p. 85, 109.)

When I decided to write about "the Greek national myths" I could not imagine where the research would arrive at. Now, to my surprise, I see that the myths, irrespective if they are national and/or Greek, they are part of our lives. They are even our lives!

Considering all the above the definition, or rather the description of "myth" is as follows: Myths are social beliefs, convictions, explanations, theories, stories which are believed by a "group" as true. This "truth" may have various validities since sometimes myths are seen as "symbols", as "allegories" as "legends", etc; but still they are accepted as closely related to reality and they are respected. A condition to call a phenomenon a "myth" is the presence of some others who do not believe in that myth. If there is no defiance then that phenomenon is perceived as "knowledge". "Myth" is the nomenclature used by those to reject a "belief". In short, one's absolute truth is the myth of the Other. Myths are closely related with mechanisms like confirmation bias, boomerang effect, rationalization, stereotyping, escapism, inability to differentiate "reality" from virtual existence, etc. – as explained in this study.

There are, however, many things we still do not know. Especially the human brain with its limitations and inclinations is still an enigma. The real explanation lies there. In the future we may learn many more characteristics of ours. At present our self-knowledge is limited.

To learn to say "I do not know the answer to this question" is a big step in the history of human knowledge and intellect, probably a bigger one than the step of Enlightenment which was based on "knowing". Humans in their haughty conviction that they know or due to the pleasure of convincing themselves that they know, or due to their fear of not knowing and remaining in the dark, they prefer to create myths to explain situations instead of saying "I do not know". Not knowing is scary.

There is, however, a hypocritical "I do not know". In the past quite often some expressed their ignorance vis-à-vis our existence to legitimize another source of knowledge which they fervently propagated as its masters. They called this source "the ultimate truth", in practice turning "not knowing" to "I know the basics". The argument that some gods and their messages and directions enlighten the unknown and the mystery of life, is a negation of the initial argument, e.i., "I don't know". By "I do not know" I mean "There is no available explanation".

When humans cope with the fear of the unknown, they may cope with myths, too. Even if they don't transcend myths they may distance themselves from many fairy tales.

***

NOTES/BIBLIOGRAPHY

(Books and articles mentioned in this volume)

Abatzopoulou, Frangiski [Αμπατζοπούλου, Φραγκίσκη]. *Ο Άλλος εν Διωγμό, Η εικόνα του Εβραίου στη Λογοτεχνία, Ζητήματα ιστορίας και μυθοπλασίας* [The Other under persecution, The Image of the Jew in literature, in history and myth-making], Athens: Θεμέλιο, 1998.

About, Edmond, *La Grèce contemporaine*, Librairie de l'Hachette et Cie, 1854.

Academy of Athens [Ακαδημία Αθηνών]. *Χρηστικό Λεξικό της Νεοελληνικής Γλώσσας* [Handy Dictionary of the Modern Greek Language], Αθήνα: Το Βήμα, 2016 (2014).

Aggelou, Alkis [Αγγέλου, Άλκης]. *Το Κρυφό Σχολειό, το χρονικό ενός μύθου* [The Secret School, the chronology of a myth], Athens: Εστία, 1999 [1997].

----. "Η κατάσταση της παιδείας στις υπόδουλες ελληνικές χώρες» in *Ιστορία του Ελληνικού Έθνους, Vol. 10*, Αθήνα: Εκδοτική Αθηνών, 1974, p. 366-367.

----. Παναγιώτης Κοδρικάς, Εφημερίδες, [Panayiotis Korthikas, Diaries], Athens: Ερμής, 1991.

Aggelopoulos, Kostantinos [Αγγελόπουλος, Κωνσταντίνος]. "Διακηρύσοντας την ελληνική ταυτότητα στα σχολικά βιβλία" [Declaring the Greek national identity in textbooks] in Kapsalis. A.; Bonidis,K.; Sipitanou, A.; (edit.), *Εικόνα του Άλλου/Γείτονα στα σχολικά βιβλία των βαλκανικών χωρών* [The image of the Other/neigbbor in textbooks of the Balkan countries], Athens: Τυπωθήτω, 2000, pp. (International congress, minutes of meeting, 1998), pp. 319-334.

Ahlis, Nikos [Άχλης, Νίκος]. *Οι Γειτονική μας Λαοί, Βούλγαροι, και Τούρκοι στα σχολικά βιβλία ιστορίας Γυμνασίου και Λυκείου*, [Our neighboring people, Bulgarians and Turks in history textbooks of Intermediary schools], Thessaloniki: Αδελφοί Κυριακίδη, 1983.

Aktipas, Dionisios & Others [Ακτύπας, Διονύσιος και άλλοι], Στα Αρχαία Χρόνια [In Anceint Years], Athens: ΟΕΔΒ, 1988.

Anastasiadou-Simeonidi, Anna [Αναστασιάδη-Συμεωνίδη, Άννα]. «Ιδεολογήματα και δανεισμός» [Ideological stories and loan word], (p. 63-71) in Haris, Yiannis [Χάρης, Γιάννης]. (Edit.) *Δέκα Μύθοι για την Ελληνική Γλώσσα [Ten Myths about the Greek Language]*, Athens: Πατάκη, 2007 (2001), pp.63-72 .

Anderson, Benedict. *Imagined Communities*. London& New York: Verso, 1990.

Asimakopoulou, Fotini & Hristidou-Lionaraki, Sevasti [Ασημακοπούλου, Φωτινή & Χρηστίδου-Λιοναράκη, Σεβαστή]. Η Μουσουλμανική μειονότητα της Θράκης και οι Ελληνοτουρκικές Σχέσεις [The Muslim minority of Thracea and the Greek-Turkish relations], Athens: Λιβάνη, 2002.

Anonymous Greek. Hellenic Nomarchy, That is On Liberty [Ελληνική Νομαρχία, ήτοι λόγος περί ελευθερίας], Athens: Κάλβος. 1980 (Italy, 1806).

Apostolidou, Venetia [Αποστολίδου, Βενετία], *Ανάγνωση και ετερότητα* [Reading and alterity], Athens: Πρόγραμμα Μουσουλμανοπαίδων, Πανεπιστήμιο Αθηνών , 2003

Apostolopoulos, Dimitris [Αποστολόπουλος, Δημήτης]. *Η Γαλλική Επανάσταση στην Τουρκοκρατούμενη ελληνική Κοινωνία, Αντιδράσεις στα 1798* [The French Revolution and the Greek Society under the Turkish rule, reactions in 1798], Athens: [private], 1989

Arendt, Hannah. *The Origins of Totalitarianism*, UK: Penguin, 1994.

Arrian the Nicomedian., *The Anabasis of Alexander*, Transl. E. J. Chinnock, London: Hodder And Stoughton, 1884. (http://www.pgdp.net)

Arrian the Nicomedian [Αρριανός]. Αλεξάνδρου Ανάβασις, Βιβλία 3 &4, [*The Anabasis of Alexander*, Books 3&4], Transl. by Kaktos, Athens: Κάκτος, 1992.

Arrian the Nicomedian [Αρριανός]. Αλεξάνδρου Ανάβασις, Βιβλίο 7, [*The Anabasis of Alexander*, Book 7], Transl. by Kaktos, Athens: Κάκτος, 1992b.

Arrian the Nicomedian [Αρριανός]. Αλεξάνδρου Ανάβασις, Βιβλία 3 - 5, Vol.1 [*The Anabasis of Alexander*, Books 3-4, Vol.1], Transl. by Γ. Ράπτης, Athens: Ζήτρος (Το Βήμα), 2004.

Arrian the Nicomedian [Αρριανός]. Αλεξάνδρου Ανάβασις, Βιβλία 6 - 7, Vol.2 [*The Anabasis of Alexander*, Books 6-7, Vol.2], Transl. by Γ. Ράπτης, Athens: Ζήτρος (Το Βήμα), 2004b.

Asdrahas, Spiros [Ασδραχάς, Σπύρος]. "Μακρυγιάννης και ο Παναγιώτης Ζωγράφος"

[Makriyannis and Panayiotis Zografos] in *Ελληνική Κοινωνία και Οικονομία, ιη' και ιθ' αιώνας*[Greek society and economy, 18th and 19th century], Athens: Ερμής, 1988 pp. 315-349

Athanasiadis, Haris [Αθανασιάδης, Χάρης]. *Τα αποσυρθέντα βιβλία, Έθνος και σχολική ιστορία στην Ελλάδα, 1858-2008* [The withdrawn books, The nation and school history in Greece, 1858-2008], Athens: Αλεξάνδρεια, 2015.

Athanasopoulou, Aggeliki [Αθανασοπούλου, Αγγελική]. "Αλβανοί και Αρβανίτες: Πολιτισμική συνάφεια και μεταναστευτική εργασία στη Βόρεια Πελοπόννησο" [Albanians and Arcanites: Cultural relevance and immigration labor in North Peloponnisos], in Papataxiarhis, Efthimios [Παπαταξιάρχης, Ευθύμιος]. (Edit). *Περιπέτειες της ετερότητας, Η παραγωγή της πολιτισμηκής διαφοράς στη σημερινη Ελλάδα* [The adventures of alterity. Production of the cultural difference in modern Greece], Athens: Αλεξάνδρεια, 2006, pp. 239-266.

Baar, Monica. "History writing" in Leerssen, Joep (edit) *Encyclopedia of Romantic Nationalism in Europe, Volume 1*, Amsterdam: Amsterdam University Press, 2018, pp. 127.

Babiniotis, Yiorgos [Μπαμπινιώτης, Γιώργος] *Λεξικό της Νέας Ελληνικής Γλώσσας* [The Dictionary of the New Greek Language], Athens: Κέντρο Λεξικολογίας, 1998.

Babiniotis, Georgios [Μπαμπινιώτης, Γεώργιος.] *Συνοπτική Ιστορία της Ελληνικής Γλώσσας*, Αθήνα: Το Βήμα, 2015 (1980).

Babiniotis, Georgios [Μπαμπινιώτης, Γεώργιος.] *Ελληνική Γλώσσα, Παρελθόν, παρόν, μέλλον*, Αθήνα: Το Βήμα, 2015 (1994).

Baltsiotis, Lambros [Μπαλτσιώτης, Λάμπρος]. *Γλωσσική ετερότητα στην Ελλάδα*, [Linguistic Alterity in Greece], Athens: Πρόγραμμα Μουσουλμανοπαίδων, Πανεπιστήμιο Αθηνών , 2003.

----.«Εθνικοί μύθοι και ιστορικές κατασκευές στις μη Ελληνόφωνες ομάδες, το παράδειγμα των Αρβανιτών και των Βλάχων» [National myths and historical constructs in the non-Greek speaking groups, the case of the Arvanites and Vlachs], in *Μειονότητες στην Ελλάδα - Επιστημονικό Συμπόσιο* [Minorities in Greece - Academic Conference], Athens: Εταιρεία Σπουδών, 2004, pp. 337-366.

----. "Οι Αρβανίτες" [The Arbanites], in Papadimitriou, Despina & Seferiadis, Serafim, (Edit.) [Παπαδημητρίου, Δέσποινα & Σεφεριάδης Σεραφείμ]. (Επιμ). Αθέατες όψεις της ιστορίας, κείμενα αφιερωμένα στον Γιάνη Γιανουλόπουλο, Athens: Ασίνη, 2012, pp. 353-376.

Billig, Michael. *Banal Nationalism*, London, Los Angeles: Sage, 2008 (1999).

Bacon, Sir Francis. *Novum Organum*, ed. by Joseph Devey, M.A. (New York: P.F. Collier, 1902). https://oll.libertyfund.org/titles/1432

Beaton, Roderick and Ricks, David. (Edit.) *The Making of Modern Greece: Nationalism, Romanticism, and the Uses of the Past (1797–1896)*, Center for Hellenic Studies King's College, 2009.

----. *Greece, Biography of a Modern Nation*, UK. USA: Penguin, 2020 (2019).

Beis, Stamatis [Μπέης, Σταμάτης]. "Όψεις του γλωσσικού ηγεμονισμού στην περίπτωση των γλωσσικών μειονοτήτων της Ελλάδας [Linguistic hegemony in cases of minority languages in Greece], [in *Μειονότητες στην Ελλάδα - Επιστημονικό Συμπόσιο*" [Minorities in Greece - Academic Conference], Athens: Εταιρεία Σπουδών, 2004, pp. 325-334.

Bietenholz, Peter G. Historia and Fabula, Myths and Legends in Historical Thought from Antiquity to the Modern Age, Leiden: E.J. Brill, 1994.

Billig, Michael. *Banal Nationalism*, London, Los Angeles: Sage, 2008 (1999).

Biris, Kostas [Μπίρης, Κώστας]. *Αρβανίτες, Οι Δωριείς του Νεώτερου Ελληνισμού, Ιστορία των Ελλήνων Αρβανιτών* [The Arvanites, The Dorians of the New Hellenism, History of the Greek Arbanites]. Athens: Μέλισσα, 1976 [1960]

Boas, Franz. *The Mind of Primitive Man*, Freeditorial, 1938.

Breuilly, John. Nationalism and the State, Manchester: Manchester University Press, 1985 (1982).

Burke, Edmund. Reflections on the Revolution in France, 1790 (https://socialsciences. mcmaster. ca/ econ/ugcm/3ll3/burke/revfrance.pdf)

CAMS (Κέντρο Μικρασιατικών Σπουδών). *Η Έξοδος, Τόμος Β* [Exodus, Vol 2]. Athens: CAMS, 1982.

Cassirer, Ernst. An Essay on Man, An Introduction to a Philosophy of Human Culture, New York: Doubleday Anchor, 1944.

----. *The Myth of the State*, New Haven: Yale University Press, 1946.

----. *Language and Myth*, (Trans. by Susanne K. Langer), New York: Dover Publications, 1953 (1946).

----. *Διαφωτισμός και θρησκεία* [Enlightenment and religion], Trans. by G. Likiarthopoulou (Chapter 4 of *Die Philosopie der Aufklarung*), Athens: Εράσμος, 2004.

Clairis, Christos (Κλαίρης, Χρήστος. "Le cas du grec" in Hagége, Claude & FODOR, Istvan (eds.), *La réforme des langues, Histoire et avenir*, Vol. 1, Hambourg: Buske, 1983, pp.351-362.

----. "Γλώσσα και πολυγλωσσία» [Language and polyglossia], in Athens: *Αντί*, September 14, 1984, (270), p.44-45. (Also in Clairis, Chr. *Θέματα γενικής γλωσσολογίας*, [Issues of general linguistics], Athens: Νεφέλη, 1990. Originally a presentation at *Université Paris 5 René Descartes* of Sorbonne in June 19, 1983.)

Clément, Olivier. «*Η αλήθεια ελευθερώσει υμάς», Συνομιλώντας με τον Οικουμενικό Πατριάρχη Βαρθολομαίο Α'»* ["The truth will set you free", Talking to the Ecumenical Patriarch Bartholomaios I], Athens: Ακρίτας, 1997.

Clogg, Richard. *A Concise History of Greece*, New York: Cambridge University Press, 1993.

Crews, Frederick. *Freud: The Making of an Illusion,* New York: Metropolitan Books, 2017.

Daskalakis, Apostolos [Δασκαλάκη, Απόστολος]. *Το πολίτευμα του Ρήγα Βελεστινλή* [The Polity of Rigas Velestinlis], Athens: Βαγιονάκη, 1976).

Dawkins, Richard. *The God delusion*, London: Bantam Press, 2006.

Decety, Jean & Ickes, William (edit.). *The Social Neuroscience of Empathy*, Cambridge, Massachusetts, London: First MIT Press, 2011.

Despotopoulos, Aleksandros [Δεσποτόπουλος, Αλέξανδρος]. *Σύντομον Πανηγυρικόν Λογίδιον εκφωνηθέν εις την 25η Μαρτίου 1821 εν τη Αγία Λαύρα*, [Short speech on 25th of March in Agia Lavra] , Patra: Έκδοση Ευ. Χριστοδούλου, 1861.

De Waal, Frans. *Good Natured, The origins of right and wrong in humans and other animals*, Cambridge, Massachusetts and London: Harvard University Press, 2001.

Diamantopoulou, N. and Kyriazopoulou, A. *Ελληνική Ιστορία των Νεοτέρων Χρόνων, 6 Grade* [*Greek history of modern times*], Textbook, Athens: ΟΕΔΒ, 1984.

Dimaras, Konstantinos. [Δημαράς, Κωνσταντίνος]. "Το σχήμα του Διαφωτισμού" [The shape of Enlightenment] in *Ιστορία του Ελληνικού Έθνους [History of the Greek Nation]*, *Vol. 11*, Athens: Εκδοτική Αθηνών, 1974, pp. 328-359.

Dimaras, Konstantinos [Δημαράς, Κωνσταντίνος] *Νεοελληνικός Διαφωτισμός* [Enlightenment of Modern Hellenism], Athens: Ερμής, 1985.

Dimaras, Konstantinos. [Δημαράς, Κωνσταντίνος]. *Ελληνικός Ρωμαντισμός* [Greek Romanticism], Athens: Ερμής, 1985b.

Dimou, Nikos (Δήμου, Νίκος) *Η Δυστυχία του να είσαι Έλληνας* [On the Unhappiness of Being Greek], Αθήνα: Πατάκη, 2013 (1975).

Doxiadis, Apostolos [Δοξιάδης, Απόστολος]. *Ερασιτέχνης Επαναστάτης, Προσωπικό Μυθιστόρημα* [Amateur Revolutionary, Personal Novel], Athens: Ikaros, 2018.

Eliade, Mircea & Couliano, Ioan, P. *Λεξικό των Θρησκειών* [Guide to World religions], Athens: Το Βήμα, 2016.

Emerson, James (Tennent). The History of Modern Greece – From Its Conquest by the Romans, B.C. 146, to the Present Time, London: Henry Colburn & Richard Bwntley, 1830.

Exertzoglou, Haris. "Shifting boundaries: language, community and the 'non-Greek- speaking Greeks" in, Athens: *Historien*, Vol.1. 1999. pp.75-92.

Fallmerayer, Jacob-Philip. *Περί της καταγωγής των σημερινών Ελλήνων* [The origin of today's Greeks], Athens: Nefeli, 1984.

Finlay, George [Φίνλεϋ, Γεώργιος]. Ιστορία της Τουρκοκρατίας και της Ενετοκρατίας στην Ελλάδα [Greece under Othoman and Venetian domination], Athens: Πυξίδα, 1958.

----. *Ιστορία της Ελληνικής Επανάστασης,* [History of the Greek Revolution], Athens: Το Βήμα, 2021 (1861).

Fleischer, Hagen. "Οι Έλληνες απέναντι στους Άλλους» [The Greeks facing the 'Others'", in The Athens Review of Books, December, 2020, Issue 123, pp. 53-62.

Fokas, Spirithonas (Φωκάς, Σπυρίδωνας]. *Ο Ζαλλώνης, οι Φαναριώτες και οι Ρουμάνοι* [Zallonis, the Phanatiots and the Rumanians], Athens: Private edition, 1989.

Frangoudaki, Anna [Φραγκουδάκη, Άννα]. *Τα Αναγνωστικά του Δημοτικού Σχολείου* [The Reading Textbooks of Primary Schools], Athens: Θεμέλιο, 1978

----. *Η Γλώσσα και το Έθνος* [The language and the nation], Athens: Αλεξάνδρεια, 2001.

----. *Γλώσσα του σπιτιού και γλώσσα του σχολείου* [The language at home and the language at school], Athens: Πρόγραμμα Μουσουλμανοπαίδων, Πανεπιστήμιο Αθηνών , 2007

----. «Η γλωσσική φθορά και οι 'μεγαλομανείς' γλώσσες» [The deterioration of language and the 'megalomaniac' languages', (p. 45-52) in Haris, Yiannis [Χάρης, Γιάννης]. (Edit.) *Δέκα Μύθοι για την Ελληνική Γλώσσα [Ten Myths for the Greek Language]*, Athens: Πατάκη, 2007b (2001), pp. 45-52.

----. *Ο Εθνικισμός και η Άνοδος της Ακροδεξιάς* [Nationalism and the Rise of Exrtreem right], Athens: Αλεξάνδρεια, 2013.

Frangoudaki, Anna & Dragona, Thalia [Φραγκουδάκη, Άννα & Δραγώνα, Θάλια]. *Τι είν η Πατρίδα μας; Εθνοκεντρισμός στην Εκπαίδευση* [What is our Home country? Ethnocentrism in Education], Athens: Αλεξάνδρεια, 1997.

Frazer, Sir James. *The Golden Bough, A study in magic and religion,* (Abridged edition) Kent:Wordworth Reference, 1993.

----. Adonis, Attis, Osiris, Studies in the History of Oriental Religion, Toronto MacMillan & Co., 1914.

Freud, Sigmund. ----. *The Interpretation of Dreams,* New York: The Modern Library, 1950.

----. *Totem and Taboo: Resemblances Between the Mental Lives of Savages and Neurotics,*. Trans. By James Strachey , New York: W. W. Norton & Company, 1990

Fritze, Ronald. Invented Knowledge, False History, Fake Science and Pseude-religions, London: Reaction Books, 2009.

Gatos, Yiorgos [Γάτος, Γιώργος]. *Πολυτεχνείο '73. Ρεπορτάζ με την Ιστορία* [Politechnic 1973, Interview with historuy], Athens: Φιλιππότη, 2004.

Gazi, Effi [Γαζή, Έφη]. *Ο Δεύτερος βίος των Τριών Ιεραρχών.Μία γενεολογία του Ελληνοχρηστιανικού Πολιτισμού* [The Second life of the Three Cappadocian Church Fathers. A Geneology of the Hellenochristian civilization]. Athens: Νεφέλη, 2004.

----. "Revisiting Religion and Nationalism in 19th century Greece" in *The Making of Modern Greece: Nationalism, Romanticism, and the Uses of the Past (1797–1896)* edited by Roderick Beaton and David Ricks, 2009, pp. 95-106.

Gellner, Ernest. *Nations and Nationalism*, Oxford: Basil Blackwell, 1983.

----. *The Psychoanalytic Movement*, Great Britain: Paladin, 1985.

Germanos, Palaion Patron [Γερμανός, Παλαιών Πατρών]. Απομνημονεύματα [Memoirs], Athens: Δημόσια Βιβλιοθήκη Δημητσάνης, 1975.

Giddens, Anthony. A contemporary critiqus of Historical Materialism, London: MackMillan Press, 1981.

----. Sociology, A Brief Critical Introduction, London: MackMillan Publishers, 1982.

Gordon, Thomas. Ιστορία της Ελληνικής Επαναστάσεως [History of the Greek Revolution], Vol. A/1, Athens: Μπαϋρον,1977 (1844)

Gordon, Thomas. *History of the Greek Revolution*, Volume 1. Edinburg and London: W. Blackwood and T. Cadell. 1832).

Graecogermania, Griechishstdien deutscher Humanisten. (1469-1523), New York: VCH Acta humaniora, 1989.

Greenfeld, Liah. *Nationalism, Five Roads to Modernity*, London: Harvard University Press, 1992.

Grigoriadis, Ioannis. Instilling Religion in Greek and Turkish Nationalism: A "Sacred Synthesis". New York: Palgrave Macmillan, 2012.

Gritsopoulos, Tasos [Τάσος Γριτσόπουλος], "Το Αμφισβητούμενον Κρυφό Σχολειό" [The

Secret School in doubt], [Journal] *Εκκλησία*, July 2004, Mentioned also in: http://users.uoa.gr/~nektar/history/3contemporary/tasos_gritsopoylos_to_amfisbhtoy menon_kryfo_sxoleio.htm

Gutas, Dimitri. *Greek Thought, Atabic culture, The Graeco-Arabian Translation Movement in Baghdad and Early Abbasid Society (8th -10th centuries)*, London & New York: Routledge, 1998.

Guys, M. de. *A Sentiment Journal through Greece in a series of letters*, Dublin: Milliken, 1773

Hand, David. "Wonderful examples, but let's not close our eyes" in *Statistical Science*, Vol.29, No.1: 98–100, 2014.

Haris, Yiannis [Χάρης, Γιάννης]. *Η Γλώσσα, τα λάθη και τα πάθη* [Language, the mistakes and the pathos], Athens: Πόλης, 2003.

----. *Δέκα Μύθοι για την Ελληνική Γλώσσα* [Ten Myths for the Greek Language], Athens: Πατάκη, 2007 (2001).

Haralambopoulos, Vasilios [Χαραλαμπόπουλος, Βασίλειος]. *Θέματα ιστορίας της Δημητσάνας* [Issues of History of Dimitsana], Athens: Αδελφότητα Δημητσανιτών, 2007.

Harari, Yuval Noah. *Sapiens, A Brief History of Humankind*, London: Vintage book, 2011.

Hassard, John. "An alternative to paradigm incommensurability in organization theory" in Hassard, John & Pym, Denis (edit), *The Theory and Philosophy of Organizations: Critical Issues and New Perspectives (Social Analysis)*. London & New York: Rutledge, 1990, pp. 219-230).

Hatzopoulos, Marios. "From resurrection to insurrection: 'Sacred' myths, motifs, and symbols in the Grek War of Independece" in *The Making of Modern Greece: Nationalism, Romanticism, and the Uses of the Past (1797–1896)* edited by Roderick Beaton and David Ricks, 2009, pp. 81-93.

Hayes, Carlton. *The Historical evolution of modern nationalism*, New York: Richard r. Smith, 1931.

Heraclides, Alexis [Ηρακλείδης, Αλέξης]. "Socialization to Conflict – A case study of the national historical ingroup-outgroup images in the educational system of Greece", in Επιθεώρηση Κοινωνικών Ερευνών, no. 38, 1980.pp.16-42.

----. *Η Ελλάδα και ο 'Εξ ανατολών κίνδυνος'*, [Greek and the danger coming from the East]. Athens: Πόλις, 2001.

----. *"Τα αίτια της αντιμειονοτικής στάσης της Ελλάδας, ορισμένες υποθέσεις για έρευνα"* [The reasons for the anti-minority policy in Greece, some hypotheses for researche], in *Μειονότητες στην Ελλάδα - Επιστημονικό Συμπόσιο* [Minorities in Greece - Academic Conference], Athens: Εταιρεία Σπουδών, 2004, pp. 43-57.

----. *The Greek-Turkish Conflict in the Aegean, Imagined Enemies*, England: Palgrave Macmillan. 2010.

----. *Το ΜακεδονικόΖήτημα, 1878-2018* [The Macedonian issue, 1878-2018], Athens: Θεμέλιο, 2018.

Heraclides, Alexis & Dialla, Ada. *Humanitarian intervention in the long nineteenth century, setting the precedent*, Manchester University Press, 2015.

Hitchens, Christopher. *God is not Great*, London: Atlantic Books, 2007.

Hobsbawm, Eric. *The Age of Revolution*, London: Abacus, 1977 (1962).

Hobsbawm, Eric. *Nations and Nationalism since 1780*, Cambridge, New York: Cambridge University Press, 1990.

Hobsbawm, Eric & , Ranger,Terence. *The Invention of Tradition,* New York: Cambridge University Press, 2012 (1983) OK

Howe, Samuel, G. *An Historical Sketch of the Greek Revolution*, New York: Gallaher and White, 1828 (second edition).

Hristidis, Anastasios-Fivos [Χριστίδης, Αναστάσιος-Φοίβος]. «Η αρχαία και η νεότερη ελληνική γλώσσα: Η αυτονομία της δημοτικής» [Ancient and modern Greek language: The autonomous Demotiki], (p. 35-44) in Haris, Yiannis [Χάρης, Γιάννης]. (Edit.) *Δέκα Μύθοι για την Ελληνική Γλώσσα [Ten Myths for the Greek Language]*, Athens: Πατάκη, 2007 (2001), pp.35-44.

Hume, David. "Of the Rise and Progress of the Arts and Sciences" appeared in 1742 in Volume two of Hume's Essays, Moral and Political. The text file here is based on the 1875 Green and Grose edition. See: Of The Rise And Progress Of The Arts And Sciences / Hume, David (infomotions.com)

Ikonomou Michail [Οικονόμου, Μηχαήλ]. *Ιστορικά της Ελληνικής Παλιγγενεσίας ή Ο Ιερός των Ελλήνων Αγών [History of the Greek reborn or the holy struggle of the Greeks]*, Athens: Δημόσια Βιβλιοθήκη της Σχολής Δημητσάνης [Public Library of the School of Dimitsana], 1976 (1873).

Iliou, Filippos [Ηλιού, Φίλιππος]. Κοινωνικοί αγώνες και διαφωτισμός, η περίπτωση της Σμύρνης (1819) [Social struggles and Enlightenment, the case of Smirna (1819)], Athens: Μνήμων, 1986.

Ioannides Aggelos [Ιωαννίδης, Άγγελος]. «Ελληνοποίησις των Συνειδήσεων, Κάθε Καρυδιάς Καρύδι...» [The Hellenization of the Consciousness], in *Η Κινστέρνα*, Vol 29, Athens, Jan.-Dec. 2019, p.51-65. (With notes by Savvas Tsilenis).

Joinville and Villehardouin. *Chronicles of the Crusades*, Trans. By M.R.B. Show, Great Britain: Penguin, 1984.

Jones, Ernest. *The life and work of Sigmund Freud* 1856-1900, Volume 1, New Work: Basic Books. 1953.

----. *The life and work of Sigmund Freud* 1901-1919, Volume 2, Ney Work, Basic Books. 1955.

----. *The life and work of Sigmund Freud* 1919-1939, Volume 3, Ney Work, Basic Books. 1957.

Kahneman, Daniel. *Thinking fast and slow*, New York: Penguin, 2011.

Kakridi-Ferrari, Maria [Κακριδή-Φερράρι, Μαρία]. «Πλούσιες και φτωχές γλώσσες» [Rich and poor languages], (p. 103-110) in Haris, Yiannis [Χάρης, Γιάννης]. (Edit.) *Δέκα Μύθοι για την Ελληνική Γλώσσα [Ten Myths for the Greek Language]*, Athens: Πατάκη, 2007 (2001), pp.103-110.

----. «Μύθοι για τη γλώσσα στην ελληνική εκδοχή τους: ιδιαιτερότητες, αντοχές, επανερμηνείες», in *Μύθοι και ιδεολογήματα στη σύγχρονη Ελλάδα – Επιστημονικό Συμπόσιο* [Myths and ideologies in modern Greece- Academic Conference], Athens: Εταιρεία Σπουδών, 2007b, pp. 199-223.

Kallivretakis, Leonidas [Καλλιβρετάκης, Λεωνίδας]. "Πολυτεχνείο '73: Το ζήτημα των θυμάτων: Νεκροί και τραυματίες," [Polytechnic School '73: The question of the victims: dead and injured], in *Πολυτεχνείο '73: ρεπορτάζ με την Ιστορία*, vol. 2, Αθήνα: Εκδόσεις Φιλιππότη, 2004, pp. 38-55. Also see: Πολυτεχνείο '73: Το ζήτημα των θυμάτων: Νεκροί και τραυματίες (ntua.gr)

Kamaterou-Glitsi, Georgia [Καματερού-Γλυτση, Γεωργία], Αρχαία Ελλάδα, Ιστορία Δ Δημοτικού [Ancient Greece, History for Grade 4], Atnens: ΟΕΔΒ, 1976.

Kant, Immanuel. *Critique of Pure Reason*, London: MacMillan, 1922.

Karabelias, Giorgos [Καραμπελιάς, Γιώργος]. *Εκκλησία και γένος εν αιχμαλωσία* [Church and naton in captivity], Athens: Εναλλακτικές εκδόσεις, 2018.

Karabot, Filippos [Κάραμποτ, Φίλιππος]. "Περί αλλοθρήσκων Εβραίων και ετερόδοξων ευαγγελικών πολιτών στο ελληνικό κράτος τον 19ο αιώνα" [On the Jews of different religion and evangelist citizens in the Greek state of th 19th century.] in Papadimitriou, Despina & Seferiadis, Serafim, (Edit.) [Παπαδημητρίου, Δέσποινα & Σεφεριάδης Σεραφείμ]. (Επιμ). *Αθέατες όψεις της ιστορίας, κείμενα αφιερωμένα στον Γιάνη Γιανουλόπουλο*, Athens: Ασίνη, 2012, pp.211-226.

Karantzola, Eleni [Καραντζόλα, Ελένη]. «Το 'απαραβίαστο' της ιστορικής ορθογραφίας» [The 'inviolability' of the historical dictation], (p.83- 91) in Haris, Yiannis [Χάρης, Γιάννης]. (Edit.) *Δέκα Μύθοι για την Ελληνική Γλώσσα [Ten Myths for the Greek Language]*, Athens: Πατάκη, 2007 (2001), pp. 83-92.

Karas, Giannis [Κάρας, Γιάννης].Θεόφιλος Καΐρης, Κωνσταντίνος Μ. Κούμας, δύο πρωτοπόρει δάσκαλοι του Γένους [Th. Kairis, K. Koumas, two pioneer teachers of the Nation], Athens: Gutenberg, 1977.

----. *Γερμανικές επιδράσεις στη σκέψη των χρόνων της νεοελληνικής αναγέννησης, Στέφανος Δούγκας ή Περί Φυσικής Φιλοσοφίας* [German influences in the thinking of modern Greek Renaissance, Stefanos Dougkas], Athens: Επ.Εταιρεία Μελέτης Φερών Βελεστίνου Ρήγας, 1993.

Katsanis, Nikos [Κατσάνης, Νίκος] "Οι Βλάχοι της Ελλάδας, Μύθοι και προκαταλήψεις" [The

Vlachs of Greece, Myths and prejudices], in *Μειονότητες στην Ελλάδα - Επιστημονικό Συμπόσιο* [Minorities in Greece - Academic Conference], Athens: Εταιρεία Σπουδών, 2004, pp. 221-231.

Katsoulakos,Theodoros and others [Κατσουλάκος, Θεόδορος και άλλοι], Ιστορία στα Αρχαία Χρόνια, Δ' Δημοτικού [History of Ancient Years for Grade 4], Athens: Πατάκη, 2020.

Kardasis, Asimakis, A. [Καρδάσης, Ασημάκης, Α.]. *Δημητσάνα, μια Δοξασμένη Πόλη* [Dimitsana, a glorious city]. Athens: (Private edition), 1988.

Kedourie, Elie. *Nationalism* (1960) (panarchy.org)

Kekavmenos, Giorgos [Κεκαυμένος, Γιώργος]. Το Κρυφό Σχολειό, Το χρονικό μιας ιστορίας [The secret school, the chronicle of a story], Athens: Εναλλακτικές εκδόσεις, 2012.

Kirtatas, Dimitris [Κυρτάτας, Δημήτρης]. "Η Κατάκτηση της αρχαίας ελληνικής ιστορίας από το Νέο Ελληνισμό κατά το 18ο και 19ο αιώνα με τη διαμεσολάβηση της Δύσης" [The possession of ancient Greek history by New Hellenism in the 18th and 19th centuries through the mediation of the West], in *Οι Χρήσεις της Αρχαιότητας από το Νέο Ελληνισμό – Επιστημονικό Συμπόσιο, 2000,* [The use of antiquity by New Hellenism Academic Conference, 2000], Athens: Εταιρεία Σπουδών, 2002, pp. 251-266.

Kitromilidis, Pashalis [Κιτρομηλίδης, Πασχάλης Μ]. *Η Γαλλική Επανάσταση και η νοτιοανατολική Ευρώπη* [The French Revolution and the Southeastern Europe], Athens: Διάττων, 1990.

----."Σκέψεις για την Κοινωνική αναγκαιότητα των Μύθων [Thoughts on the necessity of the Myths], », in *Μύθοι και ιδεολογήματα στη σύγχρονη Ελλάδα – Επιστημονικό Συμπόσιο* [Myths and ideologies in modern Greece- Academic Conference], Athens: Εταιρεία Σπουδών, 2007, pp. 175-180.

Kolokotronis, Theodoros [Κολοκοτρώνης, Θεόδωρος]. Απομνημονεύματα [Memoirs], Athens: 1964. Εκδόσεις Τ. Δρακόπουλου.

Kondoglou, Fotis [Κόντογλού, Φώτης]. *Σημείον Μέγα, Τα Θαύματα των Αγίων της Θέρμης, Ραφαάλ, Νικολάου, Ειρήνης* [The Great Sign, The Miracles of Saints Thermis, Raphael, Nicolas, Eirini], Athens: Παπαδημητρίου, 1962.

Konstantinou, Ilias [Κωνσταντίνου, Ηλίας]. *Ξένες λέξεις στην ελληνική γλώσσα* [Foreighn words in the Greek language], Athens: Τα Νέα, 2014.

Kordatos, Gianis [Κορδάτος, Γιάνης]. *Ιστορία της Νεώτερης Ελλάδας (Τουρκοκρατία),* [History of Modern Greece], Athens: 20ος Αιώνας', 1957.

----. *Ιστορία της Ελληνικής Λογοτεχνίας* [History of Greek Literature], Athens: Βιβλιοεκδοτική, 1962.

----. Ιστορία του Γλωσσικού μας ζητήματος, [History of our language issue], Athens: Μπουκουμάνη, 1973 (1943).

Kostopoulos, Tasos [Κωστόπουλος, Τάσος]. "Το όνομα του Άλλου, Από τους 'Ελληνοβούλγαρους' στους 'Ντόπιους Μακεδόνες'" [The name of the Other, From the 'Greek-Boulgarians' to the 'Local Macedonians' in *Μειονότητες στην Ελλάδα - Επιστημονικό Συμπόσιο* [Minorities in Greece - Academic Conference], Athens: Εταιρεία Σπουδών, 2004., pp.367-403.

----. *Πόλεμος και Εθνοκάθαρη, Η ξεχασμένη πλευρά μιας δεκαετίας εθνικής εξόρμησης (1912-1922)* [War and ethnic cleansing, The forgotten aspect of a decade of national venture], Athens: Βιβλιόραμα, 2007.

Koulouri, Hristina [Κουλούρη, Χριστίνα]. "Γιορτάζοντας το Έθνος: Εθνικές επέτειοι στην Ελλάδα τον 19ο αιώνα" [Celebrating the Nation: National anniversaries in the 19th century Greece], in Papadimitriou, Despina & Seferiadis, Serafim, (Edit.) [Παπαδημητρίου, Δέσποινα & Σεφεριάδης Σεραφείμ]. (Επιμ). *Αθέατες όψεις της ιστορίας, κείμενα αφιερωμένα στον Γιάνη Γιανουλόπουλο*, Athens: Ασίνη, 2012, pp. 181-210.

Kourdis, Evangelos. "The Velopoulos-Liakopoulos Phenomenon" in Lexia, 23-24, January 16, pp 225-224

Kremmidas, Vasilis [Κρεμμυδάς, Βασίλης]. "Μηχανισμοί παραγωγής ιστορικών μύθων σχετικά με μια ομιλία του Παλαιών Πατρών Γερμανού" [Mechanisms in producing historical myths related to a speech of Palaion Patron Germanos], Athens: Μνήμων, Vol 18, 1996, pp. 9-20.

----. "Προσφώνηση" [Opening Speech] in *Επιστημονικό Συμπόσιο, Μύθοι και ιδεολογήματα στη σύγχρονη Ελλάδα* [Myths and ideological constructs in Greece – Minutes of Conference], Athens: Εταιρεία Σπουδών, 2007, pp. 15-18.

----. Το *Εικοσιένα, Μύθοι και πραγματικότητες* [The 'Twenty One', Myths and realities], Athens: Καλλίγραφος, 2021.

Kuhn, Thomas. The Sructure of Scientific Revolution, Chicageo: The University of Chicago Press, 1962.

Lampsa, Karina & Simpi, Iakov [Λάμψα, Καρίνα & Σίμπη Ιακώβ]. *Η Διάσωση* [The Rescue], Athens: Καπόν, 2012.

Leerssen, Joep. Mere Irish and Fior-Ghael, Studies in the Idea of Irish Nationality, Ireland: Cork University Press, 1996.

----, *National Thought in Europe, A cultural history*, Amsterdam University Press, 2006.

----. "Nation and Ethnicity" in Stefan Berger and Christ Lorenz (edit), *The Contested Nation, Ethnicity, Class, Religion and Gender in National Histories*, Hampshire: Palgrave Macmillan, 2008, pp. 75-103.

----. "Imagology: On using ethnicity to make sense of the world", https://imagologica.eu/keytexts (httpiberical.paris-sorbonne.frwp-contentuploads201702Pages-from-Iberic@l-no 10-automne-2016-Final-2.pdf)

----. "Ethnography and ethnicity" in Leerssen, Joep (edit) *Encyclopedia of Romantic Nationalism in Europe, Volume 1*, Amsterdam: Amsterdam University Press, 2018, pp. 76-79.

Levi-Strauss, Claude. *Tristes Tropiques*, Translated by John Russell, New York: Criterion Books, 1961.

----. *The Savage Mind*, London: Weidenfeld and Nicloson, 1966.

----. *The Naked Man. Mythologiques Volume 4*, Translated by John & and Doreen Weightman, Chicago: The University of Chicago Press, 1990.

----. *Myth and Meaning*. London & New York: Routledge, 2003.

Liakos, Antonis [Λιάκος, Αντώνης]. *Πώς στοχάστηκαν το έθνος αυτοί που ήθελαν να αλλάξουν τον κόσμο* [What those who wanted to change the world thought about the nation?], Athens: Πόλις, 2005

----. *Πώς το Παρελθόν Γίνεται Ιστορία;* [How the past becomes History], Athens: Πόλις, 2007.

----. "Οι πόλεμοι της ιστορίας" [History Wars] in Papadimitriou, Despina & Seferiadis, Serafim, (Edit.) [Παπαδημητρίου, Δέσποινα & Σεφεριάδης Σεραφείμ]. (Επιμ). *Αθέατες όψεις της ιστορίας, κείμενα αφιερωμένα στον Γιάνη Γιανουλόπουλο*, Athens: Ασίνη, 2012.

Lorenz, Christ. "Representations of Identity: Ethnicity, Race, Class, Gender and Religion. An Introduction to Conceptual History", in Stefan Berger and Christ Lorenz (edit), *The Contested Nation, Ethnicity, Class, Religion and Gender in National Histories*, Hampshire: Palgrave Macmillan, 2008, pp. 24-59.

----. "Drawing the Line: 'Scientific' History between Myth-making and Myth-breaking" in *Narrating the nation, Representations in history, media and the arts,* Stefan Berger, Linas Eriksonas & Andrew Mycock (Edit), 2011 (2008). [Chapter 2, pp. 35-55]

Mackridge, Peter. *Language and National Identity in Greece*, 1766-1976, Oxford, New York: Oxford University Press, 2009.

----. "A language in the image of the nation: Modern Greek and some parallel cases". www.academia.edu., originally in *The Making of Modern Greece: Nationalism, Romanticism, and the Uses of the Past (1797–1896)* edited by Roderick Beaton and David Ricks, 2009b, pp. 177-187.

----. "The Hellenicity of the linguistic Other in Greece", in Conference "Myths of the other in the Balkans", University of Macedonia, Thessaloniki, Feb. 2011.

----. "The heritages of the modern Greeks", British Academy Review, Issue 19 (Winter 2011/12). Also: The heritages of the modern Greeks, Peter Mackridge - Academia.edu

----. "The Greek language since 1750" in Storia e storie della lingua greca, Caterina Carpinato and Olga Tribulato (Edit), Venice: Ca'Foscari-Digital Publishing, 2014 (pp.133- 164). https://www.academia.edu/10730161/The_Greek_language_since_1750

Makriyannis, Ioannis [Μακρυγιάννης, Ιωάννης]. *Απομνημονεύματα* [Memoirs], (Edit. G. Vlahogiannis), Athens: Κοσμαδάκη, [1907]. (Makriyannis, p. 22).

----.(General) [Στρατηγού Μακρυγιάννης]. *Οράματα και Θάματα* [Visions and Miracles]. Papakosta, Aggelou (Edit.), Athens : Μορφωτικό Ίδυμα Εθνικής Τράπεζας, 1983.

----. (General) [Στρατηγού Μακρυγιάννης]. *Οράματα και Θάματα* [Visions and Miracles]. Papakosta, Aggelou (Edit.), Athens : Μορφωτικό Ίδυμα Εθνικής Τράπεζας, 1985.

Margaritis, Yiorgos [Μαργαρίτης, Γιώργος]. *Ανεπιθύμητοί συμπατριώτες, Στοιχεία για την καταστροφή των μειονοτήτων στην Ελλάδα, Τσάμηδες, Εβραίοι* [Unwanted compatriots, Data about the destruction of minorities in Greece,], Athens: Βιβλιόραμα, 2005.

Margolis, Howard. Patterns, Thinking and Cognition, A Theory of Judgement, Chicago and London: The University of Chicago Press, 1987.

Maronitis, Dimitrios [Μαρωνίτης, Δημήτριος]. «Αρχαία ελληνική γλώσσα: Μύθοι και μυθοποίησης» [Ancient Greek language: Myths and mythification] (p. 15-21) in Haris, Yiannis [Χάρης, Γιάννης]. (Edit.) *Δέκα Μύθοι για την Ελληνική Γλώσσα [Ten Myths for the Greek Language]*, Athens: Πατάκη, 2007 (2001), pp.15-21.

Malinowski, Bronislaw. *Argonauts of the Western Pacific*, Wolnelektury.pl, Fundacja Nowoczesna Polska, https://wolnelektury.pl/media/book/pdf/argonauts-of-the-western-pacific.pdf

Maravelias, Xaralambos.E. (Μαραβέλιας, Χαράλαμπος. Ε). "Στις ρίζες του χριστιανικού ανθελληνισμού" [To the roots of Christian anti-Hellenism], The Athens Review of Books, Issues 102, 103 and 104, January-March 2019.

McNeill, William "Mythistory, or Truth, History, and Historians" in *The American Historical Review*, Vol. 91, No. 1, Supplement to Volume 91 (Feb., 1986). 1-10.

Mazower, Mark. Salonica, City of Gosts, Christians, Muslims and Jews, 1430-1950. London: Harper Perennial, 2004.

Metallinos, Georgios [Μεταλληνός. Γεώργιος]. *Τουρκοκρατία, οι Έλληνες στην Οθωμανική Αυτοκρατορία*, Athens: Ακρίτας, 1989.

Milios, Yiannis [Μηλιός, Γιάννης]. 1821, Ιχνηλατώντας το Έθνος, το Κράτος και τη Μεγάλη Ιδέα [Tracing the Nation, the State and the Great Idea], Athens: Αλεξάνδρεια, 2020.

Millas, Hercules (Μήλλας, Ηρακλής). "History Textbooks in Greece and Turkey" in *History Workshop*, Issue 31, Spring 1991, England, pp. 22-33.

----. *Yunan Ulusunun Doğuşu* , İstanbul: İletişim, 1994.

Millas, Hercules (Μήλλας, Ηρακλής). 'The Image of Greeks in Turkish Literature: Fiction and Memoirs', in *Oil on Fire?*, Studien zur Internationalen Schulbuchforschung, Schriftenreihe des Georg-Eckert-Instituts, Hannover: Verlag Hansche Buchhandlung, 1996, pp.79-87.

----. '1998 Yunanistan Basınında Türkiye' [Turkey in the Greek Press of 1998] in *Bilanço 1923-1998*, Z. Rona (Edit.), İstanbul: Tarih Vakfı, 1999, pp. 341-350.

----. *Türk Romanı ve 'Öteki - Ulusal Kimlikte Yunan İmajı* [The Turkish Novel and the "Other"-The Image of the Greek in national identity], Istanbul: Sabancı, 2000.

----. Εικόνες Ελλήνων και Τούρκων - σχολικά βιβλία, ιστοριογραφία, λογοτεχνία και εθνικά στερεότυπα, [Images of Greeks and Turks - Textbooks, historiography, literature and national stereotypes], Athens: Alexandria, 2001.

----. Do's and Don't's for Better Greek-Turkish Relations, Athens: Papazissis, 2002.

---- *Geçmişten Bugüne Yunanlılar, Dil, Din ve Kimlikler* [The Greeks from Antiquity to Today, Language, Religion and Identities], İstanbul: İletişim, 2003.

----. "Ιστοριογραφία ή Μυθιστόρημα? - Η μαρτυρία των ελληνικών και τουρκικών κειμένων" ["Historiography or Novels? – The testimony of the Greek and Turkish texts"], Presentation in the Conference "History at stake, forms of modern historical culture" organized by the *Historein* [Journal], Athens, 30 November - 2 December 2001b). Circulated in *Historein*, volume 4 [Journal], Athens, 2003-2004, included cd.

----. "Η δυσκολία προσέγγισης του θέματος 'μειονοτητες'" [The difficulty in approaching the case of 'minorities], in *Μειονότητες στην Ελλάδα - Επιστημονικό Συμπόσιο* [Minorities in Greece - Academic Conference], Athens: Εταιρεία Σπουδών, 2004, pp. 21-27.

----. *Türk ve Yunan Romanlarında Öteki ve Kimlik* [The "Other" in Turkish and Greek novels and Identity], Istanbul: İletişim, 2005.

----. "Tourokratia: History and the Image of Turks in Greek Literature" in South European Society and Politics, Routledge, Volume 11, Number 1, March 2006, pp.47-60. Also in

When Greeks Think About Turks – The view from Anthropology, D. Theodossopoulos (Edit.), London & New York: Routleedge, 2007, pp. 47-60. (Also in 'Tourkokratia' (http://www.herkulmillas.com/en/hm-articles/76-on-historiography/438-tourkokratia-history-and-the-image-of-turks-in-greek-literature.pdf),

----. "History Writing among the Greeks and Turks: Imagining the Self and the Other", in Stefan Berger and Christ Lorenz (edit), *The Contested Nation, Ethnicity, Class, Religion and Gender in National Histories*, Hampshire: Palgrave Macmillan, 2008, pp. 490-510.

----. Nations and Identities – The Case of Greeks and Turks, Istanbul: Bilgi, 2016.

----. *'The Imagined Other as National Identity"* in Millas, H. *Nations and Identities, The Case of Greeks and Turks*, Istanbul: Bilgi University Press, 2016, pp. 169-214.

----. "History for Nation-building: The Case of Greece and Turkey" in (Edit.) M. Carretero, St. Berger, M. Grever, *Palgrave Handbook of Research in Historical Culture and Education*, United Kingdom: Palgrave Macmillan, 2017, pp. 355-372.

----. "The Case of Greece" in *The Palgrave Handbook of Conflict and History Education in the Post-Cold War Era*, Cajani, Luigi; Simone Lassig; Maria Repoussi (Edit.), Switzerland; Palgrave Macmillan, 2019.

----. "Ποιος Ρήγας: Της Ελευθερίας ή της Ανεξαρτησίας;" [Which Rigas: Of Liberty or of Independence?] in *The Athens Review of Books*, February 2019b, issue 103, pp.59-62.

----. (edit). *Sözde Masum Milliyetçilik* [The so-called innocent nationalism]. İstanbul: Kitap, 2010. Also in Greek: *Ο Αθώος Εθνικισμός*, Athens: Alexandria, 2019c.

----. *Ανήκομεν εις την Ανατολήν – Συγκριτικά στοιχεία για την Ελλάδα* [We belong to the East – Comparative data on Greece]. Athens: Σιδέρης, 2022.

Mirabal, Voyage d'Italie et de Grèce, Paris, 1698.

Misra, Pushpa. *The Scientific Status of Psychoanalysis*, New York: Routledge, 2018.

Moshonas, Spiros [Μοσχονάς, Σπύρος]. «Η προτεραιότητα του προφορικού λόγου» [The priority of the oral language], (p. 93-101) in Haris, Yiannis [Χάρης, Γιάννης]. (Edit.) *Δέκα Μύθοι για την Ελληνική Γλώσσα [Ten Myths for the Greek Language]*, Athens: Πατάκη, 2007 (2001), pp.93-101.

Nahmouli-Gabriilidou, Karolina [Ναχμούλη-Γαβριηλίδου, Καρολίνα]. *Block 25*, Athens: Γαβριηλίδης, 2016.

Ozkirimli, Umut [Özkırımlı]. *Theories of Nationalism: A Critical Introduction*, Houndmills, Basingstoke: Macmillan, 2000.

Papadakis, Dimitris L [Δημήτριος Λ. Παπαδάκης], 'Το Κρυφό σχολειό της μονής Φανερωμένης Ιεράπετρας και η Κριτσωτόπουλα Ροδάνθη» [The Secret School of the monastery of Phaneromenis etc], Κριτική Εστία, 262-263 (January-February, 1981, p. 3-24, mentioned in (Stathi).

Papanastasiou, Yorgos [Παπαναστασίου, Γιώργος]. «Απ' τα χώματα βγαλμένοι: ένας αρχαίος σύγχρονος μύθος», in *Μύθοι και ιδεολογήματα στη σύγχρονη Ελλάδα – Επιστημονικό Συνέδριο* [Myths and ideologies in modern Greece- Academic Conference], Athens: Εταιρεία Σπουδών, 200, pp. 89-100.

Paparrigopoulos, Konstantinos [Παπαρρηγόπουλος, Κωνσταντίνος]. *Ιστορία του Ελληνικού Έθνους* [History of the Greek Nation], Vol. 5, Athens: Γεωργίου Φέξη, 1903.

Parios, Athanasios [Πάριος, Αθανάσιος] *Απολογία Χριστιανική* [Christian apologia], Athens: Εκδόσεις Γρηγόρη, 2016. (With an introduction by G. Metallinos).44

Patrikiou, Alexandra [Πατρικίου, Αλαξάνδρα]. «Να φύγουν: Οι Εβραίοι ως εχθροί της Νέας Ευρώπης στον Κατοχικό τύπο της Θεσσαλονίκης" [They should go: The Jews as enemies in the press of Thessaloniki during German occupation], in Papadimitriou, Despina & Seferiadis, Serafim, (Edit.) [Παπαδημητρίου, Δέσποινα & Σεφεριάδης Σεραφείμ]. (Επιμ). *Αθέατες όψεις της ιστορίας, κείμενα αφιερωμένα στον Γιάνη Γιανουλόπουλο*, Athens: Ασίνη, 2012, pp 245-258.

Patrinelis, Christos [Πατρινέλης, Χρίστος]. «Η Στάση της Εκκλησίας απέναντι στον κατακτητή» [The position of the Church to the conqueror] in *Ιστορία του Ελληνικού Έθνους [History of the Greek Nation]*, *Vol. 10*, Athens: Εκδοτική Αθηνών, 1974, pp. 94-98.

----. «Οι Σχέσεις της Εκκλησίας με την κυρίαρχη οθωμανική πολιτεία» [The relations of the

Church with the dominant Ottoman state] in *Ιστορία του Ελληνικού Έθνους [History of the Greek Nation]*, *Vol. 11*, Athens: Εκδοτική Αθηνών, 1974b, 123-126.

----. «Το κρυφό σχολειό και πάλι» [The secret school anew], *Ο Ερανιστής*, 25, 2005.

Pesmazoglou, Stefanos [Πεσμαζόγλου, Στέφανος]. *Ευρώπη-Τουρκία* [Europe-Turkey], 2 Volumes. Athens: Θεμέλιο, 1993..

Petrounias, Evangelos [Πετρούνιας, Ευάγγελος]. «Ετυμολογία και προέλευση του λεξιλογίου της νέας ελληνικής» [Etymology and the origin of the lexicon of Modern Greek], (p. 23-33) in Haris, Yiannis [Χάρης, Γιάννης]. (Edit.) *Δέκα Μύθοι για την Ελληνική Γλώσσα [Ten Myths for the Greek Language]*, Athens: Πατάκη, 2007 (2001), pp. 23-33.

Pinker, Steven. *The Blank Slate, The Modern Denial of Human Nature*, London: Peguin, 2003.

Politis, Alexis [Πολίτης, Αλέξης]. Ρομαντικά Χρόνια [Romantic Years], Athens: ΕΜΝΕ-Μνήμων, 2003.

Politis, Nikolas (Πολίτης, Νικόλαος). *Οι Παραδόσεις του Ελληνικού Λαού [The Traditional Stories of the Greek People]*, Vol A&B. Athens: Τα Νέα, 2013 (1904).

Popper, Karl Raimund. *Conjectures and refutations*. New York: Harper & Row, 1968.

Poulton, Hugh. *Who are the Mecedonians?*, London: Hurst & Company, 1995.

Psarras, Dimitris [Ψαρράς, Δημήτρης]. *Πώς συλλογάται ο Ρήγας;* [How Rigas thinks?], Athens: Πόλις, 2020.

Renan, Ernest. *Qu'est-ce qu'une nation?* [What is a Nation?], Paris: Presses-Pocket, 1992.

Repoussi, Maria [Ρεπούση, Μαρία]. "Το Νέο Εικοσιένα. Η ανολοκλήρωτη Ελληνική Επανάσταση στις δημόσιες επετειακές αφηγήσεις της πρώτης εκατονταετηρίδας της" [The new 1821. The non-completed Greek Revolution in the public narratives at its hundred years commemoration], in Papadimitriou, Despina & Seferiadis, Serafim, (Edit.) [Παπαδημητρίου, Δέσποινα & Σεφεριάδης Σεραφείμ]. (Επιμ). *Αθέατες όψεις της ιστορίας, κείμενα αφιερωμένα στον Γιάνη Γιανουλόπουλο*, Athens: Ασίνη, 2012, pp. 161-180.

Riess, Helen. *The Empathy Effect,* Colorade: Sounds True, 2018.

Runciman, Steven. *Byzantine Civilization*, USA: Meridian, 1956.

----. The Great Church in Captivity, a study of the Patriarchate of Constantinople from the eve of the Turkish Conquest to the Greek war of Independence, Cambridge: Cambridge University Press, 1968.

Sacks, Oliver. *The man who mistook his wife for a hat*, London: Picador,1986.

Saradi, Helen. "Byzantium and the Origin of the Modern Greek National Consciousness, as the 1992 "Constantinople and Its Legacy" Annual Lecture of The Greek Canadian Association of Constantinople, Toronto.

Sarandakos, Nikos [Σαραντάκος, Νίκος]. *Γλώσσα μετ'εμποδίων* [Language with hurdles], Athens: Εικοστού Πρώτου, 2007.

Seferis, Yorgos [Σεφέρης, Γιώργος]. "Ένας Έλληνας = Ο Μακρυγιάννης" [A Greek – Makriyannis], in *Δοκιμές, Α,* [Essays, Vol.A], Athens: Ίκαρος, 1981 (1974), pp. 228-263.

Segal, Robert A. *Myth: A Very Short Introduction*, Oxford: Oxford University Press, 2004

Seton-Watson, Hugh. *Nations and States*. Colorado: Westview Press, 1977.

Seton-Watson, H. *Nations and States*, Westview Press, Boulder, 1977.

Simopoulos, Kyriakos [Σιμόπουλος, Κυριάκος]. *Ξένοι Ταξιδιώτες στην Ελλάδα, 333-1700* [Foreign Travelers in Greece, 333-1700], Athens: (Privately published), 1984.

----. *Ξένοι Ταξιδιώτες στην Ελλάδα, 1800-1810* [Foreign Travelers in Greece, 1800-1810], Athens: (Privately published), 1985.

----. *Ο Μύθος των "Μεγάλων" της Ιστορίας,* [The Myths of the "Great" Persons of History], Athens: Στάχι, 2010.

Skopetea, Elli (Σκοπετέα, Έλλη). *Φάλμεραϋερ, τεχνάσματα του αντίπαλου δέους,* [Fallmerayer, the the tricks of the threatening opponent] Athens: Θεμέλιο, 1997.

----. *Το 'Πρότυπο Βασίλειο' και η Μεγάλη Ιδέα* [The 'Exemplary Kingdom' and the Great Idea], Athens: Πολύτυπο, 1988.

Skoulidas, Ilias [Σκουλίδας,, Ηλίας]. "Η 'Ανακάλυψη' της 'Αλβανίας': ελληνικές 'προσλήψεις' στα τέλει του 19ου αιώνα" [The 'discovery' of 'Albania': Greek 'perceptions' at the end of the 19th century] in Papadimitriou, Despina & Seferiadis, Serafim, (Edit.) [Παπαδημητρίου,

Δέσποινα & Σεφεριάδης Σεραφείμ]. (Επιμ). *Αθέατες όψεις της ιστορίας, κείμενα αφιερωμένα στον Γιάνη Γιανουλόπουλο*, Athens: Ασίνη, 2012, pp. 377-392.

Smith, Antony. *Nationalism in the Twentieth century*, Canberra: Australian National University Press, 1979

----. *The Ethnic Origins of Nations*, New York: Basil Blackwell, 1989.

----. The Cultural Foundations of Nations, Hierarchy, Covenant, and Republic. USA, UK: Blackwell, 2008, p.19, 46.

Sotiriou, Stefanos [Σωτηρίου, Στέφανος]. *Οι Βλαχόφωνοι του Ευρωπαϊκού και Βαλκανικού Χώρου* [The Vlachophones of the European and Balkan areas], Athens: Πελασγός, 1990.

Soutsos, Panayiotis (Σούτσος, Παναγιώτης). Ο Λέανδρος [Leandros], Athens: Νεοελληνική Βιβλιοθήκη Ίδρυμα Κ.Ε. Ουράνη, 1994 (1834).

Stathis, Panagiotis. (Παναγιώτης Στάθης) "Το Κρυφό σχολειό: διαδρομές του μύθου, διαδρομές της ιστορίας" [The Secret School: routes of the myth, routes of history], presentation in the Conference "History at stake, forms of modern historical culture" organized by the *Historein* [Journal], Athens, 30 November - 2 December 2001. Circulated in *Historein*, vol. 4, Athens, 2003-2004, included cd.

----. "Ιστορική κουλτούρα και κατασκευασμένη μνήμη, τα κρυφά σχολεία" [Historical culture and the constructed memory, the secret schools] in *Μύθοι και ιδεολογήματα στη σύγχρονη Ελλάδα* [Myths and ideological constructs in Greece – Minutes of Conference], Athens: Εταιρεία Σπουδών, 2007, pp. 225-258.

Steiris, Georgios, Mitralexis, Sotiris and Arabatzis, Georgios (edit) *The Problem of Modern Greek Identity: From the Ecumene to the Nation-State*, Cambridge Scholars Publishing, 2016

Svoronos, Nikos [Σβορώνος, Νίκος]. *Επισκόπηση της Νεοελληνικής Ιστορίας* [Overview of Modern Greek History, Athens : Θεμέλιο, 1985 (Original: *Histoire de la Grèce Moderne*, Paris : Presses Universitaire de Fance, 1972.

Theodoropoulos, Viron [Θεοδωρόπουλος, Βύρων] *Οι Τούρκοι και Εμείς* [The Turks and We], Athens, Φυτράκης, 1988.

Theofanopoulou-Kontou, Dimitra [Θεοφανοπούλου-Κοντού, Δήμητρα]. «Λάθη στη χρήση της γλώσσας: Αλήθεια και μύθος» [Mistakes in the use of the languages: The truth and the myth], (p. 53-61) in Haris, Yiannis [Χάρης, Γιάννης]. (Edit.) *Δέκα Μύθοι για την Ελληνική Γλώσσα [Ten Myths for the Greek Language]*, Athens: Πατάκη, 2007 (2001), pp.53-61.

Thomas, Keith. *Religion and the Decline of Magic*, London: Penguin, 1971.

Thucydides, *History of the Peloponnesian War*, Book 4, 108/4 (Thucydides, History of the Peloponnesian War, BOOK IV, chapter 108 (tufts.edu)

Toynbee, Arnold. *A Study of History, A new edition revised and abridged by the author and Jane Caplain*, New York: Oxford University Press, 1972.

Trikoupis, Spirithon [Τρικούπης, Σπυρίδων]. *Ιστορία της Ελληνικής Επαναστάσεως* [History of the Greek Revolution], Vol. 1, Athens: Οργανισμός Λαμπράκη, [2006].

Tsitselikis, Konstantinos [Τσιτσελίκης, Κωνσταντίνος], *Η μειονοτική εκπαίδευση της Θράκης* [The education of the minority in Thrace], Athens: Πρόγραμμα Μουσουλμανοπαίδων, Πανεπιστήμιο Αθηνών , 2003.

----. "Ο Κανόνας δικαίου ως έκφραση εθνικής ιδεολογίας, τα αδιέξοδα της νομικής αντιμετώπισης μειονοτήτων στην Ελλάδα» [The rule of law as expression of national ideology, the judiciary deadlock in coping with the minorities in Greece], in *Μειονότητες στην Ελλάδα - Επιστημονικό Συμπόσιο* [Minorities in Greece - Academic Conference], Athens: Εταιρεία Σπουδών, 2004, pp. 457-482.

----. *Old and New Islam in Greece*, Leiden & Boston: Martinus Nijhoff, 2012.

Tsolias, Panayiotis [Τσολιάς Παναγιώτης]. Η Κριτική της Θρησκείας στον νεοελληνικό διαφωτισμό [Criticism of religion in modern Greek Enlightenment], Athens: Προσκήνιο, 2010.

Tucker, Robert. *Philosophy and Myth in Karl Marx*, Routledge, 2000

Vakalopoulos, Apostolos [Βακαλόπουλος, Απόστολος]. "Ο Θεόφιλος, Κορυδακεύς και οι απαρχές της φιλοσοφικής διανόησης και παιδεία στις ελληνικές χώρες 1613-1670" [Knowledge and educations in Greek geographies, 1613-1670], in *Ιστορία του Ελληνικού*

Έθνους [History of the Greek Nation], Vol. 10, Athens: Εκδοτική Αθηνών, 1974, pp. 380-381.
----. Ιστορία του Νέου Ελληνισμού, Η Μεγάλη Ελληνική Επανάσταση (1821-1829), Vol. 5, Thessaloniki: [Private edition], 1980.
----. Ο Χαρακτήρας των Ελλήνων, ανιχνεύοντας την εθνική μας ταυτότητα [The Character of the Greeks, in search of our national identity], Thessaloniki, [private edition], 1983.
Vasilakis, Manolis [Βασιλάκης, Μανώλης]. Η Μάστιγα του Θεού [The Menace of God], Athens: Γνώσεις, 2006).
Veloudis, Yiorgos (Βελούδης, Γιώργος). Ο Jakob Fallmerayer και η Γένεση του Ελληνικού Ιστορισμού [Jakob Fallmerayer and the Birth of Greek historicity], Athens: Ε.Μ.Ν.Ε. Μνήμων, 1982. [Originally published as: Jacob Philipp Fallmerayer und die Entstehung des neugriechischen Historismus, Südostforschungen 29, 1970, p. 43-90.]
----. «Άνισες εξισώσεις: Η γλώσσα των νέων» [Unequal ecuations: The language of the youth], (p. 71-82) in Haris, Yiannis [Χάρης, Γιάννης]. (Edit.) Δέκα Μύθοι για την Ελληνική Γλώσσα [Ten Myths for the Greek Language], Athens: Πατάκη, 2007 (2001), pp. 73-82.
Venezis, Ilias. Μικρασία Χαίρε [Asia Minor, I Salute You], Athens: Estia, 1979 [1974].
Ventura, Lina [Βεντούρα, Λινα]. "Εθνικισμός, ρατσισμός και μετανάστευση στη σύγχρονη Ελλάδα" [Nationaslism, racism and immigration in modern Greece], in Pavlou, M. & Hristopoulos, D. Ελλάδα της Μετανάστευσης [Greece of Immigartion], Athens: Κριτική & ΚΕΜΟ, 2004, pp. 174-204.
Veremis, Thanos & Koliopoulos, Yiannis [Βερέμης, Θάνος & Κολιόπουλος, Γιάννης], Ελλάς, Η Σύγχρονη Συνέχεια [Greece, The Modern Continuum], Athens: Καστανιώτη, 2006.
Vlahoyianni, Yiannis [Βλαχογιάννης, Γιάννης]. Απομνημονεύματα Μακρυγιάννη [Memoirs of Makriyannis], Athens: Χ. Κοσμαδάκη, 1907.
Vournas, Tasos [Βουρνάς, Τάσος]. Σύντομη Ιστορία της Ελληνικής Επανάστασης [Short history of the Greek Revolution], Athens: Εκδόσεις Τ. Δρακόπουλου, [?]
Vranousis, Leandros [Βρανούσης, Λέανδρος]. Rigas Velestinlis [Ρήγας Βελεστινλής], Athens: Δευτέρα Επευξιμένη, 1963.
White, Hayden. Metahistory, The Historical Imagination in Nineteenth-Century Europe, Baltimor& London: The Johns Hopkings University Press, 1973.
Wilson, Edward O. Sociobiology, Cambridge, Massachusetts and London: The Belknap Press of Harvard University Press, 1980.
Wittgenstein, Ludwig. Tractatus Logico-Philosophicus, First published by Kogan Paul, London, 1922 (containing the original German, alongside both the Ogden/Ramsey, and Pears/McGuinness English translations (as available at http://people.umass.edu/ klement/ tlp/
----. On Certainty, Oxford: Basil Blackwell, 1969-1975.
----. Philosophical Investigations, Translated by E.M. Anscombe, Oxford: Basil Blackwell, 2001.
Wolfram, Herwig. "The Public Instrumentalization of the Middle Ages in Austria since 1945" in R.J.W. Evans and Guy P. Marchal (edit.), The Uses of the Middle Ages in Modern European States, History, Nationhood and the Search for Origins, New York: Palgrave Macmillan, 2011, pp. 221-244.
Yakovaki, Nassia [Γιακωβάκη, Νάσια]. «Η εκκρεμής συνάντηση ιστορίας και γλωσσολογίας στις Ιστορίες της Ελληνικής γλώσσας' του Τάσου Χριστίδη», in Μύθοι και ιδεολογήματα στη σύγχρονη Ελλάδα – Επιστημονικό Συνέδριο [Myths and ideologies in modern Greece- Academic Conference], Athens: Εταιρεία Σπουδών, 2007, pp.43-67.
----. Ευρώπη μέσω Ελλάδας, Μια καμπή στην Ευρωπαϊκή αυτοσυνείδηση 17ος – 18ος αιώνας [Europe through Greece, A turning point in European self-consciousness, 17th – 18th centuries], Athens: Estia, 2015.
Yiannoulopoulos, Yiorgos [Γιαννουλόπουλος, Γιώργος], Διαβάζοντας τον Μακρυγιάννη, Κατασκευή ενός μύθου [Reading Makriyannis, The construction of a myth], Athens: Πόλις, 2003.
Zallonis, Markos [Ζαλλώνης, Μάρκος]. Σύγγραμμα Περί των Φαναριωτών [Thesis on Phanariots], Athens: Επικαιρώτητα, 1972. (Original in French: Zallony, Marc-Phillippe, Essai sur les Phanariots, Marseille, 1824.

Index

www.ingramcontent.com/pod-product-compliance
Lightning Source LLC
Chambersburg PA
CBHW050350270326
41926CB00016B/3680